SUBJECT STAGES

MARÍA M. CARRIÓN

Subject Stages

Marriage, Theatre, and the Law in Early Modern Spain

UNIVERSITY OF TORONTO PRESS
Toronto Buffalo London

© University of Toronto Press Incorporated 2010
Toronto Buffalo London
www.utppublishing.com
Printed in Canada

ISBN 978-1-4426-4108-2 (cloth)

Printed on acid-free, 100% post-consumer recycled paper with vegetable-based inks.

Library and Archives Canada Cataloguing in Publication

Carrión, María M., 1959-

Subject stages : marriage, theatre and the law in early modern Spain / María M. Carrión.

(University of Toronto Romance Series)
Includes bibliographical references and index.
ISBN 978-1-4426-4108-2 (bound)

1. Spanish drama – Classical period, 1500–1700 – History and criticism.
2. Marriage laws – Spain – History – 16th century. 3. Marriage laws –
Spain – History – 17th century. 4. Marriage in literature. I. Title.

PQ6105.C374 2010   862'.3093543   C2009-906380-8

This book has been published with the help of a subvention from the Program for Cultural Cooperation between Spain's Ministry of Culture and United States Universities.

'Poem 11' from *Interpreter of Desires* by Ibn 'Arabi, translated by Michael Sells, is reproduced by permission.

University of Toronto Press acknowledges the financial assistance to its publishing program of the Canada Council for the Arts and Ontario Arts Council.

  Canada Council   Conseil des Arts   ONTARIO ARTS COUNCIL
for the Arts   du Canada   CONSEIL DES ARTS DE L'ONTARIO

University of Toronto Press acknowledges the financial support for its publishing activities of the Government of Canada through the Book Publishing Industry Development Program (BPIDP).

Contents

Illustrations

Abbreviations

Archives

AGS	Archivo General de Simancas
AHN	Archivo Histórico Nacional, Madrid
BNE	Biblioteca Nacional de España, Madrid

Collections

CCD	Cámara de Castilla, Diversos, AGS
CCPEC	Cámara de Castilla, Procesos y Expedientes Criminales, AGS
Cerv	Sala Cervantes, BNE
Cons	Consejos, AHN
CR	Consejo Real de Castilla, AGS
D Coronel	Diversos, T. F. Coronel, AHN
D Gral	Diversos, General 1, AHN
D Rueda	Diversos, Archivo de Rueda, AHN
Est Cast Esp	Estado de Castilla y España, AGS
Inq	Inquisición, AHN
OOMM	Órdenes Militares, AHN

Publications

ACerv	*Anales Cervantinos*
ANeophil	*Acta Neophilologica*
BCom	*Bulletin of the Comediantes*
BHM	*Bulletin of the History of Medicine*

BHS	Bulletin of Hispanic Studies
Cerv	Cervantes: Bulletin of the Cervantes Society of America
CompLit	Comparative Literature
CNTC	Compañía Nacional de Teatro Clásico Español
CQ	Classical Quarterly
CSIC	Consejo Superior de Investigaciones Científicas de España
EHS	Estudios de Historia y Sociedad
GLQ	Gay and Lesbian Quarterly
Hisp	Hispania
HR	Hispanic Review
IJHL	Indiana Journal of Hispanic Literatures
JEP	Journal of European Psychoanalysis
JHP	Journal of Hispanic Philology
JSCS	Journal of Spanish Cultural Studies
LC	La Corónica
MLN	Modern Language Notes
MLQ	Modern Language Quarterly
MLR	Modern Language Review
NRFH	Nueva Revista de Filología Hispánica
PH	Procesós Históricos: Revista de historia y ciencias socials
PMLA	Publications of the Modern Language Association of America
RABM	Revista de Archivos, Bibliotecas y Museos
RBAMAM	Revista de la Biblioteca, Archivo y Museo del Ayuntamiento de Madrid
RCEH	Revista Canadiense de Estudios Hispánicos
REH	Revista de Estudios Hispánicos
RevHisp	Revue Hispanique
RomF	Romanische Forum
RomRev	Romanic Review
RQ	Romance Quarterly
SCJ	Sixteenth Century Journal
TAHR	The American Historical Review
TJ	Theatre Journal
TYLJ	The Yale Law Journal
UP	University Press

Author's Note

The historical and literary materials consulted for, and cited in, this study were produced in Latin or Old Spanish; in the case of the dramatic texts, the Spanish approximates modern Spanish, but it was presented in baroque verse – a rather difficult and almost incomprehensible poetic form, even for some native speakers of Spanish. I present here all materials in English, the language in which I have chosen to write this book. To facilitate the reading of these materials, I present the quotes from the primary legal code entitled *Recopilación* and King Felipe II's deathbed confession only in English. Passages from archival legal documents as well as dramatic texts appear cited in Spanish with English translations; unless otherwise noted, all translations are mine. I have used published translations with my own annotations when the translation conveyed a meaning that did not support my argumentation; such annotations are not intended as a correction on the quoted translation, but as a point of clarification.

Quotes from lawsuits and other archival documents show the original spelling; whenever a translator used old English to convey the feel of the Spanish in the script, I have respected that usage.

When a Spanish word appears for the first time, I offer a translation; to avoid stultifying repetition, I leave such words in Spanish. I have translated the Spanish titles of nobility, but not the proper names. When in doubt, readers can consult the glossary.

Legal theory and practices in early modern Spain took place in a labyrinth of 'ambiguous laws, conflicting *fueros*, and special juridical privileges' that, as Richard Kagan has put it, became 'a hodgepodge of confused laws and competeing jurisdictions that crafty litigants exploited to their own advantage' (31). To navigate such a labyrinth,

Subject Stages uses two terms. 'Law' refers to legal codes and theories, both written and unwritten laws cited throughout this book (such as Justinian's *Institutes*, which are a crucial part of the *Corpus Iuris Civilis*; the *Nueva Recopilación de las leyes destos Reynos*, as well as the *Canons and Decrees* from the Council of Trent; or the unwritten, yet clearly scripted Spanish 'code of honour,' among others); 'law' (lower case), on the other hand, refers to the application of such legal codes and theories, or, more concretely, to acts of litigation and debate of those principles, rules, or norms of Law consulted for this study. When referring to both, 'law' will be used.

Along parallel lines, '*Comedia*' refers to the cultural, socioeconomic, and political phenomenon of the first professional theatre of Spain, dating roughly from the sixteenth and seventeenth centuries. On the other hand, '*comedia*' will be used to mean a specific instance of such *Comedia*, that is to say, to refer to a single play, dramatic text, or theatrical production.

SUBJECT STAGES

Introduction

There must be some way to locate productive discrepancies and contradictions even within an ideological framework as apparently homogeneous as that of Spain at the height of its empire ... Indeed, the culture
that emerged under Spanish Absolutism on the Iberian peninsula itself
turns out to be less the perfect mirror of state ideologies than is sometimes supposed.

Anthony Cascardi, 'Beyond Castro and Maravall: Interpellation,
Mimesis, and the Hegemony of Spanish Culture'

Theatres of early modern Spain produced a number of comic scenes of
marriage.[1] For the most part, these scenes ended a life of dramatic conflict and pretended to bring restoration to the social order. But the stages
of theatre were not the only ones where the perils and pleasures of transcendental human unions were represented: legal codes, courthouses,
and bureaucracy are a few other arenas where the sign of matrimony
was invoked as well. This book begins with the premise that marriage
circulated between the stages of theatre and the law, which in turn informed (and were informed by) stages of subjectivity in sixteenth- and
seventeenth-century Spain. The table of contents may suggest that the
way to organize such a study on marriage demands a split between law
and theatre: two chapters on legal texts; one on the birth of theatre; four
more on dramatic texts. Moreover, this division of critical labour seems
to favour theatre over law as the surface upon which marital verities
were written in early modern Spain.

   To be frank, when I first embarked in this venture sixteen years ago
such was the idea for this book, destined back then to have borne the

infelicitous titlex of *'Til Death Let Us Part*.[2] I was in part under the spell of the influential thought of José Antonio Maravall, who persuasively characterized baroque culture as a site of propaganda for the nobility.[3] But a funny thing happened on the way to that forum, which led me to revise my intentions and methods: I got hooked on the possibilities of those two strange bedfellows – comedy and litigation – and *Subject Stages* was born, instead.[4] Many years later I read Cascardi's essay and I realized how far this book had gone beyond Maravall in showing that State and Man did not wholly rule over Stage and Woman, even if the ideological framework of absolutism said so. The consequent fractured mimesis of marriage, theatre, and the law you see here is a set of different locations of culture from those in which Maravall placed what he termed the Spanish baroque.

In brief, *Subject Stages* interrogates the foundational fiction of an irrevocable union of a man and a woman of Catholic faith performed for the strict purpose of procreation as a sign of early modern times in Spain. As stipulated by Law, a church officer and two other juridical *personae* legitimized by their sound Catholic faith were to sanction the ritual drama of this union. At least two centuries passed before the Law made room for a conception of marriage not governed primarily by church Law, but during that period theatre and the law did not sit idle: subjects and stages navigated legal and theatrical venues to produce a wide variety of images differing from those representing the *institutio* of marriage founded in early modern Spain.[5] As the following chapters demonstrate, the Law's minimum cast of characters and their political theatrics became a key strategy in the production and reproduction of Spain's version of empire, the *Monarquía Católica Universal* (Catholic Universal Monarchy).[6] In turn, the heterosexual coupling and their (desired) offspring became an emblematic site for the reproduction of values of One Faith, One Race, and One Kingdom.[7]

Concurrently with the development of this formula in the stages of the Law, theatre and litigation also deployed this marital image – though they did not reproduce it literally. The dramatic literature, theatrical stages, and court documents analysed in the following chapters reveal acts of intervention that interpellate this official story of marriage performed by individuals and collectives staging a variety of subject positions strictly regulated or prohibited by the crown in private and public arenas. The central argument of the book is that in spite of the heavily codified regulations produced by the crown to control subjects with a marital formula, people in theatres, courthouses, and their homes in Spain saw a different picture – one composed with images that illustrate the discrepancies and contradictions named by Cascardi. Naturally, this alternative picture was not new; in fact, these scenes honour an old tradition of interactivity between marriage, theatre, and the law. From its beginnings as a legal and theatrical institution, marriage brought together a number of signs that through the ages were theorized, catalogued, and accepted as opposites: man and woman, public and private, heaven and hell, and so on. Students of theatre and the law know that unions of opposites (and, especially if these become contraries) need the mediation of theatrical and legal codes to channel such unions in some kind of constructive or, at least, not totally destructive manner. Such unions of opposites are also the greatest raw material for the plotting, development, and resolution of conflict, without which there are neither dramas nor lawsuits.

It makes perfect sense, then, that marriage evolved in close correspondence with theatre and the law, a point tangible in two capital texts in Western literature and society: the Greek New Comedy in the fourth century BC, and the Justinian *Corpus Iuris Civilis* (which contains the *Institutes*) in the sixth century CE. Old and Middle Comedy in ancient Greece were characterized by invective, primitive stock characters, and the bawdy, raw presence of bodies onstage, especially the ubiquitous presence of satyrs and phallic imagery, exemplarily illustrated in the scripts of Crates, Aristophanes, and Anaxandides. As Middle Comedy waned, these were replaced by love and marriage as two critical axes for the dramatic action.[8] Jan Hokenson summarizes this transition, which has continued to reverberate in history thereafter – including, as we shall see, in early modern Spain: 'Euripides' eccentric late work may have paved the way for the morally more proper forms that Aristotle endorses, but in any case the brazen fantasists of Old Comedy drop from the critical view, to reappear only much later in the Middle Ages and then again in our own indecorous times' (27). Romance was not yet flowing in the 316 BC comic air, but the scents of woman and marriage surely were. Menander's *Dyskolos* (The Peevish Fellow, also translated as the Old Grouch), the only full text extant from the New Comedy, deployed its audiovisual language to represent in grand farcical fashion the conflict created by the deity Pan, who enchanted young Sostratos with the beauty of the daughter of a misanthrope, Kemnon. By the powers invested in theatre from such an early age, the wedding desired for 'The End' became an instant success, and it morphed into not one, but two marital ceremonies.

Marriage reappeared centre stage almost ten centuries later, this time in the legal arena as a capital step in the definition of juridical 'persons' stipulated in titles IX and X of Book 1 of Justinian's *Institutes*. The union of male and female was a result ('hence,' the *Corpus* says) of the ways in which nature teaches all creatures about law. 'Hence,' issues of sex – that activity shared by humans and animals without which, technically, there is neither procreation nor rearing – and gender drove the writing of matrimonial Law: 'Roman citizens are joined together in lawful wedlock when they are united according to law, the man having reached years of puberty, and the woman being of marriageable age' (12). Title X, 'On Marriage,' actually reads like a catalogue of kin relations, spelled in painful detail to clearly stipulate which subject can marry which other, or not (12–15). This preoccupation with incest and potential mixing of bloodlines will resurface time and again in legal and theatrical scenes of marriage from early modern Spain. Menander breathed law into his comedies, and Justinian certainly incorporated high drama in the making of his legal codes; marriage became a memorable tapestry. The memory of the institution, as a result, transcended time and place, but not strictly as the site of controlled reproduction of civilization that Justinian and perhaps even Menander thought it should be. In the respective media of theatre and the law, as we shall see in the case of early modern Spain, marriage also thrived by following detours from the structures and themes of these foundational fictions; many of those sat contiguously (and, at times, perilously so, as we shall see) to the latter.

The appearance of marriage as a significant factor in the production of New Comedy and the Law yielded another side effect: a systemic foreclosure for comic theory that has kept this area of inquiry from becoming an object of study in its own right. Hokenson summarizes this critical history: once Aristotle discarded 'the rude invective of Old Comedy and tacitly endorsed the more proper, contemporary forms of Menandrine or New Comedy,' he 'consigned the madcap fantasies of Aristophanes to an inglorious past, and marked the foundational split between actual artistic history and the critical idea of comedy. For centuries thereafter, despite the popular success of "vulgar" forms, the Aristotelian conception prevailed' (14).[9] One of the most damaging of these premises, concludes Hokenson, 'is the construct of "acceptance" as the "wisdom" of all comedy (the venerable concept of comic plot as ending in harmonious acceptance of the world and its faults)' (211). Ironically, this is where Law desired to be, for as Justinian's *Institutes* states, justice – the obscure object of Law's desire – is 'the set and constant purpose which gives to every man his due,' while jurisprudence is 'the knowledge of things divine and human, the science of the just and the unjust' (3). These two premises resonate with Aristotle's reading of marriage as a means in the New Comedy to the end of articulating constructs of a harmonious acceptance of the world and its faults. *Subject Stages* seeks to show the conventional end of marriage not as a foreclosed image that merely marks 'The End' as a restoration of social order, but as an unpredictable beginning of legal and theatrical arguments that do not necessarily need to become tragic.

The importance of methodological flexibility in this inquiry cannot be understated: the subject stages that occupy centre stage in this book cannot be read with the suspicion that the truth and purity of the law separate it from the falseness and speciousness of comedy – a genre, as Hokenson has fairly lamented, theorized to represent nothing but failure. On the contrary, these subject stages begin (which, in comic fiction always means remembrance) knowing that the correspondence of theatre and the law is a primal scene in which the possibilities of the legal and the comic inform the development of this institution. Two actors in this primal scene captured by Plutarch once debated the rivalry between law and theatre, Thespis and Solon, respectively defending the beauty and truth of play (theatre) and argument (law). The result of that encounter, as Dennis Kezar notes, is that theatre and law have been encased in 'an institutional antagonism over the tenuous distinction between theatre's inconsequential fiction and the real world's socially consequential fact' (2).

The fractured mimesis of marriage, theatre, and the law in early modern Spain reveals the shortcomings of this antagonism, and as the following pages will demonstrate, there were profound theatrical dimensions in legal writings and courthouses, as well as significant legal premises in the theatre, which shaped the production of marriage. Beyond the useful but also limiting framework of genre, *Subject Stages* explores the presence of theatrical units such as characters, dramatic conflict, set design, and proxemics in legal texts; at once, it insists on analysing how marital law informs the staging of theatre. Like New Comedy and Justinian's *Institutes* before them, early modern Spanish agents and actors of marriage in society and the arts set the stage for the agony and ecstasy of juridical and theatrical marital subjects, imagining and performing multiple wedding scenes as 'The End' and a host of other strategies of deployment for marriage. A central goal of this book is to analyse the historical specificity of this correspondence.

A word about why I insist on the term 'subject' as opposed to 'individual' or 'person.' Early modern Spaniards inevitably confronted what George Mariscal has termed 'the subject of Hispanism,' the national character of man that through centuries of critical niceties and accommodation has been used to canonize the Spanish Golden Ages in exclusionary terms. Nevertheless, early modern Spanish subjects, as Mariscal proposes, were not one foreclosed entity, but 'a series of subject positions lacking any permanent closure' (6).[10] The following chapters will show subject positions that playfully produced scenes of what the Law considered intangible, invisible, or negligible in marriage. The expression *Subject Stages*, then, is designed to encompass separate yet related interpretive levels necessary to prove my argument. First, it refers to the above-mentioned subject positions; this first level could be also named 'stages of subjectivity,' designed to question the hegemonic and homogeneously constructed essential subjects of matrimony, the husband and wife (*perfecta casada*). Following Mariscal, this book shows how subject stages illustrate a continual transformation and rearticulation of material conditions and discourses of marriage.

The second level of meaning of the title refers to the stages in which law and theatre represented their business; more frequently than not these stages were subject, or compelled to submit to forces outside and beyond them. These physical spaces, as Mariscal aptly put it, were located 'within the general relations of production, systems of signification, and relations of power' that fiercely competed with each other.[11] Marriage gave meaning to courthouses, playhouses, and domestic spaces, but these spaces also gave meaning to it as they became stages where marriage was performed and represented. In some cases, the condition of subjection of these stages was such that it led to their temporary or permanent demise, as was the case of the closing of theatres, the disappearance of a wife, or the defeat of a tribunal under the power play of another tribunal. The subject stages that emerge from this second semantic field of my title take place in two referential levels: one, the material but at once intangible written surface of marriage (bound by its dual dimension of 'letter and spirit') found in legal codes, bureaucratic documents, court protocols, or dramatic texts, which preserves the primal scenes, styles, and genres demanded in their production; and two, the physical spaces of the courts, the *tablas* (wooden platforms) of the *corrales* (public theatres, those other houses also known as *casas de comedias*), court theatres, and the *coliseos*. As Cascardi proposed, only with the critical tools of interpellation can readers today understand the contradictions of early modern Spanish cultural production.

The two interactive dimensions of subjectivity considered in this book – subject positions and the frequently subjected stages where such positioning took place – will contribute to a better understanding of the fractured mimesis of hegemony and resistance in marriage, theatre, and the law.[12] These scenarios represent legal dicta, ideas, and conflicts with ingenious articulations of voice, set designs, machinery, fabric, gestures, music, and other elements of the language of theatre. The subject stages that these chapters analyse take place in four corresponding generic environments: first, the drama of honour, in which honour blinds the husband, who fails to read the character of his wife and, hence, executes her. Second, the *comedia palatina*, which represents the dramatic conflict faced when men and women belonging to different social hierarchies desire each other, thus jeopardizing blood purity. Third, the *comedia de capa y espada* (cape and dagger play), in which the identity of the *galán* (lead male character and actor) is so confused that the text also passes for a *comedia de enredos*, in which the comic confusion takes over and the stage seems to spin to no end; the cause for the confusion in this environment is none other than a smashing *mujer varonil*, a masculine/manly/virile woman who, breeched to kill, occupies the physical and symbolic space designated for a man in order to restore her shattered honour. To conclude, I consider the *entremés* or theatrical interlude, where gender regulations were somewhat relaxed. As a whole, these six chapters and the coda give readers a comprehensive vision of theatre and law as locations of culture that fostered a reception of marriage that was not as strict, orthodox, or homogeneous as the Law prescribed and desired.

Chapter 1, 'Marital Law and Order in Early Modern Spain,' and chapter 2, 'Marriage Scenes in the Archives,' consider two significant aspects of the correspondence of law and theatre, as represented in marital definitions registered in legislative texts (both codes of law and dictionaries) as well as litigation documents. Legislative codes and dictionaries sought to control subjects with words of virtual finality, binding, and irrevocability, while the formulas of bureaucracy, litigation arguments, and theatrical language became stages for other subject positions, thus opening up new questions about such processes. In making legal theory an applied event (or reality) law became critically interrelated with theatre in representing marriage – by borrowing plotlines, styles, elements of audiovisual language, and systems of theory, logic, and rhetoric that traditionally had pertained to theatre. Towering above all other voices in marriage, the king's authority voice established marital law and order in his lands, hidden behind the rhetorical constructs of the Law; after him, and at times against him, fathers made many a scene about bloodlines, successors, and transcendence, even if their anxieties threatened the crown or historical change. In other archives, men and women walked right into the arms of mind-numbing bureaucracy to play fantasies of marital order, and fathers played mother to rescue the honour of a daughter, a neighbour, or a minor.

This correspondence is further illustrated in the literal arena of theatre in chapter 3, 'The Birth of the *Comedia* and the Bride Onstage.' During the second half of the sixteenth century theatre constructed a mirror of uncanny intersubjective possibilities into which both the crown and its subjects were bound to look. The chapter analyses the subject stages represented in the symbolic, political, and aesthetic correspondences of the landmark legislative marriage regulations in Spain seen in the previous chapters. To do this, it focuses on a 1570 monumental stage production performed in Burgos by a professional troupe, which lies at the heart of the political theatrics of the monarchy. This event illustrates the central argument of this book because in reading about the production of this primitive *comedia* readers can navigate the referential maze of marriage in Spain, seeing more clearly how theatre and the law joined in ways further explored in the remaining chapters of this book.

Chapter 4, 'Foundational Violence and the Drama of Honour' explores how honour and its high drama became a theatrical convention defined by a conflict between husband and wife that sprang from the male's suspicion that the female had committed adultery. In *El médico de su honra* (The Surgeon of His Dishonour) by Pedro Calderón de la Barca, the conflict intensifies as the wife is not able to dissipate her husband's doubts, and the play ends inevitably with her death, performed literally in execution style. The *casos de la honra* (honour cases) grew to be extremely popular as audiences and critics relished the suspense of the plot and the spectacle of punishment in the courts and in society. But the *dramas de honor* (honour dramas) like *El médico* were discussed much more frequently as dramatic literature than as theatrical pieces, a critical blind spot of this drama. This chapter considers this piece as law and theatre, and examines the wife's face eerily covered in taffeta as an emblem of the woman suspended in the point of tragedy, between life and death. The reading gaze moves away from the wife's impotence and execution, and instead focuses on her lively performance of the law as litigation. The soon-to-be-dead wife deploys her litigious discourse as a tool to resist the mooring of the 'mysterious' union of man and woman, and see subject stages other than the ones demanded by this drama of marriage as a primal scene of human violence.

Chapter 5, 'Punishing Illicit Desire,' interrogates the theatrical convention of the *comedia palatina* (palatine play), which represents the legal and theatrical potential harboured by the illicit desire between a nobleman and a woman of lesser social value. Onstage, the conflict was always resolved by finding a legal way to make her his wife. However, ideologies and the legislation of *limpieza de sangre* (blood purity) severely limited the capacity of a subject to engage in marital negotiations with another subject from a lower social stratum. This was especially so if the subject in question was a female in charge of the management of a wealthy estate. *El perro del hortelano* (The Dog in the Manger) by Félix Lope de Vega stages the case of a countess who engages in sadomasochistic desire toward her secretary (who, in turn, responds to her with ample masochistic gestures). With this marriage scene, Lope subverts the generic frame of the *palatina* by underscoring the relentless attraction that brings together the lady and her secretary, which by virtue of his unclean blood constituted an illicit desire. To compose such a scene, *El perro* deploys a sequence of multiple slaps to the secretary's face that correspond symbolically to the work of a set machine called the *bofetón* (about-face machine) by provoking a public spill of 'unclean' blood from the secretary's body, which he proceeds to wipe up with a *lienzo* (handkerchief, canvas) that plays tricks with the audiences' minds. The subject stage of this chapter shows troubling genealogies and masochistic desires that turned public theatres into the magical locus of production of libidinal economies and redefined marital negotiations of property, propriety, and desire.

In chapter 6, 'Woman in Breeches,' readers explore the potentially fatal attraction that the illicit figure of a woman onstage wearing breeches exercised over audiences. In the public and courtly theatres of Spain the ultimate crowd pleaser of the *Comedia* was this *mujer varonil*, a manly woman who sought to restore her lost honour as she entertained audiences with the forbidden pleasure of showing the legs of the actress in public – an act persecuted by *moralistas* (moral arbiters) and banned by marital legislation and sumptuary laws. This chapter explores the rhetorical prowess of the subject stage represented by the woman in breeches, performed in *Don Gil de las calzas verdes* (Don Gil of the Green Breeches) written by Gabriel Téllez (Tirso de Molina) by a character who capitalizes on the spectators' desires to engage in a radical critique of marital laws and economics. The sight of the woman in breeches is even more uncanny when seen in the context of the historical evidence of women who petitioned and were granted knightly habits by the military orders, which gave them access to privileges commonly understood to be for men only. By offering readers historical, symbolic, and economic implications of sumptuary laws and practices this chapter revises one of the most popular, and at the same time, least understood characters of the *Comedia* who also contributed decisively – against the odds of the marital prescriptions of woman/wife – to further the development of the institution of marriage in Spain.

The coda, with the title of 'The Musical Chairs of Divorce,' analyses the kaleidoscopic image of divorce and music staged in the format of the *entremés* (hors d'oeuvre), loosely translated as 'interlude.' These short pieces represented the stage of bawdy dramatic representation where music, dance, foul language, desire, and sexual innuendo were unabashedly shown, staging a melting pot of transgressions of the clearly defined boundaries of marital legislation. This chapter reads *El entremés del juez de los divorcios* (Interlude of the Judge of Divorces) by Miguel de Cervantes Saavedra, whose farcical characters publicized desire and no-nonsense lack of concern with reproduction, thus representing subject stages different from the prescriptions published by the Law. The coda imagines a production of this *entremés* that capitalizes on the immense potential of the *fachada* (back stage wall) of the public theatres, imagining it as a tic-tac-toe game board, or perhaps a game of musical chairs that plays with the inaccessibility of divorce, thus inviting audiences to turn their toiling into toying and dancing with the music.

This modest sample does not represent an exhaustive catalogue of subject stages from this time and place, and as such, it is not a historical treatise of marriage, theatre, or the law. It does, however, open the door for readers to see, with Cascardi, 'beyond Castro and Maravall' and to explore new readings, sounds, and vistas of the matrimonial, legal, and theatrical worlds of early modern Spain. With these subjects and stages I invite readers to appreciate the complex circulation of marital signs in the literal and figurative halls of home, theatre, and justice. Thus, in the segment of the book where court documents are examined

– such as the bureaucratic emblems of the *facultades de mayorazgo* or petitions for a licence to found an estate or entailed property ('in front of me, the scribe') – *Subject Stages* asks readers to think about the production of a voice, a body on a stage, the making of a scene, or the unfolding of a character, all of which are key units of the audiovisual language of the theatre. Likewise, when dealing with the most consummate theatrical character – the above-mentioned transvestite who, with the design, production, and wearing of her costume created a third space that threw off balance economic, cultural, and political formulas of matrimony – this book invites readers to think about sumptuary laws and the laws governing the separation of 'man' from 'woman' in the space of theatres and in society.

Subject Stages sees otherwise the formation, deformation, and lack of formation of this primal scene of marriage, 'the couple,' and in their stead it discovers glimpses of the discrepancies and contradictions that reproduction, marital violence, masochism, queers, or divorce represent in the context of the hegemonic marital scripts of the Tametsi or the *Nueva Recopilación*, a highly evolved stage of the cantankerous predicament staged by Menander. Marriage, then, becomes the site for subjects to adopt different sexual and social positions, occupying the rhetorical stiff mould of the Law with voices that significantly break with that part of the Law that seeks to contain them, especially women. In litigation, subjects restage the newly prescribed mooring and irrevocability of marriage by performing acts of disputation, claims, suits, and other scenes of argumentation; the legal conducts will yield scenes of divorce, rape, deflowering, ownership of an estate, dishonouring, interfaith weddings, extramarital intercourse and affairs, and assault, which find uncanny resonances in scenes produced in the playhouses. The hegemonic sex-and-gender roles prescribed for a subject to be a man *or* a woman will be transformed, by the power of theatre and the law, into subjects engaging in adultery, sodomy, transvestite moves, and a variety of parental and kinship manners.

On the page of the script and in the playhouses, the designated spaces for drama and theatre, the interactive powers of theatre and the law will again make marriage morph into styles and genres as varied as comedy, *comedia palatina* (palatine comedy), *drama de honor* (honour drama), tragedy, interludes, and other artistic forms that will give marriage a topsy-turvy look. And lastly, along with the existential and spiritual plenitude promised to those entering the holy state of matrimony and its contractual bliss, readers will find a world of difference:

masochism, love, fear, desire, joy, despair and always, playfulness. 'Ceci n'est pas un mariage,' as Magritte said about the pipe in his 1928–9 painting *La trahison des images* (*The Treachery of Images*). To turn the interpretive screw once more, this book challenges readers to reconsider uncanny referential platforms such as the reality of theatre or the fictions of the law. Above all, the archaeology of knowledge that this book digs out of historical and literary palimpsests insists on the ludic dimensions of reading and writing, and on the games people can play with marriage, theatre, and the law. The choice of these textual platforms (historical, legal, dramatic, theatrical) as surfaces of participation and recreation intends to move the critical lens between the house, the playhouse, the courthouse, and the predecessor to that most political of houses, the future house of representatives of the modern state.

1 Marital Law and Order in Early Modern Spain

> On a simple reading, Christian liturgy is a poetry of citation. Its poetic effects depend on the broader range of effects in canonical Christian scriptures ... In short, liturgical texts – not to say, liturgical events – claim to multiply the possibilities of human language as they bend time.
> Mark Jordan, 'Arguing Liturgical Genealogies,' *Authorizing Marriage*

The transformation of the pair man-woman into the juridical and theatrical *personae* of husband-wife moved centre stage in sixteenth-century Spain. The strict defining lines of the Law reproduced the roles of these two subjects united in a transcendental, irrevocable relation of inequality. At the same time, some Laws were interpreted and applied ingeniously, and this paved the way for a flexible and diverse reproduction of husband, wife, and their affairs. Among many possible scenarios of marriage, this chapter considers three stages in which theatre and the law productively converged. We begin with the definition of marriage established by Sebastián de Covarrubias, arbiter of linguistic elegance, who juggled the authority of patristic discourse with semantic games, ultimately reinstating the transcendental characterization of marriage as a patrilineal affair. Then we will examine how early modern regulatory fictions of marriage staged a desire to sustain the figures of man and woman as the only subjects capable of entering the irrevocable, transcendent affair of the sacrament and legal contract of marriage. Finally we analyse the premises that guided the application of legal codes to the practice of law, an entanglement of legislative documents, lawsuits, litigants, and tribunals aptly termed a 'Cretan labyrinth' by such scholars as I.A.A. Thompson and Richard Kagan. Paradoxically, this intricate legal network was the basis not only for a structure of privileges granting power and wealth to those who worked within the system but also for a venue of disparate encounters that fostered the possibility of various interpretations of marriage Law.

The Marriage of Forking Tongues

A panoramic view of the legal evolution of marriage is economically summarized by Sebastián de Covarrubias Orozco, author of the 1610 *Tesoro de la lengua castellana o española* (Thesaurus of the Castilian or Spanish Language). Covarrubias opens his characterization of the Spanish word *matrimonio* (matrimony) with what, according to him was the 'most common' meaning for marriage at the time: 'Matrimonium est maris et feminae coniugatio, continens individuam vitae societatem' (Matrimony is the union of male and female, involving the habitual intercourse of daily life) (742). The opening sentence for 'marriage' in this treasure of *lengua castellana o española* transports readers to another primal scene in the evolution of marriage, a capital text in the legal history of this institution – the already cited *Institutes* or the *Elements* of Justinian – which, in a short chapter entitled 'De Patria Potestate' (Of Paternal Power), wrote into law the premise of power as a patrilinear affair.[1] Notoriously, Covarrubias does not cite the following *Institutes* chapter 'Title X: Of Marriage,' the longer section devoted precisely to the legal definition of the marital contract, in which Justinian's *Institutes* legalized marriage as a family affair ultimately ruled by 'natural reason':

> Roman citizens are joined together in lawful wedlock when they are united according to law, the man having reached years of puberty, and the woman being of a marriageable age, whether they be independent or dependent: provided that, in the latter case, they must have the consent of the parents in whose power they respectively are, the necessity of which, and even of its being given before marriage takes place, is recognized no less by natural reason than by law. (*Institutes* 13)[2]

The *Tesoro* chooses to leave the words borrowed from Roman Justinian Law in anonymous form and in stark contrast with the remaining sources deployed by its author to complete the ancient legal definition from the textbook of the Justinian *Institutes* – a logical choice, given that the institutionalization of matrimony in early modern Spain was equally, if not more, driven by ecclesiastical rules and regulations than by

Roman Justinian Law. Thereafter, the *Tesoro*'s own definition moves to the semantic field of marriage most common at the time, liturgy, or as Jordan aptly describes it, the poetry of citation. Covarrubias adds to the pagan, Roman legal frame of the *Corpus* the definitions coined in Christian terms by Duns Scotus, Augustine of Hippo, and Peter Paludens, thus engaging the realm of Canon Law, which, with the *Corpus*, informed the first central legal code of Iberia, the *Siete Partidas* (Seven-Part Code). With that textual strategy, the *Tesoro* inscribes the authority of these voices to reiterate the male/female union-as-quotidian-intercourse. Erudite, thorough, and with great poetic charm, as is characteristic of the entire *Tesoro*, Covarrubias fuses pagan and ecclesiastical sources to define marriage, leaving readers with images sacred and profane of a most meaningful human bond designated to incorporate two subjects in the exercise of bodily power, procreation, child rearing, and male hegemony.

The *Tesoro* expands the marital agents and actions it cites from the Roman legal code with a quote from the 27th *Distinctio* of Johannes Duns Scotus which defines the *coniugatio* (union) from the pagan text as a 'vinculum indissolubile' (indissoluble bond).[3] With this second quote, Covarrubias characterizes the thirteenth-century Franciscan theologian's changing of the ancient Roman 'habitual intercourse of daily life' into a 'mutua translatione potestatis corporum suorum se invicem facta ad procreadam prolem debite educandam' (mutual transfer of the power of their bodies, which is in turn to be done because they both owe an education to the children they procreated) (742).[4] The eleven fleeting lines in Latin with which Covarrubias fuses Justinian and Scotus capture the spirit of the protracted negotiations that unfolded through the centuries between authorities on Roman and Canon Law who sought to control the institution of marriage, one of the most complex lines of European history.[5] After inscribing the letter and spirit of marital law, the *Tesoro* strategically switches into Spanish to venture into the realm of linguistic history, telling his readers that the word *matrimonio* originated with the word *mater* (mother), 'porque está a cargo de la mujer el criar los hijos, desde que nacen hasta que tienen edad para poder ser disciplinados de su padre' (for it is the charge of woman to rear the children, from their birth until they are of age to be disciplined by their father) (742).

At this point, the *Tesoro* deploys a poetic structural parallel: Covarrubias's citation of the Roman pagan code is authorized by the use of patristic sources, and his own pagan use of the vernacular is authorized with a third Latin premise also dictated in the thirteenth century, this time by the words of Petrus Palude, the Dominican theologian from Savoy. In the Palude definition, quoted by Covarrubias, the Roman *femina* (female) is labelled with a different term, *uxor*, a female subject tentatively owned by her master: 'Et licet pater generationes sit auctor et pene uxoris dominus, tamem matrimonium, plus adscribitur matri, quam patri, quia eius officium plus apparet in matrimonio, quam officium viri' (And it is allowed that the father of the offspring be author and almost the lord of the woman, but marriage refers more to the mother than to the father, whereas her duty is more apparent in matrimony than the duty of man) (742).[6] The rhetorical gesture with which Palude seemingly empowers women is carefully organized with words of virtuality, such as 'it is allowed,' 'almost the lord,' and by the fact that the moral obligation of the woman toward the children is said to be 'more apparent' than the husband's.[7] The *Tesoro* clearly delineates the boundaries of this term, exercising a poignant delegation of authority, as the definition remains strategically contained by the parameters of patristic discourse despite Covarrubias's adventures in the linguistic and poetic realms.

This delegation of authority to patristic sources reflects the powerful rhetoric with which the Law defined marriage as an institution. In religious terms, the sixteenth century Christian liturgy, and especially the sacrament of marriage, experienced a seismic change in Europe, marking a crucial episode in the history of people's engagement of worship and public rites of celebration and prayer. This episode of ecclesiastical history was intimately connected to the development of marriage Law in early modern Spain. As Spain entered its early stages of modernity the Law froze the language of marriage in time; this is clearly staged in Covarrubias's *Tesoro*. With that, the religious component of marriage took a monumental step in foreclosing some of its other greatest possibilities – most particularly its capacity to celebrate embodiment in ways other than the remembrance of the allegorical union between Christ and his church, which matrimonial law came to interpret so economically for the crown's imperial agenda.

This chapter opens with a note about the uncanny parallels between liturgy (a core concept of Jordan's book on 'authorizing marriage'), language (as Covarrubias uses it), theatre, and the Law. These areas of spiritual, artistic, and social representation became locations of culture where subjects positioned themselves to engage canon, tradition, and critique to compose political and poetic effects of marriage. To borrow

Jordan's words again, liturgy, like language, theatre, and the Law, operates 'to multiply the possibilities of human language as they bend time' (107). The quick-and-thick linguistic palimpsest that Covarrubias wove around the concept of marriage likewise plunged into the realm of origins, traditions, transmission, and remembrance, making sure that the legal and ecclesiastical authorities occupy the place they deserve: 'Esto se ha dicho en razón de la etimología; lo demás se podrá ver en sus propios lugares' (This is what has been regarding etymology; the rest shall be seen in its own places) (742). As the following pages show, despite the clear boundaries erected by the Law, subjects composed a variety of stages in which they congregated in rituals, celebrations, and ceremonies of marriage in early modern Spain.

Law's Foundational Fictions

> Law is a crude and limited device and is circumscribed by the dominant ideologies of the society in which it is produced. Existing beliefs and assumptions shape knowledge and understandings including those about law and law reform. Therefore law reform cannot, in and of itself, be effective as a catalyst for more generalized reforms. The significance of dominant ideologies in this process on the shape and content of law and legal process makes the idea of 'progress' problematic.
>
> Martha Albertson Fineman, *The Neutered Mother*

The application of the Law, a 'crude and limited device,' as Fineman calls it, always necessitates interpretation. That step, in turn, usually encounters the difficult negotiation of what Justinian's *Institutes* separated as 'civil' and 'common' Law, necessary to rewrite the Law according to the time and place in which it is to be applied.[8] The predicament of the Law seems to be always a matter of revision and compilation. Facing overwhelming confusion about what constituted legal grounds in theory and practice under his jurisdiction, King Felipe II – much like Justinian ten centuries before him – convened several commissions through a number of years to collect, organize, and categorize laws to create a central, singular document of the Law.[9] The royal edict that authorizes the 1569 *Nueva Recopilación*, the preeminent legal code resulting from this compiling effort, says the following:

> Know that, due to the many, and diverse, laws, Edicts, orders, parliamentary chapters, and agreed writs, that We, and our ancestors the Kings of

these Kingdoms have done, and to the change, and variety that has surrounded them, correcting, emending, adding, altering their text which,
according to the difference in times, and the unfolding of the cases it seems
to have corrected, changed, and altered: and because at the same time
some of the said laws, whether because they were taken out of their ori-
ginals in ill fashion, or because of the corruption, and error of the impres-
sions, they are lacking, and diminished, and their lettering corrupt, and
wrongfully emended. And moreover in the interpretation of some others
of the said laws, doubt has emerged, and difficulties, because their words
shift with time: and because it seemed that they contradicted some others,
and that likewise some of the said laws, whichever way they are, and were
clear, and that at the time in which they were made, and published, they
seemed just, and convenient, experience has shown, that neither they can
nor should be executed; and that moreover the said laws have been, and
are divided, and scattered in various books, and volumes, and some of
them neither printed, nor incorporated in other laws, and they have neither authority nor order that is necessary, from whence confusion has been
caused, and continues to be caused, as well as perplexity, and the judges
that by them have to judge have experienced doubt and difficulty, and
contrary opinions. (*Nueva Recopiliación* Lib I, 'Ley, y Prematica que declara
la Avtoridad que han de tener las leyes deste libro' [Vol. 1, Law, and Edict
that Declares the Authority that the Laws of This Book Must Have])[10]

The need to achieve justice and, with that, to have law and order reign
in his territories drove King Felipe II, like Justinian and others before
him, to establish Law's foundational fictions: 'so that by them justice is
done, and administered, and that the good, and the just are instructed,
and ordered, and that the bad, and illicit is forbidden, and banned, and
that such is the rule and measure of all: to the good ones, so they keep,
and follow them, and to the bad ones, so they refrain and moderate
themselves' (ibid., 'Ley, y Prematica' fol. 1).[11]

Kagan correctly says that the history of *pleitos* (lawsuits) in early
modern Spain must begin with the *Siete Partidas* published in the thirteenth century as 'a mixture of procedures borrowed from Roman law
and others adapted from the usage of ecclesiastical courts' (21). In the
first decade of the sixteenth century, two secular legal compendia were
promulgated, one in Toledo with eighty laws (many of them regarding
estate property) and another in Toro, with eighty-two laws that constituted the basis for commentaries by prominent *letrados* (lettered men)
such as Antonio Gómez and Gregorio López, among others.[12] The *Nueva*

Recopilación named the *Partidas* as its primary source; other codes, such as the sixth-century Visigoth *Fuero Juzgo* (Code of Laws), the 1485 *Ordenanzas Reales de Castilla* by Alfonso Díaz de Montalvo, and the 1505 *Leyes de Toro*, informed the *Nueva Recopilación*. Even so, the legacy of the *Partidas* as the cultural grounds in which Iberia first had an encompassing legal code is articulated as a central voice of authority in the constitution of the Law, which spans four books and almost 400 folios. Title 1 of Book 2, 'De las leyes' (On Laws), says of the *Partidas* that they 'were extracted, and taken from the sayings of the holy Fathers, and from the laws, and sayings of many Wise men of Antiquity, and from the codes, and ancient costumes of Spain, so we consider them our laws' (*Nueva Recopilación* Lib 2, fol. 58).

The authoritative voices of 'the holy Fathers' and the 'Wise men of Antiquity' created a platform of legal culture that became a critical component of subjectivity's negotiation. As Antonio Domínguez Ortiz once said, belonging to a *clase privilegiada* (privileged social stratum) was a critical factor in the definition of the subject (*Las clases privilegiadas* 12). Adjudication of privilege was a virtually sacred bond with concrete implications in the legal capacity that men and women had to represent, both artistically and politically. This was a period characterized by the domination of Castilian's nobility and systematic inequality that, as Bartolomé Bennassar has demonstrated, was due to differences in privileges granted depending on the subject's material fortune, social condition, blood purity, and place of origin in the fractured geopolitical distribution of the peninsula (173–86).

The legitimacy of all Laws originated in the figure of the king, whose representatives occupied privileged positions and, unlike their powerful counterparts in the nobility, officially represented the royal persona of the king. For matters of government the king would convene the *Cortes*, an assembly of deputies from the eighteen cities holding the privilege of representation for requests, debates, and votes on taxes and other matters relevant for their constituents. Once the king made his decisions, as Bennassar illustrates, these were executed in orderly fashion: first, they were reproduced for all to know, with documents such as *cédulas*, *provisiones*, *pragmáticas*, and *ordenanzas*. Thereafter, they were upheld in the *Chancillerías* and *Audiencias*, or courts of appeals, the *corregimientos* (provincial courts), as well as *señoríos* (seigneurial lands) (59–60). The subjects who ran this complex Law-and-law state apparatus, Bennassar says, occupied a highly privileged position in society because they mediated the king's two bodies, by negotiating the mortal, earthly affairs and the ethereal, divinely invested powers of what came to be known as 'the mystical civil body' (40–1).

In this body, the *letrados* occupied a particularly privileged position, for as Diego Hurtado de Mendoza said in 1627, they became the keepers of 'the government of justice and public affairs' because they were 'middle people between the great ones and the little ones, without offending either group' (70). In the words of Jerónimo Castillo de Bobadilla's 1597 *Política de corregidores,* some of the *letrados* – like the mighty *corregidores* (constables, or royal city governors) – were associated with the work of a crown that finally brought peace to the land.[13] To be associated with the achievement of peace in Spain, a peace vehemently desired after eight centuries of relentless internal warfare in the name of religious and ethnic homogeneity, conferred upon the *letrados* the capacity to obtain a great degree of power – at least in theory.

This became a critical stage of negotiation between Law and law, which for Bennassar explains also the 'political importance of this category' (42). For *letrados,* marriage became a site of legal authorization of sexual unions and reproduction, and a way for them to write into law a defining sign of the Catholic Universal Monarchy. Nevertheless, the institutionalization of marriage yielded results less homogeneous than those stipulated by the Law.[14] Further research that cuts across ideological, methodological, and chronological lines, from its preliminary stages in the *Partidas* to its most recent instalments – such as the union of Príncipe Felipe with divorcé Letizia Ortiz – is necessary to fully understand the impact of such institutionalization.[15] Although *Subject Stages* does not encompass the full scope of such research, it takes one step in that direction by exploring ways in which legislation, litigation, and theatre intersected during the most forceful period of the constitution of marriage as a capital unit of government, culture, and society in Spain.[16] In the sixteenth century, Spain experienced a massive move to institutionalize marriage coinciding with, on the one hand, the loss of the *Sacro Imperio Romano-Germánico* (Holy Roman Empire) and, on the other, its growth as an imperial power competing with England.[17]

In publishing the Tridentine marital rules, the crown focused on a course of matrimonial reform that granted the Spanish monarchy the power of an ever-present male gaze closely related to the Inquisition's *panopticon,* declaring those subjects not abiding by its principles worthy of prosecution, eternal punishment, and excommunication.[18] Civil laws in the *Nueva Recopilación* begin with the same focus as the Trent legislation – the regulation and control of clandestine marriages, a crime severely punished by the Law:

> We order, that whomever was married, according to what the Church defines as a clandestine union, with a woman, that for that same act he, and those who were involved in it, and those who were the witnesses of such marriage, lose all their property and assets, and are subject to our *Cámara* (Royal Council) and *Fisco* (Treasury), and are exiled from these our Kingdoms, in which they cannot enter under penalty of death. (*Nueva Recopilación* Lib 5 Tit 1 Ley 1 'De los casamientos' [On marriages])

'Marriage Civil Law,' compiled in Book 5 of the *Nueva Recopilación*, was motivated mostly by the desire to regulate the material components of marriage: dowries, *arras* (wedding coin sets), and jewels; single and married women, and the licence they needed from their husbands; wills and their executors; *luto* (mourning); *mejoras de tercio y quinto* (meliorations of the third and fifth); *mayorazgos* (estates); inheritances and their distribution; profits between man and wife; donations; and sales, purchases and other redemptions, by means of patrimony or *abolengo* (ancestry) (Lib 5, titles 1–12).

Ecclesiastical law, on the other hand, written in the 24th Session of the Council of Trent held in 1563, was occupied with regulations pertaining to the doctrine of the sacrament of matrimony, twelve canons, and a decree of reformation for marriage, with ten chapters, respectively, on the form and protocols of the ceremony and contracting, spiritual relationship, public honesty, affinity arising from fornication, prohibited degrees, abductors, vagrants, concubinage, liberty of marriage, and the prohibition of solemn celebrations of marriage at certain given times of the year (*Canons and Decrees* 177–86). The legitimacy of marriage in early modern Spain was, in theory, divided, scattered, prone to confusion, and destined to be rewritten; but the deus ex machina of the king's voice arguing for one single legal code filled in the gap for this social contract, placing 'la Fè Catolica' and the Tametsi Decree centre stage in the *Nueva Recopilación*.[19] The subjects of law may have been different, but as foundational fictions, civil and ecclesiastical Law worked as one source of legitimacy in early modern Spain, a social contract that rested on the premise that the Spanish subject, as George Mariscal said, was essentially a *cristiano viejo*.[20]

Underscoring the overwhelming power that ecclesiastical Law had in the process of the institutionalization of marriage, Eukene Lacarra

Sanz proposes to consider two legislative events as the most significant for the study of marriage Law in the Iberian Peninsula – the 1215 Fourth Lateran Council and the 1563 Council of Trent:

> In the first council the Church made provisions concerning marriage as an ecclesiastical ceremony and attempted to identify by exterior signs all groups it considered dangerous to the Christian way of life, including prostitutes. The latter was especially important in Spain because the reception of the doctrine relative to clerical and lay mores and the intense pastoral activity that attempted to implement it signaled and defined the Catholic Counter-reformation. (xi)

The overlap, fusion, and confusion of Roman and Canon Law is a central issue in the study of marriage in Spain. As Marina Brownlee has argued, understanding cultural authority in early modern Spain begins with considering 'the context of the central (and centralized) government of sixteenth- and seventeenth-century Spain,' a side of the cultural authority firmly inscribed in the writings of the rhetorical powerhouses of the Law, 'in which myths of origin and legitimizing historiography play the crucial roles' (x). We have seen how Covarrubias negotiated the lack of authority of poetic and linguistic games with the historiography of marriage. Patristic discourse, in the end, was the source of legitimacy for the roles of husband and wife – a garden of forking tongues that informed the foundational fictions of marriage in the sixteenth century in Spain.

The inflexibility of these roles and what they represented for the institution of marriage is aptly described by Juan A. de Jorge García Reyes, who sees the official publication of the 1564 Royal Decree (affirming the Decree of Tametsi from the Council of Trent as law, which chapter 3 will analyse more closely) as inseparable from the establishment of the principle *cuius regio, eius religio* in the 1555 Peace of Augsburg. Thereafter, Civil Law came to define every European territory as a place of one religion – that of its regent. According to García Reyes, this double-take strategy translated into 'the consecration of the Catholic factor as exclusive in our nation, a consequence of our historical heritage and the need for religious unity as a means to consolidate the Monarchy born in the Modern Age. All things a-Catholic, then, will be illegal' (116). Subjects aligned with what García Reyes calls 'all things a-Catholic' were cast outside the Law and faced encounters with the law.[21]

This civil and ecclesiastical legal body found a highly effective supplement in what Emilia Navarro termed 'manual control' – a massive dissemination of fictions based on Law's marriage principles that sought to regulate gender and sexuality. The sixteenth century was, in fact, a period during which conduct handbooks became bestsellers, a vast archive of normative narratives about marriage, sex, and gender that remained for centuries in Spain's collective imaginary. As Navarro correctly points out, new economic practices during the Renaissance generated by the creation of an urban middle class were at the heart of this first literary boom and its relation to law: 'Within this context, it is easy to understand the necessity, the proliferation, and the power of the "how to" books of conduct, which added yet another layer to the regulatory fictions already extant, namely the legal, medical, and religious texts, and their prescriptive and proscriptive discourses' ('Manual Control' 18). A number of humanists granted a key role to Catholic marital politics. For instance, in the first quarter of the sixteenth century Juan Luis Vives dedicated his *Institutio foeminae christianae* (Instruction of the Christian Woman) to Catherine of Aragón, advising her on the preparation of her daughter Mary Tudor, the future queen of England, for Catholic marriage, a text that he complemented with the rules for the perfect husband, entitled *De Officio Mariti* (On the Duties of the Husband). Luis de León, on the other hand, wrote *La perfecta casada* (The Perfect Wife) after Trent, building a perfect container for the potentially unruly woman.[22] Undoubtedly the rhetorical collaboration of these two handbooks with the legislative texts contributed to their reaching canonic status in Spain's cultural and political history.

These and other conduct handbooks were ostensibly designed to discipline Woman for the betterment of society and pitted – to borrow Navarro's expression – the 'variety of rubrics' offered to gentlemen with an ideology of 'spatial and bodily boundaries' that brought women to social and existential stasis ('Manual Control' 18). For Mariscal, these politics of exclusion were crucial to the formation and preservation of the essentialized, unsubstantive, and reified national subject of the *cristiano viejo* mentioned above (23). However, these acts of exclusion in humanist texts were not performed in monolithic or homogeneous fashion. There are fundamental differences (of time, form, and content) that separate the ways in which Desiderius Erasmus, Juan Luis Vives, John Knox, Juan de Molina, Juan de Espinosa, and many others chose to represent marriage and spousal characters in their treatises. Despite these differences and the fact that they were significant enough to constitute a core point in the development of the great Schism, these regulatory fictions shared a categorical mandate about marriage, especially in their representation of the wife, an image of woman in submission that does not differ significantly from the way the law represented her transnationally. Only in the 'twisted plots and critical turns' – to borrow Matthew Stroud's apt words – of theatre and litigation does one find the roles of husband and wife differing from this standard-ized version, making the subjects who staged them represent acts of resistance and intervention that in their redefinition of the strict marital parameters forecast modern revisions of this institution, even when the law remained unchanged.

The works of Erasmus and Vives became landmarks in this mapping of the humanist marital training, and they both dedicated their respective *Institutii* on marriage to the still-married Catherine of Aragón, wife of Henry VIII of England. Vives's text of 1523 predicated at length the fun-damental mores for Woman to lead a Christian life. Woman's duty was to be prepared from cradle to altar for this job: to not read 'evil books,' to learn to write by copying the letters of the 'saint males,' to develop good domestic skills such as being silent when the husband punished her physically, and, above all, to stay away from public office, which could translate into a dishonour for Woman and her family, since Nature did not equip her for government. The text elicited highly contradictory read-ings: for example, although Marcel Bataillon considered this golden cage for Woman 'an environment of scrupulous purity' (*Erasmo* 633–4), Valerie Wayne has appropriately deconstructed this view and termed Vives's text a 'sad sentence' that hinders women's freedom and creative forces (21–2). However, the handbook was translated and read extensively throughout Europe and the Americas, becoming a capital reference book for four centuries of women's education.[23]

The essentialist constructs of the 'two sexes' in and outside of marriage, as Constance Jordan has noted, became textual strategies that during the Renaissance had highly problematic implications for women's political actions vis à vis their womanhood. Furthermore, as Navarro also demonstrates, these conduct handbooks – agreed upon among men to regulate Woman – diversified occupations for men in society while they 'underscored gender, and elided class' in their rep-resentation of Woman ('Manual Control' 19), an impossible crossroads for women. In the stages of drama, seventeenth-century audiences of the *Comedia* read this subject stage of the ruling wife in the text of *El Conde Partinuplés* by Ana Caro, in which the character of Rosaura of Constantinople, who successfully represented the absolute dominant role of empress, faces the threat of rebellion on the part of her people were she not to be married, and decides to postpone marriage until she can domesticate her future husband with magic tricks, cross-dressing, riddles, and a rewriting of the ancient myth of Psyche and Cupid.[24]

Marital litigation, with theatre, opened the door for subjects to resist the exclusionary ideologies of closure omnipresent in civil and ecclesiastical Law. As María José Muñoz García points out, the writers of the *82 Leyes de Toro* resolved the contradictions of the different sources that informed their text (the *Forum Iudicorum*, the local *Fueros*, the *Siete Partidas*, and the *Ordenanzas reales de Castilla*, for instance), interpreted them, and, at the same time, dictated new laws in Castile (91). But the relief from dominant ideologies that these laws afforded subjects in Spain, especially in issues pertaining to the new areas of legislation and to women's rights, was relative. For instance, the *Nueva Recopilación* (Lib 5, Tit 3, Leyes 54–61) regulated the relations between husband and wife, which as Muñoz García argues, limited 'married women's capacity for action' at such a fundamental level that she needed a 'licencia' (marital licence) without which she was not legally able to take any action that might have an impact upon the marital union (95–6).

Rhetorical claims of marriage Law sought to control very closely this area of cultural and political production, particularly the capacity and power that women and subjects other than the *cristiano viejo* had to perform their own versions of marriage on- and offstage. However, as Richard Pym says, such claims did not 'map unproblematically onto the complex topography of everyday life, or the immediate experience of Spaniards' (*Rhetoric* ix). Voices of scepticism, subversion, irony, and ultimately, a variety of experiences of resistance demonstrate, according to Pym, 'the extent to which these rhetorics and the ideology they helped to construct or underpin reflected, or, just as commonly, failed to reflect, the realities of social, economic, and cultural practice in early modern Spain' (*Rhetoric* ix).[25] Far from controlling and organizing the existence of all subjects, marriage Law translated into a sense of alienation evident in the application of the legal codes to the practice of law. The complete history of this litigation falls beyond the scope of this study, but the following pages will show how certain subjects and stages capitalized on the possibilities of theatre to develop effective tools to represent marriage in courthouses and playhouses.

Inside/Out of the Cretan Labyrinth

The process of formation of the Law as discourse and discipline during this period of Spain's cultural history was defined in no small part, as we have seen, by the close interaction between church and state, which dominated not only religious and political discourses, but other aspects of culture as well. As a result, theological reflection and Counter-Reformation dogma exercised great influence over the production of legal idioms, protocols, and discourses. As Francisco Tomás y Valiente ('Delincuentes y pecadores') and Bartolomé Clavero ('Delito y Pecado') have shown, even the legal definition of 'transgression' was often lost in the confusion between 'delito' (crime) and 'pecado' (sin). This lack of clarity signalled the permeability of the different discourses involved in the formation of Spanish culture, a factor terribly difficult to control by state and church – particularly in stages where any given subject's performance could redefine certain terms of political meaning and significance, as in theatre and litigation. As a result, legal theory and its application formed discrete, separate units, and as we shall see in the next chapter, litigation and theatre allowed subjects to speak in open dissent against marital Law, especially in areas where socio-economic control and regulation was a tangible issue.

Mary Elizabeth Perry describes a key point in the administration of law and order in Seville, which she calls 'the Great Babylon of Spain':

> Crime at this time was defined by a ruling alliance of the Crown, aristocracy, and Church. Royal ordinances regulated many local activities, from selling food to carrying weapons. Through the city government, aristocrats decided who should be allowed to beg and how prostitution could be legally practiced. The Church censored public performances and preached a morality that condemned adultery, homosexuality, and abortion. Officials who enforced the laws and punished offenders were named by the Crown, aristocracy, or Inquisition. (*Crime* 1)

Anyone seeking to play with these crimes, laws, and punishment had to navigate a host of institutional structures best studied by Kagan, who aptly cites Thompson in calling them 'a Cretan Labyrinth' (21–78).[26] A litigant's dramatic life (comic, but not funny at all) was characterized, according to Kagan's economical summary, by travelling between piles of briefs, testimonials, proofs sealed by a notary, ambiguities, and contradictions in the Law, with overlapping jurisdictions, inefficiency, bureaucracy, corruption, greed, and inordinate amounts of energy, money, and time that more often than not ended up being wasted (22). Different from the medieval dispute tradition, which allowed the judge to make a legal decision guided by his *albedrio* (will) and based on what he himself deemed right or wrong, proper or improper (*ex aequo et bono*), magistrates in the Castilian *pleito* (lawsuit) that Kagan examines were to strictly adhere to the Law (22). The point of such procedure, then, was not to determine what was right and proper or not, but to have the judge – 'subject to the higher authority of the law, which only the monarch, as the servant of God, could make' – establish which party was 'able to prove his case with arguments drawn from the law' (23). If the rhetoric of the Law was to be persuasive in absolute fashion, there would be no evidence for *Subject Stages*; and, as Kagan recognizes, 'knowledge of the law was therefore an essential ingredient in winning a lawsuit' (23).

As seen, Law was rhetorically strong, but as Kagan himself says, it was also 'so ambiguous, confused, and misleading that it did little to promote just and equitable decisions' (23). A separate royal *Cédula* published in 1564 declared the decisions from the Council of Trent to be Law in Spain, and the 'Ley, y Prematica' that opens the 1569 *Nueva Recopilación* called that legal code the law of the land. However, as Kagan notes, the structural disarray that characterized the compilation of the 1569 code, with the king's 'refusal to promulgate the *Recopilación* as law, which meant that laws not included in the collection were not abrogated,' created a state of chaos that led contemporaries to decry in virtually unanimous fashion 'the evils of allowing magistrates so much room to pick and choose what law to apply' (26). To that it must be added that there were special *fueros* (codes) that were invoked to seek exemption from royal jurisdiction for members of a particular community or group: thus, for instance, people from Vizcaya, clerics, students, soldiers, veterans, members of the military orders, inquisitors, and others formed what Kagan aptly observes was 'a web of jurisdictional refuges which many used to escape prosecution and to delay proceedings in the king's courts' (29–30).

The labyrinth of the Law found ample correspondence in the confusing maze of what Kagan terms 'its institutional analogue: an array of law courts and legal tribunals so bewildering that lawsuits regularly became lost in a confused jurisdictional morass' (32). Litigants used this confusion to their advantage whenever possible, a high legal drama that was seldom resolved and made this navigation an ocean of corruption. As Juan de Hevia Bolaños established in his *Curia philipica*, ecclesiastical courts were designed to see cases regarding 'orders, benefits, patronages, tithes (*diezmos*), first fruits, oblations, burials, marriages, and legitimations, as well as cases involving the sacraments, papal bulls, apostolic letters, and criminal charges against the clerics' (quoted in Kagan, 34).[27] But marriage travelled, subjects and stages in tow, through ecclesiastical and secular courts. Documents pertaining to payment and restitution of dowries, for instance, can be found in a variety of tribunals, and as Kagan notes, although ecclesiastical Law 'stipulated that such disputes belonged to the church, widows attempting to recover dowries from their husbands' estates generally sought secular justice. This particular conflict was never resolved; accordingly, many cases involving dowries flip-flopped between the two sets of courts' (34).

The confusion contributed to a proliferation of legal events and their unavoidable outcome, paperwork, which, Kagan observes, was aggravated by the 'corruption and greed of the court officials responsible for the copying and transcribing of legal documents' for which they collected fees and engaged in such fraudulent practices (38). These, Kagan notes, included but were not limited to charging by the page – which they filled with large lettering – acceptance of 'donations,' bribes, gifts, and other kinds of payments under the table, fake documents, false witnesses, appeals, recusations, imposed delays, turnover of magistrates, royal edicts of suspension of a trial, and the division of labour between *abogados* (advocates), *procuradores* (attorneys), and *solicitadores* (solicitors) that at once catapulted the cost of litigation and plunged its reputation to levels perceived to be those of state-sanctioned robbery (38–42).

It made perfect sense, then, that the privileged standing of *letrados* noted by Bennassar met a very different fate at the hand and pen of Francisco de Quevedo y Villegas, who brilliantly connected the dots of this labyrinthine legal landscape:

> If there were no *letrados*, there would be no arguments; and if there were no arguments, there would be no lawsuits; and if there were no lawsuits, there would be no attorneys; and if there were no attorneys, there would be no lies; and if there were no lies, there would be no crimes; and if there were no crimes, there would be no constables; and if there were no constables, there would be no prisons; and if there were no prisons, there would be no judges; and if there were no judges, there would be no favoritism; and if there was no favoritism, there would be no bribery. Look at this display of infernal vermin produced by a single, young graduate who pretends to have a beard and whose authority comes only from his lawyer's cap. (translation quoted in Kagan 73)

This satire against *letrados* and the legal system is, no doubt, deeply conservative in the ways in which it thrashes the new structures of privilege that were substituted for old nobilities.[28]

While Quevedo's burlesque sonnets – which I associate with this invective against the *letrados* in their pornographic dimension of questioning authority in radical fashion – could be read as a 'desire to restore the glory of feudal aristocracy' along the lines proposed by José Antonio Maravall, I concur with Barbara Simerka in reading them also as manifesting 'an embryonic stage of a new hegemony, one based upon economic rather than military success, or it may be polyphoned – relying on the reception of the (early) modern reader for its meaning' (179). As Kagan notes, Cervantes considered the *escribanos* (scribes) 'satraps of the pen,' parasites living off great power (like the provincial governors from the Old Persian etymology) and disloyalty (38). The way they abused the little power they had helped them profit from the new hegemony of economic success that Simerka proposes. Their penmanship and voices joined another group of subjects inside/out of the stages of the Cretan labyrinth: those composing the fictions in the bureaucratic and litigation archives, the subject stages of the next chapter.

2 Marriage Scenes in the Archives

As with language, culture offers to the individual a horizon of latent possibilities – a flexible and invisible cage in which he can exercise his own conditional liberty.

Carlo Ginzburg, *The Cheese and the Worms*

By 'fictional' I do not mean their feigned elements, but rather, using the other and broader sense of the root word *fingere*, their forming, shaping, and molding elements: the crafting of a narrative.

Natalie Zemon Davis, *Fiction in the Archives*

Between the years of 1588 and 1589 Doña Elvira Enriquez de Almansa y Borja, widow of Don Álvaro de Borja y Castro Marquis of Alcañices, faced a violent legal struggle to retain control over her persona and possessions. A certain Don Enrique Enrriquez and his brother Don Antonio bribed members of her family and servants to infiltrate the sanctity of her house, gradually penetrating her property and honourable home with the intent to force her to marry Don Enrique. Doña Elvira slapped Don Enrique with a lawsuit to stop the violation and deter the forced marriage. Her words of deposition offer us a glimpse into the case:

Ambos propusieron que V.S. diese un poder para que se dispensase el voto que tengo hecho de castidad, y que no importaua nada, porque si algun tiempo me diese gusto casarme, lo pudiese hacer: y riyendome dello como cosa de pasatiempo, todauía porfiauan que le auía de dar, y que no se auían de yr sin el. E dixo el dho don Enrique, ha de ser, V.S. le ha de otorgar, y no ha deauer otra cosa: y en estas platicas entro un escriuano,

ante el qual passo un poder que no tiene sustancia ninguna, con lo qual me
parecio que me podia despedir de sus importunidades: y el dia siguiente
por la mañana entro el dho don Antonio en mi aposento con mucha os-
sadia y me dixo, mucho deue V.S. a mi ermano porque la tiene mucho re-
specto, porque le dixo cierta cosa, y me respondio, esso no, porque he
miedo de enojarla; y tras el entro D. Enrique y me dixo, toda esta mañana
me ha estado persuadiendo mi hermano D. Antonio á que haga cierta
cosa, y yo dixe que no quería enojar á V.S. y el d. Antonio respondio, que
antes por aquel camino se auian de llevar las mugeres principales, porque
no auian de dar voces, y que ya auia dho que me ternia por las orejas; que
fueron cosas de que quede tan espantada y amedrentada, que no hay
palabras para encarecerlo: y en este mismo dia a la noche boluio aentrar el
dho d. Antonio en mi casa en tiempo que mis criados eran ydos á Zenar, y
el dho dEnrique su hermano quedaua atras, y me dio un papel que fir-
mase, que era cierta instrución de lo que se auia de pedir a Sa., diciendo
que el poder no valia nada sin aquel papel, presupponiendo que yo dedia
dispensacion del voto y tambien del parentesco para me casar con el dho
dEnrique: de lo qual me sobresalté de ueras, y lo resisti todo quanto me
fue posible. (*Sobre el violento casamiento*, CCPEC, Leg. 1604, Fol. 1)[1]

(They both proposed that Your Sanctity granted an exemption from my
chastity vow, which didn't really matter, because if at any time I wanted to
marry, I could do it: and hence, laughing at it as if it were pastime, they
still swore that you should grant it, and that they would not leave without
it. And the said Don Enrique said, perforce, Y.S. must grant it, nothing else
will do: and in these talks there was a scribe, in front of whom a power
passed without any particular substance, which made me feel that I could
say goodbye to all these importunities: and the next morning the said Don
Antonio had the audacity to enter my room and said to me, Y.S. is in great
debt with my brother because he respects you a great deal, because you
said certain things to him, and he responded, not that, because I fear to
upset you; and the said D. Enrique entered behind him and said to me,
this entire morning I have been persuading my brother D. Antonio to do
something, and I told him that I did not want to upset Y.S. and the D.
Antonio responded that noble women had to be guided to follow the right
path, because they were not supposed to scream, and that he had said that
he had me by the ears; all those things left me so horrified and intimidated
that there are no words to underscore that: and in that same night the said
d. Antonio entered my house again when my servants were out to dinner,
and the said dEnrique was left behind, and he gave me a paper to sign,

with instructions of what had to be asked of your Honour, saying that the
power was nul and void without that piece of paper, presupposing that I
was asking for dispensation from the vow and also from the bond of consanguinity to marry said dEnrique: which truly shocked me, and I resisted
all I could.)

The conscious, vocal protestation of a woman to the threatening words
and actions of two men, resisting, as she says, 'all I could' is a peculiar
sight in Spanish early modern history.

Her act of resistance reveals something else: a lady making a marriage
scene. Her performance, with plenty of props and high drama, voices
a subject otherwise expected to control her tongue and be in compliance of norms stipulated by Law since antiquity. This social drama is
perhaps the reason why voices like hers have not found meaningful
resonance until recently in Spain's cultural history. Although Doña
Elvira's marriage scene and position of privilege vastly differ from
Menocchio, the miller from Friuli whose cheese and worms inspired
Carlo Ginzburg to devise new ways to read the stories of subjects associated with popular culture, her word and persona are seemingly
unintelligible.[2] For she, like Menocchio, forged herself a cage. The fact
that these subjects related to dominant ideologies in contradictory or
difficult ways does not justify relegating them to places of awe or oblivion. Their voices need a particular reading guide to be heard across
time and space. As Marta Vicente and Luis Corteguera note, such was
the case with women in early modern Spain, for they negotiated authority and textuality with strategic deployments of language, femininity, subordination, obedience, role-modelling, madness, authorship,
collaboration, and performance in legal, political, and religious spheres
in ways that are poorly understood (1–15).

As Vicente and Corteguera add, performance was a critical tool for
women to negotiate such compliance and submission, which in marriage meant two very specific roles:

Women found opportunities to claim authority by invoking models that
may appear at first only to reinforce women's subordination to their male
relatives or authorities. For example, the ideals of the obedient wife and the
devoted mother did not necessarily divest women of all authority ... By
performing these two models of femininity and adapting them to their circumstances, women found certain forms of authority privately and publicly. Privately, the 'good wife' and mother could claim moral authority that

allowed her to have a say in the running of the household and the daily lives of its members. (3–4)

These performative roles, as Vicente and Corteguera point out, were not merely narrative devices, for women composed them with 'stage design, the actors' gestures, wardrobe and body language' (9). Moreover, as the following pages will reveal, women were not alone in this; men found themselves playing the role of a mother or a wife, usually to defend a woman in a particularly vulnerable position.

In court, as in her household, Doña Elvira played the roles of wife and mother. As the above quote also proves, she knew how to impersonate the authority voice of her husband who had passed away eight years before the date of the lawsuit. The death of Don Álvaro sixteen years after their wedding (1564–80) left Doña Elvira a considerable fortune and a great name. He was, after all, the descendent of Saint Francisco of Borja, cousin of Emperor Carlos V and Rodrigo de Borja – also known as Pope Alejandro VI and the father of the notorious Borgia progeny. As it was not uncommon in upper social echelons of early modern European societies, Doña Elvira was related to Don Álvaro, her uncle. Her marriage and subsequent widowhood left Doña Elvira in a privileged position to raise seven children, which she did until 1592 when she remarried – as she promised – not when forced but when she wished to do so.[3] Paradoxically, this same power was also her greatest liability because it placed her in a position – like Penelope in Homer's *Odyssey* – of having to fend off suitors who sought to occupy her husband's place.[4]

The scene from the case file *Sobre el violento casamiento* quoted above clearly shows the great theatrics of the case: bodies inside and outside the house; virginity, laughter, and screaming; dispensations and home invasions; a paper and a power; threats, compliance, and above all, resistance, comic resistance. One could argue that this was serious stuff, and that the theatricality of litigation is hard to read because that is the nature of historical legal records found in early modern Spanish archives. Moreover, as Renato Barahona says, this massive body of documentation is not consistent, it lacks uniformity, and files only rarely house the totality of documents from a case – from filing to verdict and sentencing (169–70). All that said, Barahona adds, even if discrete inquiries are not conclusive, such research helps 'advance our understanding of early moden customary engagements, matrimonies, and sexual practices' (xx). The written and unwritten legal codes seen in the previous chapter were translated into practice as marriage scenes; these are, in turn, present in Spanish archives that this chapter explores.

In order to more clearly define these scenes, the following pages will consider two different scenarios: bureaucracy and litigation. As we shall see, the first one – a forensic genre if there is one – imposed severe limitations on subjects' possibilites of representation of marriage.[5] Nothing funny should happen to anyone on the way to the bureaucratic forum; and yet, as we shall see, a few voices made themselves heard. The second stage is what I call spectacles of the law, a series of 'fiction in the archives'– to borrow Natalie Davis's words – formed, shaped, moulded, and crafted by means of performative language (*Fiction* 3). These laws' spectacles unfold in acts of litigation, in which the most openly theatrical rendition of the marital roles were performed and preserved in the archives by means of the way in which they related to objects and other subjects – called props, proxemics, and kinesics in theatre.

The Tall Order of Marital Bureaucracy

The incessant reiteration of marital formulas in bureaucratic documents made material the static collective imaginary of marriage stipulated by the Law. Documents pertaining to the execution of the estate of the Marquis of Valladares perfectly illustrate the relentless chorus of 'transaction, liquidation, adjustment, and settlement of the assets, estate, and miscellanea …' (*Transacción* D Gral Leg. 241 and D Gral Leg. 248). In the archives, the rex/deus ex machina appears as the monologic voice of the partilineal affair stipulated since Justinian's time, framing the subject stages of bureaucracy. The regulated union of man and woman for strict purposes of procreation, reiterated in the formulas voiced by the officers of the Law, was the principle upon which marital subjects were destined to share their lives in a prefabricated ideological house of marriage. This was stamped in the collective memory of Spaniards under the guise of bureaucratic forms with which they were to become acquainted, since the Law stipulated that they were bound to register their married personas with the pertinent authorities. Men and women were engaged in this system, collaborating with a fantasy of marital order interesting to read as much for its coherence and uniformity (unlike the messy litigation documents) as for its occasional contradictions and inconsistencies.

Two types of documents best exemplify the logic of bureaucracy that gradually inflicted the trauma of a muffled version of marriage on future generations: dominant husband, accessory wife, offspring. The first one is the *capitulación matrimonial* (prenuptial agreement), a contract stipulating a priori clauses of property, and conditions for cohabitation, child rearing, and other family issues relevant to the forthcoming marital union. The second one is the *facultad de mayorazgo* (licence to found an estate or entailed property). The *capitulaciones* represent a rhetorical and stylistic frame in which the identification of legal objects with/and subjects occupied the majority of the text – great proxemics, high drama. The dynamics between the contractual parties (church, state, man, woman) and the objects and processes in question (assets, liabilities, child rearing, custody, and so on) also offer valuable data for studying marital issues during this period. The semantic field of the verbs that define these contracts – *ayuntar* (join), *asentar* (settle), *concertar* (arrange), *tratar* (contract) – reveals the rigidity that characterizes the marital irrevocability stipulated by Law.

This rigidity permeates another genre, the *escrituras de censo* (census deeds) where formulaic expressions of marriage abound. Don Alonso Palacios and Catalina de Cantalapiedra, for instance, appear in one such deed making their marital union known, and including the licence given by Mr Palacios to Ms Cantalapiedra to 'ayuntar' (join) him (*Escrituras* D Rueda Leg. 114 Fol. 4). Fixed expressions such as 'Let it be known by this public deed,' 'town jurisdiction,' and 'with licence and expressed consent' legally authorized the state of marriage, validating its contractual nature (ibid.). In another *escritura* (deed), the marriage scene is clearly delineated as a tableau vivant in which every person fits a particular character: Don Juan Perez Asensio and Catalina Perez viuda de Alonso Poçero appeared 'in front of me, the scribe,' as witnesses (ibid.). The juridical personas of this case are named virtually as a cast of characters: along with their first and last names, they are identified as the scribe; the witnesses; the widow; the single lad and legitimate son; the legitimate daughter, and so on. Furthermore, proxemics plays a role in the making of the scene (alas, a more constrained one than those in the stages of litigation and theatre) as seen, for instance, in the formulaic expression 'in front of me, the scribe.' Kinesics is even more limited, although it could be argued that the expressions 'appeared as witnesses,' 'sustain the weights and obligations of matrimony,' and 'give and deliver' imply a certain kind of movement, as they are all verbs of action.

The documents related to the *mayorazgos* and their *facultades* reiterate this contractual marital mantra differently from the *capitulaciones* and *escrituras* because their language focuses on issues of foundation and origin, not on the division or distribution of assets. The *facultades* do not reveal positions of open resistance to the marital roles; in the *facultades* father still knows best. But the desire to perform such a paternal role oftentimes shows with a flair for drama that betrays a ghost in the fatherly subject's machine. The blind spot of this anxiety of origin becomes evident in the historical fate of the legal institution of *mayorazgo*, a contradictory subject in Spain's cultural history if there ever was one. On the one hand, these fathers sought to make their lineages transcend time, while on the other, such transcendence translated into a freezing of such time for Spain. For Antonio Domínguez Ortiz, the advantage of the *mayorazgo* was precisely its capacity to secure the title, production, or profit generated from the land, territory, or assets owned by the core members of the lineage, through generations forever after, for as long as such family remained intact, which he praises as the successful strategy of nobility to guarantee historical continuity (*Sociedad y Estado* 329).

Bartolomé Clavero, studying the *mayorazgo* as a juridical institution, argued instead that political and sociocultural pressures lead to the development of this feudal territorial property at the expense of economic advancement (*Mayorazgo* 408–14). Other scholars have driven this point home more forcefully, reasoning that the genealogical drive of the *mayorazgo* institution anchored Spain in a widely disseminated feudal system of socio-economic organization that can be tied to this country's falling off the economic and cultural development bandwagon of modernity. Jesús Cruz, for instance, says that although the *mayorazgo* lasted well into the nineteenth century, since the eighteenth century it 'often became more of an obstacle than a benefit to landowners' (101). By that time, David Ringrose says, 'despite the stultifying institutions of *mayorazgo, señorío jurisdiccional, manos muertas,* and *propios municipales,* a remarkable amount of land was already changing owners and modes of exploitation' (166).

The transcendence of this institution no doubt was related to the compulsive preoccupation in both the founders and the negotiators with the recognition and preservation of a founding moment, a palpable desire in the marriage scenes of the *mayorazgo* archives. The limiting and reiterative language of these *facultades* established a formulaic, stagnant marriage infrastructure that supplemented that of the *capitulaciones.*[6] This stands in open contrast with the supple envelopes enclosing the *mayorazgo* documents, of which the delightful *cuadernillo* with elegant calligraphy in sepia ink holding the *Título* (Title) of the *mayorazgo* de Vela de los Cobos is a great example (*Título* D Gral Leg. 157 No. 1). The introduction reflects the anxiety of the voice desiring to freeze time and lock meaning in the formula:

> Titulo al maiorazgo, que en el ultimo dia del mes de febrero del año pasado de mill quinientos sesenta y quattro fundaron los señores Dn. Francisco Vela de los Cobos, y Da. Catthalina Mexia, su muger en favor del Sor. Dn. Diego Vela de los Cobos su hijo, y sus suszesores. (*Título* D Gral Leg. 157 No. 1 fol. 1r)

> (Title of *mayorazgo* that in the last day of the month of February of the past year of 1564 Don Francisco Vela de los Cobos and Doña Cathalina Mexia, his wife, founded in favour of Don Diego Vela de los Cobos their son, and his succesors.)

Following this typical notarial formula the title proceeds to stage another formula, this time closer to the citational poetry of liturgy: marriage is the union of two subjects in the name of the Holy Trinity and the Virgin. The emblems of the ecclesiastical and political actors who were, by Law, allowed to stage the legal union of the church with the state inscribe the paternalistic family structure reiterated incessantly throughout the remaining of the *Título*. The family's *facultad* grants its subjects, the country, and the people related to them the prosperity needed to move into the future. At once, this segment of the *Título* expands exponentially the theatrical elements involved in the production of this record:

> En el nombre de Dios Padre, è Hixo, y Espirittu Santo tres personas, e una esencia Dios verdadero, Haze donde todas las cosas de quien todos los bienes prozeden, que bibe sin comienzo, ê Hina sin fin è dela gloriosissima virgen Santa Maria nuestra señora Madre de Dios, â lo qual suplicamos que lo contenido en esta Escriptura conserue … y conseruar los linages que vienen eporque las cosas, que esttan suxettas â dibision facilmentte se consumen, è diminuien, èporque de derecho natural, ê dibino, è posittibo se permitte, è puede fazer conbuena conciencia. (*Título* D Gral Leg. 157 No. 1 fol. 1r)

> (In the name of the Lord Father, and the Son, and the Holy Spirit, three persons and one essence, the true God makes all things from whence all goods proceed, who lives without beginning, and without end, and of the

very glorious Virgin Saint Mary our lady Mother of God, to all of whom we implore that what this deed contains they preserve … and to preserve future lineages, and because things that are subject to division are consumed easily, and diminish, and because natural Law, and divine Law, and positive Law all allow this, it can be done in good conscience.)

In the notarial speech of the *mayorazgo* marriage was performed forever after according to Catholic dogma, and the family's wealth was devoted to the service and defence of its 'kings and natural lords.' Bureaucracy sought on the one hand to preserve family members and their clean lineages and, on the other, to avert the destruction of those who live in division – that is to say, subjects outside the boundaries of marital legislation. At once, the mixing of juridical and theatrical personas in this scene of marriage is patent: the Holy Trinity and the Virgin Mary descend into a scene of imploration, integrity, clean lineages, township, brotherhood, and outcasts. As the *Título* progresses, the rhythmic lull of successors, lineages, and assets recedes to yield a different scene in which don Francisco Vela instructs his heirs to build churches in the *zaguanes* (front porch) of their various villas and to found and maintain the Santo Domingo hospital, charity house, and church with the wealth of his estate (*Título* D Gral Leg. 157 No. 1 fols 20v–7r).

The *mayorazgos* became an apt bureaucratic vehicle to preserve the marital prescription of patrilinear power from ancient Roman times. It is hardly a surprise, then, to see that as a rhetorical structure the language of the *facultades* placed male subjects as the personas capable of executing the holding, possession, and succession of the title and property of the estate.[7] Thus, for instance, when Don Diego Vela de los Cobos, son of Don Francisco Vela and Doña Cathalina, is granted the entrance to (possession of) the *mayorazgo*,

> ttodos los dias de vuesttra vida, ê despues de vos vuesttro hijo varon maior ligitimo, y no ligitimado salvo si no fuese por subsiguiente mattrimonio, y despues del su hijo y nietto, y visnietto varones ligittimos maiores de dias, y ansi de uno en ôttro de varon, en varon perpettuamentte para siempre jamas sin diferenca de quartta, ni quintta generacion, ni de ôttra alguna, ê àfalta de vuestros hijos varones legittimos, queremos, y es nuestra voluntad, que suzeda en estta dicha donacion è maiorazgo vuestra hija maior ligitima la qual goze del usofructo del dicho maiorazgo por sus dias, y en fin de ellos suzeda el hermano sigundo de vos el dicho Don Diego Vela nuesttro hijo si fuere vivo, è si no lo fuere susceda su hijo varon

maior lexitimo prefiriendo en este caso el tio maior, que fuere bivo ô su hijo varon maior a los hijos, ô hijas de la dicha su sobrina vuesttra hija, è nuesttra nietta porque la dicha vuesttra hija, que suscediere en estte maiorazgo por falta de varon, queremos que solamente sea usufructo-mania del dicho maiorazgo por sus dias nomas. (*Título* D Gral Leg. 157 No. 1 fols 15r–16v)

(every single day in your life, and after you, your oldest legitimate son, and not legitimated except for the subsequent matrimony, and after him his son and grandson, and great-grandson all legitimate males of legal age, and so forth and so on from one male to the other, in male perpetually forever and ever without difference of either fourth or fifth generation, or any other, and if there was a lack of legitimate male sons we want, and it is our will, that in this donation and *mayorazgo* our oldest legitimate daughter becomes the heir, who will then enjoy the usufruct of such said *mayorazgo* for the rest of her days, and at the end of them she is to be succeeded by the second brother of yours, the said Don Diego Vela our son, were he to be alive, and if not may his oldest legitimate male son, preferably in this case the oldest uncle who were alive, or his oldest male son, succeed the sons or daughters of the said his niece, your daughter, and our granddaughter because such said daughter of yours, who would be the heir to this *mayorazgo* if there is no male for it, we wish that she receives the usufruct of the *mayorazgo* for the remaining days of her life and not any longer.)

The frequency with which these narrative and performative voices re-iterated the desire that their *mayorazgo* transcended time was in full compliance with the patrilinearity stipulated by Law. At the same time, if the male subject in possession of a powerful *mayorazgo* was to marry the heir of another powerful *mayorazgo*, such union may pose a threat to royal interests. Hence, the foundation, holding, title, and possession of an estate had to be approved by the crown.

Having the king's authority voice appear in a bureaucratic document pertaining to a *mayorazgo* was a sine qua non to perpetuate compliance with the Law. Interestingly enough, though, some marriage scenes in the bureaucratic archive show the voice of the king or his representa-tive disrupting at least in appearance the homoerotic partilineal affair of family Law, offering instead an alternative genealogical scheme. Thus, for instance, the case of the *mayorazgo* belonging to Don Francisco Hernandez de Córdoba y Benavides, who received confirmation of his estate on June 1567 by virtue of a royal edict by King Felipe II (*Real*

Cédula D Gral Leg. 229 Caja 26 No. 19). After several folios listing the property of this *mayorazgo*, the king speaks in the first person about the transcendence of wealth, property, and legal conditions:

> E en tal manera que esta manda de bienes que yo alli hago de todas estas sobredichas heredades que nunca sean partidos ni se puedan partir ni uender ni enagenar sino que todavia sean juntas todas las dichas here-dades como dicho es y que la aya uno y uposde otro segun las condiciones sobredichas. (*Real Cédula* D Gral Leg. 229 Caja 26 No. 19 fol. 8v)

> (And this order of assets that I give about all the above said estates is given in such a way that such said estates must remain all together as said, and that one owns them, and thereafter another, according to the above said conditions.)

The narrative voice proceeds thereafter to alter the rule of patrilinearity in this *mayorazgo*:

> mando que lo aya y herede la fila mayor del dicho garci fernandez mi hijo y falleciendo la fila mayor del do garci fernandez sin auer filos legitimos mando que lo ayan las otras sus hermanas toda via que lo aya y herede la mayor segun y con las condiciones sobredichas. (*Real Cédula* D Gral Leg. 229 Caja 26 No. 19 fol. 8r)

> (I order that the older daughter of the said Garci Fernandez, my son, en-ters the state of possession and inherits it, and upon the death of the older daughter of the said Garci Fernandez without having given birth to legit-imate children I order that the other sisters enter the state of possession of it, in such a way that the oldest inherits it according to, and with the above said conditions.)

The entitlement of these women in this *mayorazgo*, as the rest of the *fac-ultad* explains, is quite literally the exception. As happened in the vast majority of *facultades*, the narrative voice provides an exhaustive list of potential succession scenarios, always favouring the male heirs first and then, as a last resort, the daughters. The case of Garci Fernández, no doubt, is an exception that proves the partilineal rule, for a daughter was a better body than nobody, which would leave a *mayorazgo* dismantled.

Besides the few instances in which a daughter was named the hold-er of a *mayorazgo* title, these documents also staged a few voices seek-ing to make marriage scenes. In the closing segment of that same 1567

Cédula (Royal Edict) confirming Don Franciso Hernández de Córdoba y Benavides's possession of the *mayorazgo*, the royal 'I' switches later to the 'I' of Doña María Alfonso, who initiates a lawsuit against the mayor, Martin Alfonso, 'sobre rrazon de los bienes y herencia de a mi me pertenecie auer de los dichos mis padres' (pertaining to some goods and inheritance that belonged to me from my said parents) (*Real Cédula* D Gral Leg. 229 Caja 26 No. 19 fol. 17v). These acts of memory turn the stiff narrative of the *mayorazgo* into a series of stages in which the juridical personas move and shift with the pronouns, thus creating a scenario reminiscent of a *comedia de enredo* (comedy of errors). The first persona of yet another narrative voice remembers the thick palimpsest of litigation that has already taken place over this *mayorazgo*:

> e otrosy yo el dicho fernan lopez queria otrosi mouer contravox el dicho alcalde martin alfonso y vos contrami algunos pleytos y questiones en Razon delos bienes de los dichos alcalde lope. gutierrez y doña ynes nuestros padres dexaron en la razon del su finamiento asi sobre los dichos bienes deque a vos fueron fechas las dichas mandas como por Razon de los otros bienes y herencias de los dichos nuestros padres y por mostrar nos todos los sobredichos doña maria alfonso y alfonso Fernandez y fernan lopez y ruylopez de los dichos pleytos y contiendas que entrenos auemos y pdriemos auer sobre todos los bienes y herencias de los dichos alcalde lope gutierrez y doña ynes nuestros padres y sobre los frutos y rentas dellos y sobre cada una codas de los dichos bienes ... (*Real Cédula* D Gral Leg. 229 Caja 26 No. 19 fols 17v–18r)

(Moreover, I, the said Fernan Lopez wanted to also begin some lawsuits and questioning against you the said Mayor Martin Alfonso, and you against me, with regard to the goods of the said Mayor Lope Gutierrez and Doña Inés, our parents, left us when they died. And so about the said goods, for which you received certain grants made by virtue of the other goods and inheritances of our said parents and to show all of us the above said Doña Maria Alfonso and Alfonso Fernandez and Fernan Lopez y Ruylopez of the said lawsuits and disputes that we have had between us and we could have pertaining to all the goods and inheritances of the said Mayor Lope Gutierrez and Doña Inés our parents, and over the profit and rents of those goods and over each coda of such goods.)

Bureaucratic documents reveal a few subjects whose 'flexible and invisible' cages, as Ginzburg said, allow them to tell the story of marriage differently from the formula prescribed by Law. However, it will be in the arena of litigation where this diversity of voices will make the strongest mark, which in turn corresponds more clearly with the representation of legality and marriage in the playhouses.

Spectacles of the Law

> Michael Fried's opposition between theatricality and absorption seems custom-made for this paradox about 'performativity': in its deconstructive sense performativity signals absorption; in the vicinity of the stage, however, the performative is the theatrical.
>
> Andrew Parker and Eve Sedgwick, *Performance and Performativity*

The clockwork bureaucratic machine of marriage constituted, as shown, a most efficient space of citation and bureaucratic poetics of marriage in early modern Spain. These documents developed a historical memory of patrilineage, gender disparities, and the static roles of wife and husband across the peninsula that, by virtue of its powerful citational rhythm, remained locked in archives designed to reproduce the domestication of subjects in the imperial frame. A different, if related, archive of the cultural history of marriage has recently been opened, one that Eukene Lacarra Sanz characterizes by the 'changing boundaries of licit and illicit unions [that] reflect the arbitrary definitions' that the Law imposed on marriage (187). The boundaries of sex and gender used by jurists in Spain to characterize concubinage and prostitution evolved since the latter Middle Ages as a moving legal cartography that elicited protest and argumentation from the voices of authority as well as sectors of the citizenry.

But one need not resort to cases of violation of the Law, such as prostitution and concubinage, to find resistance to the institution of marriage. Spain's archives hold ample evidence that there was substantial intervention to redefine the strictures of marriage as a space to domesticate subjects, especially women. The marital roles stipulated by the Law locked men and women in a game of inequality in which a dominant husband was expected to find a woman to play an accessory role as wife, a container where he would come to reproduce himself, his property, and his name.[8] Enter the subject stages of litigation, where men and women played with marriage and raised conflicting, sensuous voices that argued with, and interrogated, the presumed logic of the straight, paternalistic line of the written legal texts of the institution of marriage.[9] In the words of Parker and Sedgwick, in the vicinity of the stage, performativity, or the

Law, becomes the theatrical. These voices, pushing the tight bureaucratic envelope found in the Law and bureaucracy of marriage, created spectacles of law, events of performance and litigation that in creative ways staged the subject(s) of marriage otherwise.[10]

These spectacles, in comic complicity with legislation, bureaucracy, and theatre, show marriage to be a sacred legal institution that subjects engaged in to exercise various degrees of agency. By locating marriage in such an unstable position the producers of these marriage scenes debated, negotiated, and argued about marriage, underscoring the tailoring of its fabric and interpellating the mere idea of *prête a porter* husbands and wives.[11] In this highly theatrical process, subjects argued with the reality of marriage Law and favoured agency and pleasure as truth over the products and contradictions of compliance and submission. Developing a voice became a key issue for the actors who sought to interpret and apply the Law.[12] For Francisco Tomás y Valiente, this is part of the cultural life of the law:

> Las normas en las que el Derecho consiste no agotan su realidad en el momento lógico de su aparición, sino que cobran vida, o la prolongan y enriquecen, al ser interpretadas y aplicadas. La sociedad en cuyo seno han surgido unas normas jurídicas no acoge éstas pasivamente, sino que las corrige, amplía su significado o lo restringe, adopta ante ellas una actitud favorable o, por el contrario, tiende a rechazarlas, las entiende de un modo o de otro. (*Manual de Historia* 25)

> (Legal norms do not exhaust their reality in the logical moment of their appearance; instead, they come to a life prolonged and enriched by their being interpreted and applied. A society that has produced juridical norms does not receive them passively, but rather corrects them, amplifying or restricting their meaning, adopting a favourable attitude with respect to them or, on the contrary, it could tend to reject them, to understand them in one way or the other.)

I use the word 'entiende' following Tomás y Valiente, as an understanding of marital law different ('de un modo o de otro') from the formula of the pair husband-and-wife as a mirror of the union of Christ and *his* church; my understanding – lost in translation – adds to Tomás y Valiente's 'difference' the dimension of queerness, which will be further explored in chapter 3.[13] Such, as I see it, was the role of marital legal theatrics in early modern Spain.

The subject stages of litigation gradually broadened the scope of theatrical language and discourse engaged in the courts. Some of the props, like the power and the letter seen above in the case of Doña Elvira, varied in size and proportion. In a letter from Cardinal Manrique, archbishop of Seville, to Empress Isabel of Portugal, a deus ex machina hung over 'el pleito matrimonial' (the matrimonial lawsuit) between Duchess Doña Ana de Aragón and Don Alfonso Pérez de Guzmán when the cardinal overruled the request for being 'cosas santas' (saintly issues) (*Carta* CCD Leg. 39 Fol. 39). Dowry assets, naturally, became a great prop in marital litigation, as shown in the 1544 lawsuit between Doña Beatriz de Figueroa, Doña Maria Manrique, duchess of Terranova, and Doña Leonor Manrique against Don Garcia Hernandez Manrique, Count of Osorio; the character flaws of Mr Garcia make him lose all dowries and 'frutos y rentas' (earnings and rents), for which he was ordered to observe 'perpetuo silencio' (eternal silence) with regard to the said Doña Beatriz, her daughters and heirs (*Sentencia en el pleito ... 1544* CCD Leg. 39 fol. 45 Fol. 1). A 1552 dispute between the Osorio and Alba de Liste families shows two entire townships constituted as a monumental prop in their legal drama of matrimony (*Escritura de concierto* CCD Leg. 39 Fol. 46 fol. 1). At times, the *mayorazgos* were used as props for acts of litigation, as in the 1580 case of Arias Gonzalo de Avila, Juan Arias de Avila, his son Don Pedro Arias de Avila, Don Antonio Arias de la Cerda, and Don Juan Arias de Puertocarrero, Count of Puñonrostro, 'sobre posesión de bienes del Mayorazgo de este nombre' (over possession of assets belonging to the Estate of that name) (*Sentencia en el pleito ... 1580* CCD Leg. 39 Fol. 48).

At times, actual human beings showed up as props in cases of marital litigation, as in the case of Juan Pérez de Marquina, who forcefully moved his daughter Catalina Marquina out of a convent to marry her to Martín de Leguizamo in 1522 (*Pleito de Juan Pérez* CR Leg. 128 Fol. 6), or in the case of Rodrigo Pacheco, who sued his brother for kidnapping his son to force him to marry (*Pleito de Rodrigo Pacheco* CR Leg. 83 Fol. 1). Other records focus on actions pertaining to marriage, rather than in the strict aspect of material objects or props. Such are the cases, for instance, of disputes over abuse, cited in the lawsuit of the Infanta Doña Mencía de la Vega against the Infante Don Fernando de Granada (*Pleito de la Infanta* CR Leg. 41 Fol. 15); over the alleged crime of adultery, as Pedro de Bilbao alleged that Provost Ochoa de Salazar was committing (*Pleito de Pedro de Bilbao* CR Leg. 93 Fol. 1); over bragging about sexual relations with a relative, as Juan de Amores claimed in his suit against

Juan Pérez (*Querella* CR Leg. 136 Fol. 25); over impotence as María de la Cruz alleged about her husband (*Pleito de María de la Cruz* CR Leg. 47 Fol. 8); or over refusal to engage in marital sex as Aldonza de Guevara did, alleging that her husband's other wives still lived (*Pleito de Iñigo López* CR Leg. 26 Fol. 13).

Some cases represent supple histrionics that can transport readers to the fictional worlds that Davis sees in the archives: see, for example, the late sixteenth-century case in an Inquisition tribunal, which stages a rich marriage scene between Beatriz de la Palma and Gaspar Suárez (*Alegaciones* Inq. Lib. 1225 fols 179–92). The narrative voice, framing the 'alegaciones de la causa … sobre matrimonio' (allegations about the legal cause … about marriage) between these two subjects, acknowledged that Mr Suarez confessed to having had sexual intercourse with Ms de la Palma – 'habuit copulam carnalem cum ea' – and that three scopophilic witnesses with names eerily reminiscent of literary characters (Elvira de la Torre, Elvira de Color Negra, and Ysabel de la Cruz) testified that the lovers 'se vidisse eos in horto domus solos et jacentes simul ex quibus liquido probatur copula inter eos nam ex quo probatur' (were seen in the home's garden alone and lying down together, of whose liquid the copulation between them can be proven) (*Alegaciones* Lib. 1225 fol. 179v).

Sexual transgressions, as Lacarra said, are a particularly fertile legal ground in which to read the arbitrary definitions of the Law. This is certainly true as well of the process of reading how men and women performed marital roles in cases of litigation. In this respect, the above-mentioned study by Barahona on sex crimes in Vizcaya filed in the Chancillería de Valladolid, and Scott Taylor's inquiry into honour-related violence in Yébenes filed at the *fiel del juzgado* (judge) in Toledo are two significant contributions to this field of inquiry.[14] A third collection could be mined from penal cases filed at the Alcaldía Mayor (Town Hall) of the township of Rueda. In one of the many cases found in that collection a certain Juan Mateo, 'mozo soltero natural de la villa de Bohadilla' (single lad born in the town of Bohadilla) is accused of the *estupro* (rape or ravishment) of Catalina de Torres, 'donzella onesta y recoxida' (honest and shy young woman), a minor, both serving in the house of Luis Jimenez in the year of 1678 when the suit was filed (*Procesos: heridas* Div Rueda Leg. 100 Fol. 35 fol. 1r). Mr Mateo, tricking people over the real function of marriage like the many Don Juans roaming the Vizcaya and Toledo cases cited by Barahona and Taylor, made a great marriage scene soliciting Catalina and offering her words of marriage, 'jurando que dios le faltase si faltase a la palabra que la daba de ser su marido' (swearing that if he were not to fulfil his word of marriage to her, God may as well abandon him) (*Procesos: heridas* Div Rueda Leg. 100 Fol. 35 fol. 1r).

With that trick, Mr Mateo ravished Ms de Torres using all the force that the language of rape communicates: 'la gozo y quito su virginidad continuando el esto en virtud de dicha palabra' (he enjoyed her and stole her virginity, continuing to do so by virtue of such promise) (*Procesos: heridas* Div Rueda Leg. 100 Fol. 35 fol. 1r). As the dramatic conflict intensified and the plot thickened, mimicking the greatest *comedias* of the time, Mr Mateo 'dilataua el cumplir la palabra esqusandose con muchas fribolas' (delayed in delivering to her the promised goods, excusing himself with lots of frivolities and so Ms de Torres confronted him (*Procesos: heridas* Div Rueda Leg. 100 Fol. 35 fol. 1r).[15] He scorned her, but she defended herself – again, with the tools of performance best exploited in the *comedias* – by denouncing him: 'la suso dicha dio quenta a su ama Ana Gonzalo muger del dicho Luis Gimenez y asi mesmo al susodicho' (the said Ms de Torres told her owner Ana Gonzalo, wife of the said Luis Gimenez, and also told him) (*Procesos: heridas* Div Rueda Leg. 100 Fol. 35 fol. 1r). Mr Gimenez scolds Mr Mateo, who later in the same sentence appears passing through his boss's 'heras' (fields), a move that adds to the dramatic suspense because he does not go there to ravage another woman, but to escape – thus subverting the usage in *estupro* lawsuits of what Barahona identifies as 'the barren and uninhabited places' favoured by perpetrators of assaults (69–70). In the escape, Mr Mateo intensifies the drama of his scene by telling another servant in Gimenez's house, son of Juan Navarro, that they were trying to force him to marry Catalina but he did not wish to do so. The fugitive, whose actions emulate the deplorable marriage scenes performed by the Tenorio, does not miss the opportunity to declare publicly 'que era verdad había dormido con ella muchas veces' (that it was true that he had slept with her many times) (*Procesos: heridas* Div Rueda Leg. 100 Fol. 35 fol. 1v).

The narrative voice in this case is Antonio Ramirez, neighbour of Rueda and legal guardian of the person and possessions of Catalina de Torres, daughter of Pedro de Torres, deceased, and Catalina Polo. Mr Ramirez plays the roles of father and mother by scolding Mr Mateo and defending Catalina: 'en todo lo cual el susodicho ha cometido grave y atroz delito' (in all of which actions the above named Mateo has incurred a grave and atrocious crime). Furthermore, the parental role adopted by Mr Ramirez drags his legal tongue to strike a pose at the judge himself:

> porque en dicho nombre de dicha mi menor me querello y acuso criminal-
> mente en lo mejor que haya lugar de derecho con el dicho Juan Mateo y pido
> sea condenado en las penas que hay en que ha incurrido executando las en
> su persona y bienes ya que inzidentalemente cumpla la palabra de casa-
> miento que tiene dada a la susodicha en quio efecto se executen las penas en
> que ha incurrido en su persona y bienes para que le sirva de castigo y a otros
> de en gemplo. (*Procesos: heridas* Div Rueda Leg. 100 Fol. 35 fol. 1v)

> (because in the name of such a minor I accuse with criminal charges ac-
> cording to the best possible legal circumstances and sue the named Juan
> Mateo and I ask that he is sentenced with the appropriate punishment for
> his actions, his persona and property, and that incidentally he fulfils the
> word of marriage that he gave the above-named Catalina de Torres in
> whose representation the appropriate sentence of the charged defendant,
> and his property, so he receives his punishment and others see this case as
> an example.)

The pretend father/mother, managing the household like the 'women in the text' analysed by Vicente and Corteguera, folds humbly but firm-ly as he addresses the judge hearing the case:

> pido y suplico admita esta querella que sumo en forma y para su gustifica-
> cion Vmd. se sirva de recibir su declaracion a la dicha menor y con vista de
> ella por el riesgo que corre la dilacion mandar prender al susodicho y para
> otra querella pidimiento o conclusion ... pido justicia. (*Procesos: heridas* Div
> Rueda Leg. 100 Fol. 35 fol. 1v)

> (I ask and beg that you accept this lawsuit that I present formally, and to
> justify it Your Highness please receive the deposition of the above-named
> minor and, with her in mind because of the risk that a delay may entail,
> arrest the above named defendant, and for another suit, request, or con-
> clusion ... I ask for justice.)

The *Nueva Recopilación* ordered that no slave or servant would marry against his/her will: 'We order that none of the lords of our kingdoms, nor any person who has servants push any owner or young woman to marry against her will with any person ...' (Lib. V Tit. 1 Ley xi). However,

Mr Mateo's playing with the institution of marriage, like an amateur Don Juan, provokes high legal drama, as this Law collides with the legal stipulations of *estupro*. The caregiver of the minor, playing motherly with her, should have been played by Catalina Polo, her biological mother; unfortunately for the girl, Ms Polo/Mrs Torres plays no other part than the bureaucratic entry of a 'mother's name,' disappearing thereafter. In her stead, perhaps the father of the girl, Pedro de Torres, may have cared for her; again, the tale's reversal of fortune finds him dead. The case then turns to the girl's legal guardian Antonio Ramírez, who plays the part that naturally would have belonged to the biological mother of Catalina de Torres. Interestingly enough, Mr Ramírez's wife, Ana Gonzalo, is absent from this legal drama of dishonour, save for the fleeting moment onstage as the minor's confidant, which she shares with her husband.

The Rueda collection also registers several cases of *amancebamiento* (cohabitation) – a sex crime defined in the *Nueva Recopilación* as a public sin perpetrated by the unlawful cohabitation usually of a cleric or married man and a *barragana* or mistress (Lib. 8 Tit. 19 Leyes i-viii).[16] In the township of Rueda Mayor Bayon stated on 23 September 1645:

> Sebastian Botinete vezino de la dicha villa, con poco temor de Dios de su conciencia faltando a las obligaciones del matrimonio, muchos dias ha es publico amancebado con geronima Hernandez, moça soltera, que en esta dicha villa se ha seguido grande escandalo. (*Procesos: injurias* Div Rueda Leg. 98 Fol. 25 fol. 1r)

> (Sebastian Botinete, neighbour of the township of Rueda, with little fear of God in his conscience and not fulfilling the obligations of marriage, has for many days now lived unlawfully and publicly with Geronima Hernandez, a single young lass, which in this township has caused great scandal.)

Ms Hernandez and Mr Botinete were both servants in the house of Father Basilio Poçero, a cleric well known for housing only people characterized by their 'todo recoximiento y onestidad' (complete devotion and honesty) (*Procesos: injurias* Div Rueda Leg. 98 Fol. 25 fol. 1r).

There is no shortage of histrionics in this legal file. The priest expelled Ms Hernández from his house, after which Mr Botinete 'se la llevo a la villa de Tordesillas adonde por mas de seys meses ha continuado el dicho amancebamiento en la misma forma que antes' (took her to the town of Tordesillas where for over six months they continued their unlawful cohabitation the same way as they did before) (*Procesos: injurias* Div Rueda Leg. 98 Fol. 25 fol. 1r). Botinete, playing the good *amancebado*, was married to Isabel Leonardo, who became aware of the situation by the public nature of her husband's affair. The comedy of errors takes a decisive turn when Mr Botinete decides to take Ms Hernandez into the legal residence he shared with Mrs Leonardo, where the good wife lay on her deathbed:

> y la tuvo en su casa en su aposiento della algunos dias de donde por el inconveniente de estar su mujer mala y no poder estar conformidad la paso a una casa de la villa donde la tiene y trata y casa con ella de dia y de noche con notable escandalo de la vecindad y de sus parientes. (*Procesos: injurias* Div Rueda Leg. 98 Fol. 25 fol. 1v)

> (and he had her in his house and in her bedroom a few days, from whence by virtue of the inconvenience of his wife being ill and not being able to agree, he moved her to a house in the town where he has her and sees her and weds with her day and night to the notorious scandal of the neighbourhood and his relatives.)

The transfer of the *barragana* (concubine) from one scene to the other yields ample opportunity for great set design, on which Mr Botinete capitalizes to outdo the abandonment performed by Mr Mateo (who merely went to 'las heras') and soar to the mythical level of don Juan, who performed his illicit theatrics in Naples, the coast of Tarragona, the fields of La Mancha, and Seville. Although a much more modest proposal, the move between Rueda and Tordesillas signals the dramatic mobility that characterizes Botinete.

The narrative voice of Mayor Rafael Bayon clarifies that Mr Botinete actually has overdone himself in another scenario: he is, indeed, a bigamist *amancebado*, but Ms Leonardo and Ms Hernandez are not his only victims, for he has bounced from town to town

> pretendiendo ser señor a muchas mujeres asi doncellas como casadas donde notable escandalo y es de natural inquieto amigo de ruidos y pendencias inclinado a andar continuamente de noche muy a deshora ocupandose de hacer semejantes delitos. (*Procesos: injurias* Div Rueda Leg. 98 Fol. 25 fol. 1v)

> (pretending to be the husband of many women, both single and married, causing great scandal, and he seems to naturally be prone to making noise

and quarrelling, being inclined as he is continuously to roam very late at night to perform such crimes.)

The character of the mayor in this marriage legal drama perfectly fits his public servant duty, because 'para que averiguada la verdad' (in his search for truth) and for the 'quietud de la dicha villa' (for the sake of the town's order) he seeks to find them guilty so that these scandalous and disruptive crimes can be punished. At once, in the process he finds a way to engage rhetorical and stylistic tools to articulate a scene of pleasure, chaos, and plural desires that no doubt speaks of resistance to the institution of marriage. Mayor Bayon condems Botinete's roaming libido, an impeccable performance as representative of the law that voices the fatherly figure who remembers the first Law of matrimony: ye shall marry not in clandestinity. But the rich texture of Botinete's marriage scene also reveals moments of homoerotic pleasure in the voice of the mayor, a representation of same-sex flirtation tangible in the details of the transfer of sex that, as Harry Vélez-Quiñones has noted, represents 'alternative configurations of desire' (*Monstruous* 92).

Subjects invested in expressing their opinions and arguing their cases about marriage produced a wealth of bureaucratic and litigation documents, many of which fall outside the scope of this study. Such is the case of the dispensations to marry despite illegal (by both ecclesiastical and civil standards) degrees of consanguinity, a rite of passage for many a subject regardless of their status or standing in society. Catholic Princess Isabel of Castile and her husband-to-be, Prince Fernando of Aragon, for instance, found themselves in this situation in order to consummate the marital union that would strenghthen their precarious union. The Catholic king and queen, like Doña Elvira and many other nobles in the early modern society of the peninsula, had to petition for a *dispensa* (dispensation) to marry, which was granted so they could marry despite being cousins. Rome found no objection, especially in the face of a monarchic plan that would defend the Catholic faith and fight heresy. Marriage scenes abound in the bureaucratic and litigation archives, but as the next chapter will show, the subject stages of the *comediantes* also tried a different variety of marital law and order to play with the institutional development of marriage in Spain since the early sixteenth century. In the last three decades of the century marriage, theatre, and the law intensified to produce terrible situations, dramatic conflicts, and some marvellous artefacts, objects d'art of marriage that the remaining chapters will examine.

3 The Birth of the *Comedia* and the Bride Onstage

In that mishmosh blockbuster allegory of global corporate capitalism (either that, or academia), Spain (in the Roman sense, Hispania, Iberia) is the great disruptor, the unstoppable emissary who insists on demonstrating that the emperor, empire itself, is a big cheater.

Mary Gossy, 'Uncannily Queer Iberia:
The Past and Present of Imperial Panic'

Despite its small size, the town of Alba de Tormes occupies a rather visible place in Spain's historical imaginary. The Mudéjar churches of San Juan and Santiago, the unfinished basilica, and its numerous convents and monasteries hold treasures such as the façade of the Dueñas, oil paintings by Luis 'el Divino' de Morales, or the V-shaped relics of St Teresa's arm and heart, exposed next to her incorrupt body. Atop its tallest hill the Armory Tower stands as a vivid reminder of what once was the imposing house of the first Duke of Alba, Garci Alvarez de Toledo; inside the ruins of the palace-castle a guide recites a brief history of the Albas, one of the most powerful families in Europe. Perhaps inspired by the fact that tiny Alba is the keeper of such substantial pieces of Spain's historic patrimony, the guide risks a categorical affirmation that the origin of Spain's theatre occurred in that very same home, where plays were staged for the duke and duchess before they began to be produced elsewhere in the peninsula. I heard this recorded tale of the origins of Spanish theatre during a visit to this monument in the summer of 2004. Desperately trying to put together my own beginnings with the study of the *Comedia* – Spain's first professional theatre and arguably the most encompassing literary and cultural production of the Renaissance and baroque in the peninsula – I asked the guide if she was referring to the oft-quoted stagings of Juan del Enzina's *Cancionero*, published in 1496. My voiced doubt about her story brought the conversation to an abrupt end; the guide quickly sank in puzzlement, and humbly acknowledged that she, too, had to find out more about this matter.

Once the core of Hispanism and a greatly abused measure of Spain's history, the *Comedia* has been the subject of a vast array of scholarly publications and heated debates, frequently limited by registers of nationalisms and other turf wars. Cultural and literary critics, philologists, historians, and journalists from a number of nations have argued about how, when, and where this theatre originated, agreeing only on the point that the *Comedia* is the product of many sources that should be read with a variety of lenses considered simultaneously – some are more important than others, depending on who is speaking. For a guided tour of the Armory Tower, emblematic of the thousand and one stories industrially repeated every day throughout the peninsula, the story of the birth of theatre in Spain as an event that took place within the boundaries of the great past of the House of Alba is a convenient, rather economic narrative.

However, to suggest that such theatre began in Spain by virtue of a relatively small series of plays published by one author and represented in a place of exclusionary politics does not quite paint the whole picture. The *Comedia*, in the end, deconstructed the political theatre of empire, and even when it occupied the space of the court, as in the case of the dramatic productions of del Enzina, Lope, or Calderón, it did not do so merely to extol the virtues of monarchy and the noble *estamentos*. In 1976 Charlotte Stern proposed that the *Coplas de Mingo Revulgo* signalled the beginning of a 'conscious exercise in political satire and social moralizing' long before del Enzina staged his nativities in the House of Alba ('The *Coplas*' 314). Without a doubt her theory marks a different starting point than the celebratory one I heard in the Tower. My aim, too, is to explore a new beginning, to rehearse another first impression of the *Comedia* – that of the interactive correspondence of marriage and theatre which, in bringing together a bride, a queen, and their subjects to experience a public feast of the senses, significantly connected actors and audiences in a novel fashion.

By the end of the sixteenth century the tradition of wedding ceremonials began to reproduce not only under the shape of 'real' matrimonial unions, but as a host of major theatrical productions as well.[1] This chapter focuses on the 1570 representation staged in Burgos among a number of performances devised to celebrate Anna de Austria's voyage to the altar.[2] The chronicles portraying the events say that the future queen was received with a grand festival in which the more properly theatrical segment – a primitive *comedia* loosely based on the *Amadís de Gaula* – was represented 'with a few other fun interludes' that led to a jumble in which chaotic jousting turned into a mob and the sacking of the virtual city of London, a scenario that burned down to ashes, including the two wooden castles built for the occasion (*Relación* Burgos ms R 4969 fol. 52v).[3] Concurring with the chronicler in that this monumental fiesta celebrating the arrival of the new queen to Spanish soil 'greatly amused and delighted everybody' (*Relación* Burgos ms R 4969 fol. 52v), I see this as the moment when theatre, a lettered ritual of gathering of people, was born in Spain.[4]

The Birth of the *Comedia*

Since the beginning of the twentieth century scholars have used a variety of terms to explore the primitive stages of theatre in Spain. In 1909 Hugo Rennert offered a rather comprehensive overview of the Spanish stage 'in the time of Lope de Vega,'while in 1930 J.E. Gillett appointed Torres Naharro the 'first dramatist,' and in 1939 the word for C.V. Aubrun was *début*. In 1966 Stern's thoughts were focused on 'the early Spanish drama' ('Some Thoughts'), a proposal that she reiterated in 1996 when she argued that it all started in the fifteenth century (*The Medieval Theater*). In 1969 Margaret Wilson (*Spanish Drama*) explored 'the beginnings' (5–23) of the *Comedia*, while Shergold (*A History of the Spanish Stage*) sought to appeal to those interested in more copious and elaborate archival data, a gesture reiterated – more synthetically – two decades later by Melveena McKendrick in her panoramic view of theatre in Spain's two golden centuries (*Theatre*). In 1984 Javier Huerta Calvo traced the evolution of medieval theatre from tropes and liturgical drama to *autos*, to paratheatrical and court spectacles, court theatre, populist and elite theatre, ending with the *prelopistas* or the small cohort of playwrights known to have published their pieces before Lope de Vega (*El teatro* 11–72). A decade later he explored the concept of 'the new world of laughter,' tracing the roots of the *Comedia* to units of the *teatro breve* such as the ancient *comedia*, mimes, orality, dialectology, festive madness, erotic language, and Italian

influences offering his readers a few incisive inquiries from the relationship of farce, ridicule, and subalterity to the making of theatre in early
modern Spain (*El nuevo* 18).

In 1979 Ronald Surtz alluded to 'the birth of a theatre' as the critical
metaphor that could explain the development of dramatic conventions
from Juan del Encina to Lope de Vega. Although this book deploys this
same expression, I am, rather, being critically queer (after Judith Butler's
usage of the term in *Bodies That Matter*) by insisting on the correspondence of 'birth' with Edward Said's 'notion of *beginning* as opposed to
origin, the latter divine, mythical, and privileged, the former secular,
humanly produced, and ceaselessly re-examined' (xii–xiii). Concurring
with Said, who proposed for his own studies on literature and society
not to seek further celebrations of imperial design and domination, my
search for the birth of Spain's theatre seeks to underscore the possibilities of the reproduction of political and aesthetic difference at a time
and place where difference was strictly prohibited. Such a critique of
imperial design and domination ought to bear in mind the cross-
disciplinary nature of this theatre, a point that some critics have considered a significant factor in determining its origins; for instance, in a
1965 study on Fray Iñigo's *Vita Christi*, Stern explored 'relationships
between drama and ritual, between drama and music, song and dance,
between the comic interlude and the serious play, between the sacred
rite and the secular farce' ('Fray Iñigo' 198).

Three decades later Miguel Ángel Pérez Priego asked readers not to
limit the definition of theatre in medieval Spain to dramatic literature
(of which there is very little), but to consider it as a happening that includes scripts, ritual, liturgy, parody, and other 'forms of theatrical
spectacularity' that should be studied as part of the question of beginnings (9). In 2000 Margaret Greer challenged *Comedia* scholars again,
and argued for a more effective engagement of critical methods in this
area of intellectual inquiry, in order to pursue a substantial revision
that, among other factors, should reconsider the question of origins. To
that end, Greer proposed that the study of this theatre should also pay
'attention to the full range of dramatic production, considering how the
images of the human subject represented in diverse theatrical venues
may interact, reinforce, or counterbalance one other' ('A Tale' 393–4).

My intentions and methods seek to render visible hidden aspects of
political and aesthetic representation involved in the theatrics of matrimony in sixteenth- and seventeenth-century Spain. To that end, I begin
with an exposition of the tactics that a particular group of *comediantes*

deployed in their performative text to raise substantial questions about the institutionalization of marriage and the critical role it played in the global economy of its time; the remaining chapters will likewise focus on the relations between dramatic literature and its production onstage. The Burgos representation dramatized the story of a future empress rejecting matrimony, a plot to be staged in front of the very eyes of the future queen of Spain and her new subjects (until then only married by proxy, with the king *in absentia*). I read this theatrical happening as an act of oppositional reception, an instance of what José Muñoz has called disidentification.[5] For Muñoz, disidentification encompasses and moves between production and reception, and is a way for disempowered subjects in a representational hierarchy to decode the cultural field that so encodes them (25). These subjects employ this hermeneutical performance as a 'survival strategy ... to resist and confound socially prescriptive patterns of identification' (28). Muñoz moves between various registers of 'minority' subjects (queer, Hispanic, black, coloured) that have a history of encoding which I do not pretend to impose on the *comediantes*. Despite the differences in historical specificity that separate the Spanish *comediantes* from the Latino-American queers of colour, to whom Muñoz refers, noting areas of aesthetic and political representation common to these two groups can benefit the reading of their respective instances of cultural production.

With this particular performance the *comediantes* decoded in queer fashion the hierarchical structure of marriage, signalling that their public show was an event in which theatre – and not the biological, legitimate child of *cristianos viejos* desired by the crown – could be a product of matrimony. Theatre, in this case, shared the theoretical, social, and cultural space of queerness in that it opposed what Lee Edelman has termed 'reproductive futurism,' an ideological establishment that privileges heteronormativity and favours the figure of 'The Child' that, in this particular ceremony, referred to the future of the bride as a vessel of the heir to the Spanish crown. In Edelman's view this uncanny and contradictory naturalization of infancy constitutes 'the repository of variously sentimentalized cultural identifications' and 'has come to embody the telos of the social order and come to be seen as the one for whom that order is held in perpetual trust' (11). The *comediantes* represented in this ceremony the negative image of this child, a critical gesture that Edelman recognizes in the exercise of queerness.

Borrowing from the story of the ancient birth of the novel staged by Apuleius, in which baby Voluptas ludicrously appeared after her folks were shoved literally and figuratively through premarital hell (her arrival marking at once the 'real' sign of the wedding ceremony, and 'The End' of the myth of Psyche and Cupid in 'The Sixth Book' of *The Golden Ass*), the *comediantes* presented Anna de Austria with a tightly bound wedding gift: the likewise voluptuous, pleasurable brainchild of theatre.[6] Their dramatic gesture shares James C. Scott's theory of engagement of politics and performance between dominant and subaltern subjects, in which those belonging to the former group speak among themselves – and to their allegedly owned subjects – through a public transcript, while the latter communicate by virtue of the hidden transcript, a discursive event that takes place 'beyond direct observation by power holders' (1).

In this case the queen sat in a privileged place in the audience, where the *comediantes* knew she would be, surrounded by her wedding entourage. The troupe addressed her and her subjects with a dramatic speech, which they articulated in certain terms that were literally illegible by means of the direct observation of the (absent) king and his representatives. The hidden transcript of the *comediantes* referred members of the audience to a highly publicized code deployed in the process of the institutionalization of marriage, and palpably designed to silence wives and render them invisible in public spaces. In considering how this code also unintentionally turned brides into a dramatic spectacle and how these *comediantes* played with such contradictory subjects, theatregoers were able to see how this staging of the *Amadís* erected a queer image of the cheating emperor (empire itself, as Mary Gossy says in the epigraph) for all the members of the *vulgo* there present to ponder.[7]

Instituting Marriage

The most successful stage in the process of institutionalization of matrimony in sixteenth-century Europe came about with the Decree of Tametsi (as it came to be known), approved in Session 24 of the Council of Trent, dated 11 November 1563 and entitled 'Doctrina sobre el Sacramento del Matrimonio' (Doctrine on the Sacrament of Marriage). In 1564 King Felipe II promulgated the canons and chapters of this session as law in a *Real Cédula* that commanded all his subjects to abide by the principles approved by the Tridentine Synod 'to end the heresy and errors that in these times in Christianity have propagated so much, and for the much-needed reformation of the abuses, excesses, and disorders' (Tejada 1).[8] By virtue of that legislative document, the king sided with Pope Pius V in expressing his wish to have these normative principles become positive law in the peninsula. At the same time, he faced oppostion from Inquisitor Espinosa and others in the Holy Office, who, as Pedro Rodríguez notes, sabotaged the first translation into Spanish of the *Catecismo Romano*, the handbook for prelates to administer sacraments – a document that was not translated until two centuries later (15). In an effort to control Catholic Reformation controversies, the king granted substantial power to institutions such as the Patronato Real, which Ignasi Fernández Terricabras defines as 'the set of rights to *patronato* (board, council, sponsorship) attributed to a particular monarch ... Philip II' (174), and the Cabildos, 'a community of clergymen endowed with juridical personality and whose essential role is to solemly worship in a cathedral or school church' (291).

These and other political institutions were critical in the dissemination of the Tridentine documents in Spain, for, as the *Cédula Real* ordered:

> Thus we entrust and order the archbishops, bishops, and other prelates, and the generals, provincials, priors, guardians of the monastic orders, and whomever else this affects and concerns, that they make public, and publish in their churches, districts, and dioceses, and in other parts and places where it would be necessary, the Holy Council (of Trent), and that they keep it and obey it, and make others keep it and obey it, and execute it with the care, zeal, and diligence that any business in the service of God, and the church's welfare, require. And we orderd those in our council, and the presidents of our courthouses, and governors, magistrates, and any other justices, that they offer and grant all favour and help needed for the execution and obedience of such Council (of Trent) and its laws. (Tejada 2)

For Fernández Terricabras, King Felipe's *translatio* of the principles of the Council to the idea and praxis of government in Spain was a key piece in his constitution of a 'secular clergy.'[9] Despite the king's political intent, the juridical, economic, and social application of these institutions was complex and laborious and, as Fernández Terricabras demonstrates, was received with much protest and argumentation (173–380).

Ultimately, the words of the brief chapter wedded the language and ideology of Spain's Law with the emergent powers of European legal

discourses, while, at the same time, they redefined the marriage ceremony, until then a rather private affair.[10] As stipulated in the Tametsi,
the performance of the rites of union of one man with one woman for
the strict purposes of reproduction became a spectacular event, in the
sense that the foundation for the legal and religious arguments behind
the Tametsi was the issue of an audience. The chapter ruled that
marriage would only be valid – legally, religiously – if a priest and at
least two other witnesses were present at the ceremony. This audience,
the witnesses, served a naturalizing function for the institution insofar
as their presence at the ceremony ratified the legitimacy of the 'I' who
agreed to the marriage.

Andrew Parker and Eve Sedgwick theorize that this ceremony takes
place assuming relative meanings of the first person subject: 'The subject of "I do" is an "I" only insofar as he or she assents in becoming part
of a sanctioned, cross-gender "we" so constituted in the presence of a
"they"; and the I "does," or has agency in the matter, only by ritually
mystifying its overidentification with the powers (for which no pro-
noun obtains) of state and church' (10).[11] As Sedgwick argued in an
earlier study, in such performativity context queer subjects are those
'whose subjectivity is lodged in refusals or deflections of (or by) the
logic of the heterosexual supplement; in far less simple associations
attaching to state authority; in far less complacent relation to the wit-
ness of others' (4). These refusals or deflections were tangible components of the arts of resistance developed by the *comediantes*, whose work
agrees with Parker and Sedgwick in the premise that 'marriage isn't
always hell, but it is true that *le mariage, c'est les autres*: like a play, marriage exists in and for the eyes of others' (11). In the singular case of
early modern Spain, these 'eyes' were ostensibly appointed as ecclesiastical subjects, represented in formulaic terms by first-person pronouns allowed within the boundaries of the Law.

The Tametsi stipulated that the signatures of such members of the
officiating audience, stamped in the parish register forever after, in turn
represented the people of the parochial congregation who, for days,
had heard and read the bans publicizing the event:

> Those who shall attempt to contract marriage otherwise than in the pres-
> ence of the parish priest, or of some other priest by permission of the said
> parish priest, or of the Ordinary, and in the presence of two or three wit-
> nesses; the holy Synod renders such wholly incapable of thus contracting
> and declares such contracts invalid and null, as by the present decree It

invalidates and annuls them. Moreover It enjoins, that the parish priest, or any other priest, who shall have been present at any such contract with a less number of witnesses (than as aforesaid); as also the witnesses who have been present thereat without the parish priest, or some other priest; and also the contracting parties themselves; shall be severely punished, at the discretion of the Ordinary. (*Canons and Decrees* 180–1)

'Those who shall attempt to contract marriage' thus became actors on the world's great stage of matrimony designed by the Catholic monarch and his political allies to exercise monopolizing ecclesiastical and legal control over marital contracts in Spain. This overwhelming stage of performativity was masked with the institutional promise that this contract, when signed according to the Tametsi, would help such actors escape from the place of abjection deserved by those who chose clandestinity, and from the ensuing severe punishment – the severe punishment also promised in the decree.

Given the context of this political economy of marriage, one can conclude that the Tridentine marital reforms were clearly and categorically intended to position the church as the executor of what James Scott calls the 'public transcript as a respectable performance' (45–69), a remarkable show of heteronormative political and juridical theatrics scripted to engender an imperial body constituted and reproduced by subaltern subject positions. Such hierarchy is clearly established in the microtext of the union of man / woman, defined as a perpetual union that translates into one sacred body, 'bone of my bones, and flesh of my flesh' (*Canons and Decrees* 193).[12] Ironically, Tametsi's prescription for publicized and spectacular weddings – intended to erect another angle of the crown's panopticon – paved the road for subjects to escape ecclesiastical and political control by turning wedding ceremonies into an ideal site of resistance to the ideologies of closure stipulated by Law, an essential script for all Spaniards seeking to achieve the legal state of matrimony after 1564.

Visible Bride, Mysteries of Marriage

Despite the widely disseminated literature of control that prescribed new ways to contain women in 'patriarchal territories' or 'bodies enclosed,' to borrow Peter Stallybrass's terms, Counter-Reformation brides experienced an uncanny surge in popularity that moved them from a familiar environment of anonymity and submission to an uncharted locus of cultural and social attention. With this I do not mean to imply that suddenly all women became visible in the cultural and political landscape of Spain. On the contrary, despite the tremendous efforts made by the *comediantes* and other media moguls of these two centuries to ride the wave of spectacularity for women, these subjects continued to occupy a place of alterity and poor visibility in Spain that only recently has begun to be properly explored and analysed. The question of evidence for women in this period, as Navarro has demonstrated in her astute reading of Cervantes' *El celoso extremeño* (*The Jealous Extremaduran*), arises when the correlation of gender and genre is considered far more unstable than critics have been willing to acknowledge. If, as Joan W. Scott says, the evidence of experience for women and other marginalized subjects can only be expressed faintly, then the reading of such evidence, as Navarro's reading demonstrates, is key in rewriting history. In the specific case of post-Tametsi brides, as stipulated by Law, these women were expected to engage performances of prominence, eloquence, and spectacular possibilities that, by definition, threatened the canonized *perfección* of the married woman as a silent, ordinary, and pure object – the vessel of legitimate biological and ideological reproduction.

That uncanny prominence gave spectacle lovers much to play with, and the frequent queering of these subjects in artistic media, especially the theatre, constitutes evidence of the desire on the part of artists and audiences to destabilize the spectacle of control and manage representation of a man turning into a ruling husband and a woman turning into someone's *mujer*.[13] One of the characteristics of early Spanish drama is its departure from the strict Elizabethan regulation that only allowed boy actors, but not women, to appear onstage; in this respect Sidney Donnell has noted that the transvestite drama of the early modern period in Spain generated copious signs of a crisis of masculinity in the imperial design, most visible in the manic feminization of the enemy that was substantially played on- and offstage by the *comediantes*. The queering of the roles of husband and wife by the *comediantes* is tangible in a number of ways that make the classical theatre of Spain a great performance of *impostoría* (imposture), especially in the multiple wedding scenes.[14] As Donnell argues persuasively, confusing this ubiquitous finale of many *comedias* with a sense of closure is conflating story and discourse, finishing the tale in a way that perverts the falling of the curtain; instead, he proposes to leave these comic scenes 'unresolved even though a closed, symmetrical narrative structure remains in place' (33).

In this particular context, the sacramental and dramatic dimensions of the *misterio* of marriage began to take shape collaboratively. Theological writing had not specified different sex or gender rights or responsibilities in its scrupulous consideration of the discrete units that made marriage a *misterio y signo*. As José Rincón shows, the fundamental premise for this theological evolution, ratified by Bruno el Cartujano in the eleventh century, is the transcendence of the sign of matrimony as sacrament, a sacred representation of the union of Christ with the church: 'marriage is the *sacramentum*, that is to say, the sign; the union of Christ with the church is the *res sacramenti*, which is the same as that which is signified. Signification is so important for him that she (it, the church) alone constitutes sufficient motive for the celebration of the nuptials' (407). This point of signification as a staging of the sacred bond of Christ and the church in the bodies of a man and a woman was driven by two characteristic traits that would be central to the categorical definition of marriage, over which the church proclaimed to have sole jurisdiction: the bond was designed exclusively for the purpose of procreation, and it was indissoluble. The transgression of these sacred premises did not only warrant earthly prosecution but it was considered grounds for eternal condemnation. Since the end of the fifteenth century the management of this jurisdiction moved to the church, which became the final authority in charge of the administration of marriage, as was the case with royalty and nobility petitioning for dispensation for reasons of consanguinity, estate administration, and property law, among others.

The concept of marriage as a sacrament was forged, as Rincón demonstrates, between the ninth and the thirteenth century, when Alexander of Hales and his disciple in Paris, St Bonaventure, correlated the sacred union of man and woman with that of Christ and the church (8). For St Bonaventure this *misterio* was a sign that the church authorized by virtue of its own permanent union with Christ, and not by the actual words of consent: 'unde cum signatum in hoc sacramento, sit conjunctio Christi et Ecclesiae et conjunctio non potest melius significari quem per conjunctionem exteriorem' (whence with the seal in this sacrament, it is the conjunction of Christ and Church, and this union cannot be better signified than by the exterior union) (quoted in Rincón, 306). By the sixteenth century, the Tametsi Decree incorporated this *misterio* into the legal institutionalization of marriage:

Husbands love your wives, even as Christ also loved the Church, and delivered up himself for it; adding shortly after, *This is a great sacrament, but I speak in*

Christ and in the Church. Whereas therefore matrimony, in the evangelical law, excels the ancient marriages in grace, through Christ; with reason have our holy Fathers, the Councils, and the tradition of the universal Church, always taught, that it is to be numbered amongst the sacraments. (*Canons and Decrees* 177)

Between the thirteenth and the fifteenth centuries copious representations of the *misteris* of the Passion circulated around Europe, especially in England, France, and Germany. The rhetorical prowess of these religious *misterios*, which would eventually incorporate matrimony as a critical piece, had a significant impact on the evolution of theatre. As Shergold demonstrates, a tradition of *misteris* developed very early in Barcelona, Mallorca, and Valencia, with the staging of biblical episodes and events from the life of Christ yielding a trove of early evidence of the use of wooden platforms and fountains, stage props and signs that became centrepieces in the celebration of matrimony on- and offstage (52–84). Some of the *consuetas* were divided, as Shergold recognizes, 'into a number of scenes, each called a *pas*' (64). This, undoubtedly, would have a critical impact on the *pasos* that would constitute one of the earliest recognizable dramatic forms of the Spanish sixteenth century.

Wedding Belles in the Place of Theatre

In time and through all these different stages of marriage, theatre, and the Law, the promise of a wedding came to entice audiences much larger than the modest threesome imagined by the authors of the Tametsi. In fact, crowds of church- and theatregoers came to expect, both in texts and in performances, the production of remarkable dramatic conventions based on the *institutio* of marriage; likewise, wedding ceremonies gradually became events in which the drama was a key component. Real and virtual wedding ceremonies became increasingly more complex and meaningful, and the *comedia* benefited from playing with that scenario, both materially and ideologically. As a result the place of theatre as a culturally productive environment capitalized on the spectacularization of marriage by corresponding in playful manner with it. Unfortunately, critics have not considered this a significant factor in the analysis of this theatre and have read the *mujer varonil* seeking to restore her honour, the final multiple wedding scene, or the mock trials and punishments of adultery as dramatic moments largely unrelated to the substantial changes operated in the marital institution.

Administrators of *corrales*, *cofradías*, and *compañías de teatro* made substantial decisions pertaining to their running of the theatres with the regulations of the sacred institution of marriage very present in their minds;[15] for instance, they incorporated the rule that all their actresses had to be married as part of their constitutions when it was the law; they divided the members of the audience according to their sex and marital status, as it was prescribed by law; and they lived with the power granted to the *alguaciles* to scrutinize and regulate sexual and gendered behaviour in the theatre. This led to a series of steps in the professionalization of theatre that Joseph Oehrlein and Melveena McKendrick ('Representing') have compared in three particular contexts: the *cofradías*, the administration of theatres, and society. With this historical evidence about the conjugal life of actors, Oehrlein concluded that theatre developed in Spain framed by a 'double moral system' (216–21). Rather than succumbing to the contradictions and uncertainties that such a moral system entailed for them, the *comediantes* played with these rules and regulations. Thus, for instance, the cross-dressed men documented by Ruano, by virtue of their costuming, gained access to the forbidden paradise of the actresses's dressing rooms and became wedding belles in the place of theatre ('Noticias').

Ruano has crafted virtual reconstructions of the space of the *corrales*, some of which give a good idea of the gender-based division of these urban spaces and the obstacles erected to avert the violation of the marital institution by controlling the circulation of gender and sexuality. His images of 'the women's staircase,' 'the theatrics of representation from the *cazuela*,' and 'the dressing rooms' illustrate this negotiation of laws and their presence in the physical structure of the public theatres and in the life of the *comediantes* (*El Corral*). Despite these physical and institutional barriers (discussed further in chapter 4), playwrights, *autores*, actors, and other members of the production crews played with the spectacular dimensions of marriage, much to the grief of the *moralistas*. The *comediantes* upstaged the absurdity of the *cazuela* and the supposed privacy of the *tertulias* and the *desvanes*. They would not hesitate to have one married actress play a saint in one scene and the exact same married actress impersonate a prostitute in the next. On occasion, a male actor would show up in drag in the *cazuela* or in the women's *vestuario*; and, in general, they displayed tremendous solidarity – or, when their dramatic lives required it, blatant treason – when their fellow *comediantes* became involved in complex extramarital affairs.[16]

Some, like La Calderona, radically transformed the political and theatrical imaginaries of Spain, affecting sacred imperial marriage and its likewise sacred relationship to rulership, when the king banished the mother-actress to a convent and her bastard son, Don Juan José de Austria, appropriated the power of the crown.[17] The critical reception of the *Comedia* has amply documented the spectacular nature of wedding processions, *toros* (bullfighting), entertainments, *juegos de cañas* (equestrian games), and other celebrations, a correspondence of 'nobility and theatrical spectacle' (to borrow Ferrer Vals's title) in which the primitive *comediantes* played a critical role.[18] The representation of these opportunities for artistic intervention became commonplace in the cultural production of the baroque, offering readers and spectators the opportunity to engage in critical reception of the ideological coup performed by the crown during the sixteenth century. Despite this evidence, it has not been until recently that these brides have appeared meaningfully represented in the literary and cultural history of this period in Spain.

Symbolic Power, Ceremonial Style

As María José del Río has argued in her examination of Madrid as an *urbs regia*, royal wedding *ceremoniales* became a marketplace of monarchic power in which princess- and queen-brides were a most coveted currency. For del Río, Anna de Austria's entrance in Madrid was a landmark in the constitution of this city 'as the capital city of a monarchy that saw itself as the most powerful in Christendom, and that liked to use the title granted by Alexander VI to the Catholic king and queen, and that wanted to create a powerful image of itself by means of an elaborate ritual that crosssed the walls of the court to disseminate through a great part of the city that served as its political seat and religious see' (10). Del Río also notes that, although the establishment of Madrid as the ceremonial capital city of the Catholic Universal Monarchy would take time, Anna's entrance in Madrid, shortly after her stay in Burgos, marked the beginning of a legacy that had a significant influence on literature, politics, culture, and the Law (60–4). In her analysis of the official account of this entrance, published by the chronicler Juan López de Hoyos, del Río detects the influence of the Italian *festaiuoli* (festivals) and the *borgoñona* (Burgundian) etiquette, as well as the constitutional symbolism of the future queen's entrance to the capital city. The ceremonial style of these brides entering key points of Spanish territory

> dramatized the transition of succession, underlining the continuity of the political order. Hence, the ceremony included frequent exchanges of good

will, harmony and good government, while at the same time it mobilized onstage the legal notions centered in the attributes of the king as ultimate source and guarantor of justice, in ritual acts of recognition and submission of the bearers of public appointments, liberation of local prisoners or confirmation of local (municipal, cathedral ...) jurisdictions with a public oath of the privileges and liberties granted by their predecessors. (64)

No doubt the *comediantes* in Burgos both engaged and questioned this constitutional sense of the ceremonial entry of Queen Anna de Austria in Madrid, and played with what Fernando Bouza has labelled the 'image and propaganda' that King Felipe II carefully designed to establish his political absolutist regime. These productive tensions of marriage, theatre, and the Law are particularly tangible in the Burgos event because they marked the eruption of a primitive *mujer esquiva* in Spain's political and theatrical imagination. For this highly ritualized approach of the princess-bride to the epithalamium, a theatrical company built a pretend fleet to enter the town square, a complex set of monumental artefacts and machinery designed to set the future queen and her audience in the midst of a world of sheer premarital fantasy. In the portable naval battle, a dramatic reflection of Anna's recent travels to Spain, another regal bride and future queen, Oriana, experienced a dramatic metamorphosis that took her from the role of damsel in distress that she played in the popular chivalric tale, the *Amadís*, to a scene out of *Waterworld*, a monumental disappearing act elicited by her bold, dramatic refusal to marry Emperor Patín.

This intersubjective theatrical mirror presented audiences, and especially the future occupants of the *cazuelas*, with a clear opportunity to argue with the real. The spectacle, no doubt, invited them to reply with the question, 'what is theatre but a sustained argument with the real?' The dramatic argument means to critique, with Judith Butler, the foundational premise that the Real is the law of castration (*Bodies* 200–1); or, in Freud's words, that 'in the psychical field the biological factor is really the rock-bottom' (*Bodies* 271). In Burgos, as I see it, the rock-bottom got flooded in front of Anna's eyes: Oriana disappeared instead of living miserably ever after, leaving Patín and his crown without a 'Real' heir – meaning a royal heir by her. The artistic and political effect of the Burgos monumental show of illusory waters runs parallel with Virginia Woolf's parodic figuration of the English court as a 'whole gay city' fractured in the 'huge and massy fragments' of ice 'burst asunder' by the 'sulphur spring' (62). As the court sank, Orlando, the gentleman poet who represented the future of that England sinking in the 'race of turbulent yellow waters' of the thawing river, gazed at the scene, as he faced the reality of the disappearance of Sasha the Muscovite princess in the night forever after (62). By insisting on the point that women like Anna, Oriana, Woolf, Sasha, and the future Orlando, those in the *cazuelas*, and readers in general, can stage a significant event by gazing at and reading each other actively, visibly, from different sides of the dramatic looking glass, I propose that in marriage and theatre, the historic princess-bride Ori/Anna was not – does not have to be – a phantasmatic pawn in a masculinist fantasy show.

In addition to that it could be argued that the bedrock of subjectivity for Anna, other queens, and women in general was their function of procreation, as prescribed by a variety of dissemination venues of the marital dogma. King Felipe II, in fact, betrayed this phallic ghost in his deathbed confession to Dr Francisco Terrones:

> We searched all Europe to find a princess whose family seemed prone to guarantee fecundity, and we found it in the imperial princess Anna de Austria, my relative, who accepted immediately my propositions ... Anna accomplished her mission unselfishly and gave me five children; among them, four boys, of whom only King Felipe (III) survives. (De la Cierva 104)

This confessional text also reveals an understanding that this bride, in the kings' severely limited relational language, brought a different meaning to their marriage:

> But she achieved something that for me was as important as securing my offpsring; she knew how to give me, for the first time since Isabel of France died, and even more than her, a family life ... She encouraged me to buy soldiers and dolls for my sons and daughters, and to inspire in them a fondness for my walks in the country, and to take care of my birds. (De la Cierva 104)

It is well known that King Felipe's decision to marry Anna was anything but the simple family affair that this confession may intimate, and this symbolic power was certainly inscribed in the ceremonial style with which Princess Anna's road to the altar was designed.

At first, Anna was to be married to Prince Carlos, King Felipe's son. Archduke Carlos de Estiria left his brother Maximilian's court to offer Anna's hand to Carlos. Upon his arrival in Spain he learned that both the prince and Isabel de Valois were dead. Catalina de Habsburgo-Lorena notes that 'given the new situation, as soon as he set foot in Madrid on December 18, 1568 Archduke Carlos received instructions to offer Anna's hand to Don Felipe' (123). As Henry Kamen illustrates, the king framed this decision within the context of a triple alliance between Spain, Austria, France, and Portugal that would translate into 'peace and universal quiet to all Christendom, hurt the Turk our common enemy, and extirpate heresies everywhere' (*Philip* 125).[19] Closing a year of laborious pan-European negotiations King Felipe II signed the *capitulaciones matrimoniales* with Anna on 24 January 1570. He thus formally rejected the offer sent to him by Catherine de Medici exactly a year earlier, inviting him to marry her daughter Marguerite de Valois. Luis de Lorena, Cardinal Guisa, officially representing the French queen, brought the offer to him at the end of January 1569 – but King Felipe preferred not to marry her, given that she was the sister of his recently deceased wife, Isabel.

The king followed the word of his advisors, who argued that the Valois women could not bear male children, and on 2 March 1569 he conveyed to Francés de Alava his desire not to marry Marguerite de Valois, because 'I have such scruples about marrying two sisters, that I could never agree to it' (quoted in Kamen, *Philip* 125). In a letter dated March 1569 the king admitted to his trusted advisor Cardinal Granvela that, although 'I would so much rather prefer to remain in the state in which I find myself,' he also understood his royal duty to give the imperial crown a successor, 'my duty to God and to my subjects, which must always be put before my own happiness' (quoted in Kamen, *Philip* 261). In exchange, he promised in matrimony his beloved daughter Isabel Clara Eugenia, then two years old, to the king of France, whose daughter, Marguerite, in turn, was to marry the king of Portugal.

The marriage between the Austrian princess, twenty-one years of age, and the Spanish emperor, then forty-two, was first celebrated on 4 May in the castle of Prague, with Spanish ambassador Luis Venegas de Figueroa as proxy. Anna was to travel to the peninsula via Genoa, but the threat of Turkish fleets attacking the convoy made this a risky path in times of imminent holy war; instead, she disembarked on the northern coast of Spain. From Andalucía King Felipe ordered that Maximilian escort his daughter to Espira and then send her to Flanders, where Fernando Alvarez de Toledo, third Duke of Alba, would join her and decide the maritime route to follow. Alba determined that the future queen was to travel to Laredo, but the weather forced the fleet to detour to Santander, where she arrived on 3 October, accompanied by her two brothers, Albert and Wenzel. There, a colossal reception of two thousand people awaited the bride, among them, a group of over one hundred musicians, who continued to entertain her for the remainder of her travels. The wedding protocol was rivalled in its complexity and pomp by the festivities celebrated in the various stopping points of Anna's intricate journey to the altar. After Santander she travelled to Burgos and Valladolid on her way to Segovia, where the ceremony with the bride and groom was to take place.

Royal receptions, common at the time, had been elevated practically to an art status. As early as 1526 Princess Isabel de Portugal solemnly entered Seville to meet her future husband King Carlos I de España. The duke of Calabria, the archbishop of Toledo, and the duke of Béjar had met the princess at the border of Spain and Portugal, between Elvas and Badajoz, where the official delivery ceremony took place. Diego Ortiz de Zúñiga describes the Sevillian reception to the future queen in the Puerta de la Macarena, where a triumphal arch had been built in carefully choreographed design with other arches marking her way to the Alcázar, where the wedding ceremony would take place: 'The senators and civic officials of Seville came out to meet Her Majesty the Empress, all in rich and radiant costumes, with the assistant Don Juan de Ribera and the very illustrious duke of Archos, the chief mayor of Seville' and were joined by high-ranked clerics, knights, scribes, merchants, and other folks, 'all richly and seductively disguised' (354). In 1543 people in Salamanca gathered in the streets to greet Princess María de Portugal (in the city to marry Prince Felipe) to see two clouds descending from a triumphal arch that, in turn, opened to reveal a choir of children singing in tune with musicians. In 1548, twenty-two years before Anna marched in Burgos, the Palace of Valladolid was decorated for the representation of a comedy based on another text by Ariosto. As Cristóbal Calvete chronicled it, the event was staged 'with all the theatrical apparatus and scenes that Romans used to represent such events' (1:5). The stage was designed as part of a plan of festivities to welcome Prince Maximilian to Valladolid on the occasion of the prince's marriage to the infanta María. The elaborate scenario, Roman style, marked a first in the history of the Spanish theatre, if the use of bombastic displays to celebrate royal alliances was not new.

Here Comes the Real Bride (Burgos 1570)

The chronicle printed in Seville describes the *comedia* as an elaborate blend of props, people, and places. In the Burgos 'Infantry Square,' says the chronicler, 'eleven galleys' were pushed by 'two-hundred and eighty twelve-year-old children,' a fleet that lodged 'forty armed knights' (*Relación* Seville ms 34.182 16, n. p.). The Roman *cavalleros* eventually met the army of knights of Amadís, who stood on a 'firm island' and confronted King Lisuarte when he pressed for Oriana to marry the emperor (*Relación* Seville ms 34.182/16 n. p.). The father ignored Amadís and delivered his daughter to the Romans, who 'smuggled her in a ship,' an assault that the 'knights of Amadís fought until they rescued the lady and broke the lateen' (*Relación* Seville ms 34.182/16, n. p.). The duel of the two armies morphed the fleet into flames, a *palenque* (fenced game area), and a knightly tournament, which in turn evolved into the *folla* (mob) that ended the fiesta with fireworks. The Burgos chronicle, on the other hand, gives exquisite detail about the fleet, vividly underscoring the pomp of the audiovisual language used to put together the spectacular show:

> The galleys were fifty-two feet long, and the galleon was over sixty, and the frigate twenty-five, with well-proportioned prows and sterns. Each one of them had fifteen benches per side, thirty galley slaves each, dressed in the colours of their respective galleys, and the oars painted likewise. (*Relación* Burgos ms R 4969 fol. 51v)

The ensemble included *cómites* (galley captains) dressed in crimson satin, little trumpets, banners, taffetas, silks, war drums, and flutes, a bombastic fleet that paraded around the square, before a 'well-dressed scoundrel' declared the purpose of the performance 'with a very well composed ballad' (*Relación* Burgos ms R 4969 fol. 51r).

The Seville chronicle depicts how Lisuarte hollered to Oriana that she had to marry Patín; instead, the Burgos chronicler writes that 'those Romans asked King Lisuarte and his advisors, King Arbán of Norgales and Sr. Grumedán, for the hand of Princess Oriana for Emperor Patín, their liege' (*Relación* Burgos ms R 4969 fol. 52v). The advisors counselled King Lisuarte not to deliver his daughter to the Roman army, but he was determined to 'give her away' (*otorgarla*) in order to keep his word (*Relación* Burgos ms R 4969 fol. 52vr). The Burgos chronicle denotes the impact that this bizarre historical fusion of marriage and *comedia* must have had on the audience: 'and in refusing Oriana this marriage, and in the solace and hope that Mabilia and other characters brought to her, and other amusing interludes that this comedia had, many good things happened' (*Relación* Burgos ms R 4969 fol. 52v). What took place there was 'good things' for Anna, the members of the audience, and Oriana, who, after being embarked 'virtually by force' in the galleon, disappeared forever after in the *plaça* without having to succumb to an undesirable marital altar.

The commemoration of Anna's arrival, welcoming the future bearer of the imperial crown's successor to Spanish soil after three 'unsuccessful' marriages by the king, was singularly characterized with a clear and present sense of Spanish history, the first time in Spanish pageantry that audiences witnessed the grandeur of Spain's historical memory. Effigies of nobles and kings gave this stage a visual presence of figures past. The planners focused on its most formidable component: the live performance of the *Amadís de Gaula*, and set their stage in one of the city's squares, where the chroniclers say they built

> a perfect edifice portraying a perfect city, composed with excellent perspective, in its streets, houses, and square, and the windows so very well distributed that although it was a small place, this problem was compensated by the subtlety, draftsmanship, and great skill of the architect and painter. On one side you could see the compartments, and in them, the shops of mechanical crafts. On the other, the temples and churches with their towers and capitals, and in the highest point the clock, which gave the entire edifice the great lustre and clarity that characterized it. (*Relación* Burgos ms R 4969 fol. 33r)

The threshold for this city sported a sixty-two-foot-tall statue of Neptune with a monumental fountain around him so overwhelming that one of the chroniclers said 'its mere sight terrified' (*Relación* Burgos ms R 4969 fol. 34v).

In fact, the masters of ceremonies spared no detail, evoking the highly ritualistic and legendary entertainments employed by Elizabeth I of England in Kenilworth and other British courtly spaces to build her single, imperially pregnant *figura*. This was surely a familiar (and, in more ways than one, rival) performance and plot for Anna, her husband-to-be, and their subjects, and the dramatic recreation of Burgos, in open dialogue with Elizabeth's *imago* of the Virgin Queen, placed the issue of eschewing marriage at the centre of its histrionic mirror. Offstage, under the scrutiny of her new subjects as she watched Oriana's fate, Princess Anna advanced on her way to become the fourth and last wife of King Felipe II, the next queen of the Catholic Universal Monarchy, and its last hope to remedy the crown's lack of succession. Onstage players entertained the princess-bride with the story of Queen Sardamira, Prince Salustanquidio, and a battalion of knights imagining themselves invincible, a galleon, a frigate, and two galleys, all on wheels, a scoundrel passing for court jester, and an ocean of Romans who discharged their artillery to ask for the hand of Oriana, their daughter, to have her marry Emperor Patín, their lord. She herself refused the petition from the Roman envoy 'crying because of this force,' which denotes both the violence of the coercion of her father and the abduction, as well as her own fortitude and that of Amadís and his knights as they resisted imperial forces (*Relación* Seville ms 34.182/16 n. p.).

In the end, Oriana embarked in a galleon, mirroring a move from the *Amadís* to the *Decameron* or, perhaps, from Anna's experience only a few days earlier with the Spanish envoy driving her away from her homeland on the voyage to Spain. Back onstage the armada retired (eighteen years too early to feel like a 'real' defeat) and subsequently ran into eight galleys, after which the soirée ended with a naval battle and the disappearance of Oriana into oblivion. No doubt this forecasts both Anna de Austria's successful marriage to King Felipe II as well as the numerous appearances of *mujeres esquivas* that theatregoers saw onstage in commercial and public theatres, in the *corrales*, *alcázares*, and *coliseos* throughout the peninsula. Whether or not this double entendre was the intent of the masters of ceremonies and the players, the fact remains that they publicly staged the voice and agency of a lovable princess as the epicentre of a worldwide political and military storm, all on wheels. Oriana's potential to reflect the real persona of Anna de Austria is crucial to the historical reading of Spain's imperial endeavour, but it is also a breakthrough in the development of marriage, theatre, and the law in the cultural production map of sixteenth- and seventeenth-century Spain.

Anna de Austria and the Bride Onstage

Unfortunately, in the busy marketplace of royal female bodies in Europe, Anna is oftentimes remembered as a particularly desirable princess – not because she might have learned a different kind of queenly performance in the staging of Oriana, but because she was twenty-two years younger than her husband-to-be, healthy enough to conceive the crown's successor (as she did), and because her physical features were deemed striking. Kamen's act of historical capture of the face of the young queen, perhaps designed to add some spark to his otherwise somber biography of King Felipe II, is very telling – a rather revealing *flannerie* that betrays another masculinist ghost: 'Philip was enchanted with his new wife and fell deeply in love with her. Petite, elegant, with a strikingly white complexion, deep blue eyes and flowing blonde hair, Anna could not have been more different from Elizabeth Valois' (*Philip* 136–7).[20] Lacking, as it happens in the case of many women, her own account of this historical tale, there is really no telling what Anna thought of Oriana, her predicament, and her disappearance. She certainly fulfilled her queenly duties, which as Laura Bass says, included counselling the king, securing alliances, being a model of piety, and producing an heir that would secure the crown for the future (*The Drama* 95).

Anthonis Mor, the Flemish painter, captured her likeness in 1570 as a keepsake of her journey; the painting shows her dressed to travel, her gloves and feathered hat on (*Anna von Österreich, Königin von Spanien*, Kunsthistorisches Museum, Viena). In 1616 the Spanish painter Bartolomé González painted the queen against the exact same composition in which Mor placed her; González's portrait, however, shows Anna richly dressed, in a white damask with gold trim and organza bows, although she still sports the same dark brown gloves with which she holds the white silk handkerchief (*Ana de Austria*, Museo del Prado, Madrid. Fig. 1). The gold trim in the 1616 portrait evokes the dress she wore to sit for a similar portrait painted by Claudio Sánchez Coello, which in turn placed the hat from Mor's portrait on the queen's head (*Ana de Austria*, Museo Lázaro Galdiano, Madrid). Seeing this sartorial symphony one could imagine, perhaps, that she might have seen how the play of Oriana and Anna (O-RIA-ANA) interpellated normative fictions of spousal roles, while the *comediantes* did what they knew how to do best, 'enseñar deleitando' (to show, and teach, with pleasure). No doubt, the imperial feast of marriage in Burgos constituted a queer sight to be remembered by the princess-bride and her subjects as a forecast of other queer subjects such as Angela in *La dama duende*, Rosaura in *El Conde Partinuplés*, and Leonor in *Los empeños de una casa*, among other *comediantas*.[21]

What the historical documentation amply proves is that for all *comediantes* the staging of theatrical events like this one at royal wedding ceremonies certainly became a 'muy buena cosa' (very good thing). As Shergold says, by 1599 a more or less clear pattern of festivities surrounding these occasions had formed, marking 'the beginning of a new royal interest in the drama which enabled the court theatre of the seventeenth century to be created' (245). In 1613 Lope de Vega, the king

Figure 1 Bartolomé González, *La reina Ana de Austria, cuarta esposa de Felipe II* (Queen Ana de Austria, fourth wife of King Felipe II), c. 1616. Oil painting, 108.50 cm x 87 cm (Madrid, Museo del Prado).

of public theatres, published his playwrighting manifesto, the *Arte nuevo*, which poignantly captures the political and artistic gains (and potentially devastating losses) of the *Comedia*:

> Elíjase el sujeto y no se mire
> (Perdonen los preceptos) si es de reyes
> Aunque por esto entiendo que el prudente
> Felipe, rey de España y señor nuestro,
> En viendo un rey, en ellas se enfadaba
> O fuese el ver que al arte contradice,
> O que la autoridad real no debe
> Andar fingida entre la humilde plebe.   (291)

> (Select the subject and don't be dismayed –
> Forgive these rules – if kings must be portrayed.
> Though as for that I understand our lord
> Philip the Prudent, king of Spain, deplored
> Seeing a king in them, either because
> He thought it went against artistic laws
> Or did not want authority to show
> Before an audience so mean and low)   (140 Carlson trans.)

Despite the Prudent King's resistance to seeing his 'autoridad real' manipulated by *comediantes* and 'fingida entre la plebe,' by the 1600s Madrid was the *capital ceremonial* and, as Lope suggests, any subject could appear onstage regardless of its point of origin or circumstances of birth: 'elíjase el sujeto y no se mire, / (perdonen los preceptos) si es de reyes' (291). In the end, many questions remain for readers who wish to visualize more clearly those real brides walking down the aisle. This book shifts the ground of this cultural history from the premise of marriage as a conclusion – where brides walk down the aisle to become mere patriarchal territories, bodies enclosed – to a different understanding of these women's figures. Anna de Austria and the other brides, radiant as they walk down the reading aisle, will raise new questions about the theatre of sixteenth- and seventeenth-century Spain and, hopefully, will get other bizarre, spectacular turns at the altar of interpretation.

4 Foundational Violence and the Drama of Honour

> Natural hatred is a greater evil in marriage than the accident of adultery.
>
> John Milton, *The Doctrine and Discipline of Divorce*

The violence with which Don Gutierre Alfonso de Solís directs his anger against Doña Mencía de Acuña, his wife, is perhaps nowhere more exemplarily represented in *El médico de su honra* (*The Surgeon of His Honour*) than when he orders Ludovico, the bloodletter, to execute her:

> Que la sangres,
> y la dejes, que rendida
> a su violencia desmaye
> la fuerza, y que en tanto horror
> tú atrevido la acompañes,
> hasta que por breve herida
> ella espire y se desangre. (198)

> (That you should bleed her, but in such a way
> That strength, surrendering to loss of blood,
> Will gently swoon away. Through this ordeal
> You are to keep her company, in there
> Till she has bled to death, and breathes no more.) (72)[1]

This staggering moment when the husband tersely spells out the details of his wife's capital punishment brings to fruition the plot he has designed to restore a masculinist order.[2] The combination of wonder and terror he instils in Ludovico and, by extension, in the spectators stems from the severity – part content, part form – that informs his words, a contorted spirit that animates the language shrewdly chosen by Pedro Calderón de la Barca for this particular version of the play.

The lapidary command seems to respond to a need and desire to cure the gentleman's ailing honour, as the title implies; at once, the order emulates the king's conclusive style of judicial administration.[3] Indeed, as Don Gutierre conveys to the shaking Ludovico, his urgent utterance leaves no room for interpretation:

> No tienes a qué apelar,
> si buscas en mí piedades,
> sino obedecer, si quieres vivir.   (198–9)

> (Do not reply, nor hope for pity from me.
> Only obey me, if you wish to live.)   (73)

Don Gutierre's categorical speech act constitutes verbal evidence that he is, as is King Pedro, literally willing to erase the boundary of life and death; he thus simultaneously inspires a sense of marvel and dread because his speech act emblematizes the violence of the letter, in the Derridean sense, the possibility that an entity – an idea, a character, a theme, or a situation – can perform a trace that remains in memory (101–3).[4] He wraps up this astounding performance by delegating to the executioner, as his scribe, the task of carrying out the manual labour of writing on his wife's body what he considers to be the letter of the Law.

Tortured by rage, jealousy, and blindness, he delivers a memorable staging of a husband, his hands paradoxically bearing the signature of Doña Mencía's blood forever.[5] The fact that he is aware of the chilling transcendence of the script that he interprets, i.e., that of a lawfully wedded man, becomes fully legible when, charged with uxoricide and quickly judged and acquitted, the king commands him to give his hand again in matrimony. The royal decision seeks to restore Doña Leonor's honour, forcing Don Gutierre to revoke in public his previous decision to abandon her because of what he once read as an act of infidelity. In a perverse twist of fairness, the king's final verdict also gives Don Gutierre the chance to symbolically undo Doña Mencía's execution by giving him a second opportunity to read and write the plot of marriage. However, his words show no evidence of self-reflection as he offers his hand in matrimony to Doña Leonor while he recites the most macabre wedding vows to his new bride:

Mas mira, que va bañada
en sangre, Leonor ...
Mira que médico he sido
de mi honra: no está olvidada
la ciencia.   (214)

(But mark well,
Leonor, that this hand is stained with blood ...
You see I am the Surgeon of my honour.
It is a science I do not forget:
An art I have not lost.)   (82)

Don Gutierre, indeed, offers readers ample proof that he has mastered the art and science of honour – which in this play, tragically, entails mastering the art of violence. Convinced that both Doña Leonor and Doña Mencía have been unfaithful to him, he tries to break away from them. He once abandoned Doña Leonor, not yet his bride, leaving her to suffer the living hell of dishonour while he moved on to seek an honorable life; the second time around, though, the indissoluble bond of matrimony does not allow him to abandon Doña Mencía. His illegal decision to execute her is nonetheless approved by the king himself, an act of compensation as categorical and inexcusable as Don Gutierre's two judgment flaws. As readers can gather if they wish to do so, the accused has been deceived on both counts not by the women whom he suspected, but by the fragility of the evidence he has chosen to ignore in his attempt to prove that the two women had behaved dishonourably toward him. Irony is the only textual unit that, in the end, speaks eloquently, as the law-abiding Don Gutierre agrees to wed Doña Leonor in sheer submission to the royal decree. As 'The End' approaches, Don Gutierre's figura stands beside the king who watches his every move, Doña Mencía's cadaver brutally representing the only remaining evidence of his first marital scenario, and Doña Leonor embodying a second marriage waiting to be written with his bloody inkpot.[6] The rhetoric of irrevocability and the categorical style employed by these two men, supplemented by the inertia and submission of the two women, present readers with a dramatic tapestry in which characters weave unbearably thick performances of marriage, violence, and the Law.

But Doña Mencía's execution and the previous death threats uttered by the king and Don Gutierre are by no means the only way in which violence circulates in this text. *El médico*, as a matter of fact, engages a variety of rhetorical strategies of violent domination that, because of their forcefulness and impunity, rarefy the terms of poetic and political representation of the play and virtually demand that readers resist such an environment.[7] It is no coincidence that characters in the play constantly react by sublimating violence, seeking ways to read and write their stories otherwise. My contention is that *El médico de su honra* employs violence as a rhetorical strategy to articulate a critique of the public linguistic and discursive systems designed to manage and control the institutionalization of marriage, particularly those seen in the previous chapters which pertain to the application of legal theory and writing to the everyday practice of marriage in the domestic sphere. As this chapter argues, this rhetorical strategy advances a view of marriage and the law that, by virtue of its predetermined annihilation of the wife's character, forebodes one of the most resilient aspects of marriage as an institution incompatible with modernity. After analysing aspects of the foundational violence of marriage, this chapter proposes to hear arguments by a variety of characters about the drama of honour and its relation to violence in marriage, from whence the wife's character, Doña Mencía, will emerge as an audible voice. In the tragic point between life and death, her persona asks audiences to understand the paradox of listening to silence in order to understand her predicament and perhaps find meaning (and solutions) to this violence.

Foundational Violence

Heavily invested in shaping a unified, orderly culture and society, the emergent absolutist 'nation / state' of Spain generously and efficiently sponsored careful scrutiny of certain institutions, among which marriage stood out. Within this context, Georgina Dopico Black (*Perfect Wives*) argues that *El médico* critically engages inquisitorial practices, and that Calderón therefore stages the procedures and protocols of the Holy Office as tools designed to reproduce sophisticated ways to contain and 'perfect' women, simultaneously condemning and condoning them. However, as the previous chapters have shown, the brand of justice devised and executed by the Holy Office represented only one piece – albeit a mighty one – in the puzzle of *fueros*, tribunals, venues, and idioms that constituted Spain's emerging legal system. The different discourses of marital regulation that proliferated in Spain from the middle of the sixteenth century, and the language on which they were all based, evident since its inception in the twelve Tridentine canons on marriage, constituted an essentially self-contained cultural unit that proved to be utterly resistant to change in Spain.

This was due in great part, as Navarro noted, to the quick dissemination of Counter-Reformation dogmas by virtue of the revolution of the press and the new modes of reading. As the previous chapters have shown, the sense of existential mooring and finality that the letter of Canon Law imprinted on marriage, and that was so effectively publicized throughout the land, was ratified by the appended rule that not complying with it warranted excommunication. Furthermore, the confluence of these ecclesiastical ideologies on marriage and sexuality with secular publication and legislation translated into a widespread interpretation of the married couple as an association constituted by two specific, static roles: a dominating husband and a duly submissive wife. The end result, for Ruth El Saffar, is that 'the marriage structure, based on a model of dominance and submission, produces in the one called to assert his control a terror and anxiety that only makes of this would-be paradise a torment,' a context in which Calderón 'probes the terror that possesses the one whose gender role requires that he dominate and subdue another' (866). However, this inequality also translated into one of the most heated legal debates of that time, which discussed the vitiation of the marital contract by means of violence (*vis*) or fear (*metus*), or how acts falling under either of these two legal categories could translate into corruption or falsification of consent.[8] Legal theoreticians, as well as various litigants, argued punctiliously points of will, veracity, intention, identity, and hierarchy in marriage, generating crucial semantic distinctions for the word 'violence' that reflected the clear emergence of a dissident consciousness.[9]

In 1564, as seen in earlier chapters, King Felipe's *Real Cédula* stipulated the religious character of marriage, while the *Decreto de Reforma* established the manner in which ceremonies were to be carried out, granting, as Pilar Tenorio Gómez says, a public status to marriage that substituted what until then had been a rather private affair (44). The issue of violence in the private sphere quickly appeared in the widely publicized and disseminated regulatory fictions of marriage, many of which articulated narratives that could be read as inciting a husband to violent behaviour toward his wife. In 1569, the *Nueva Recopilación* pre-scribed that 'if the married woman were to commit adultery, she, and the adulterer are both at the disposition of the husband, who can make of them what he pleases' (Lib 8 Tit 20 Ley 1). Following previous legal codes, the *Nueva Recopilación* says that the husband could kill both perpetrators and not leave one of them alive, but that if he were to kill them, he could keep neither her dowry nor the property of the adul-terer (Lib 8 Tit 20 Ley 1).

In 1598 Diego Gómez Cornejo reiterated this principle in his com-mentary to the eighty-two Laws of Toro: in matters of adultery, legisla-tion in Spain – following the *Siete Partidas* – entitled the husband to take any action he deemed just, as long as he acted in the name of the com-mon cause of justice. Although in principle Gómez Cornejo seemed not to support the husband, denying him rights to property owned by him and his wife, the commentary quickly restores the integrity of the hus-band who acts in the name of the Law:

> The man who killed by his own authority the adulterer and adulteress, even if he catches them in flagrant commission of the crime, and even if the killing is performed justly, will take neither the dowry nor the goods of those who he kills; except in the case he kills or condemns them by virtue of the authority of our justice, in which case we order that the law from the *fuero* (code of law) that apply to this case is observed. (*Opus* fol. 396)

The stress that this public condition of marriage added to the sphere of domestic relations is patent in many of the copious treatises for hus-bands and wives that proliferated throughout Europe, most of which reiterated the marital engagement of husband-master and wife-servant. Juan Luis Vives clearly articulates this rhetoric of foundational violence and submission with his prescription that the wife must observe resig-nation and silence when confronted with the husband's physical pun-ishment, further suggesting that perhaps his drive to assault has been incited by her wrongdoing:

> And, if out of vice or a fit of madness, he were to lay hands on you, think that it is God who punishes you, and that this happens because of your sins, for which you do penance ... Devour your pain at home and don't crow about it outside, don't complaint to other women about your husband, never let it seem that you place a judge between you and him:

confine your domestic troubles with the walls of your house; don't let them go out in the street or circulate around the village. (*Manual* 1094)

The language used by lawmakers and authors of conduct handbooks who sought to regulate marital relations found its way into the contractual arena and signalled a categorical finality in the legal production of married subjects.

The above-mentioned lawsuit filed by Doña Elvira Enriquez against Don Enrique Enrriquez illustrates the complex negotiations of marital issues in the courthouses, and how those involved in such litigation faced substantive social and personal controversy.[10] Don Enrique alleged that Doña Elvira had given him signs of matrimonial engagement but, despite the evidence presented by him and his violent intent and argumentation, in the end the judge decided that she was not bound to marry him. The violence of the language employed in this case was generated primarily by the force with which don Enrique attempted to take over the dead marquis's estate, and his performance of this violence was so notorious that it appeared explicitly in the title page: 'File about the Violent Marriage Attempted between Doña Elvira Enriquez Widow of Don Alvaro de Borja, Marquis of Alcañices, and Don Enrique Enrriquez' (*Sobre el violento* CCPEC, Leg. 1604, Fol. 1). In fact, the violence tangible in these court documents would become characteristic of the negotiations of this estate. The *mayorazgo* continued to be disputed in court by many others after Doña Elvira, until the house of the Count-Duke of Benavente won all appeals and earned the entitlement of the Ducado de Gandía in 1800. Doña Elvira, heir to the substantial fortune left to her by her deceased husband, employed significant amounts of force to contest the case, particularly the strongest piece of evidence presented against her, a paper signed by her that bore the proof that she had agreed to marry Don Enrique:

> me hicieron firmar mucho despues de auer publicado en esta corte el dho casamiento con malos terminos y actos deshonestos, pareciendoles que por una vía y otra me auian de obligar a que contra mi voluntad me casase con el otro don Enrique. (*Sobre el violento* CCPEC, Leg. 1604, Fol. 1)

> (they made me sign a long time after having published in this court such marriage with bad terms and dishonest acts, for they thought that one way or another they would force me to marry the other Don Enrique against my will.)

Don Enrique, on the other hand, refuted the allegation, saying:

> le dio ella la palabra delante de una altar auiendo testigo al Señor Sant Antonio de que se casaría con el y le llamó muchas vezes marido y le dijo que quanto a lo espiritual lo era y que lo demás se aria en casando ella su hija y acabando ciertos negocios que tenía. (*Sobre el violento* CCPEC, Leg. 1604, Fol. 1)

> (she gave him her word in front of an altar, having Lord Saint Anthony as her witness that she would marry him, and she called him her husband many times, and told him that in a spiritual sense he already was and that the rest would take place as soon as she married her daughter and finished some pending business she had.)

Despite Don Enrique's fabrications and forceful argumentation, the judges found in favour of Doña Elvira and ordered Don Enrique to desist.[11] The presence of this violence remained, though, like Doña Mencía's blood on Don Gutierre's hands, for her and others after her to read. The tension between the processes of legislation and litigation exposed a troubled relationship between the sacrament of marriage and the intense negotiations of material property that were part of the secular performance of marriage, a wealth of referents that play-wrights utilized to manage politics and poetics in the composition of their texts.

The Drama of Honour

In the *Comedia* the word 'honour' became one of the most reiterated terms of dramatic engagement. Lope de Vega captured this point in his defence of the new art of writing *comedias* cited earlier: 'Los casos de la honra son mejores, / porque mueven con fuerça a toda gente' (Best are those plots where honour has a part, / These stir profoundly every hearer's heart) (*Arte Nuevo* 293, 143). Two reasons guided the stirring force with which Lope deemed that these scenes of marriage could move: on the one hand, the violation to a sense of honour that caused the dramatic conflict, and on the other, the fact that such violation (usu-ally encoded as the crime and sin of adultery in the honour dramas) could not merely be shown, but punished onstage. Francisco Bances Candamo's 1689–90 *Theatro de los theatros de los passados y presentes siglos*

(Theatre of Theatres of the Past and Present Centuries) captures the delicate balance with which subjects and stages were faced when involved in a *caso de la honra*:

> There is not a single one among all the Castilian *Comedias* that ends with an adultery, although there are some that begin with one and end in the tragedy of vengeance, because it is an indispensable rule that one shows the crime without its punishment, in order not to give a bad example, and because one is supposed to show horror in adultery rather than to incite anyone to commit it; and, in an example that is preached in church, to tell the punishment it is imperative to tell the sin. (34)

In the theatre, honour evolved in highly sophisticated terms that, by the end of the seventeenth century, as Bances Candamo notes, had built an artistic mirror in which the blame for adultery and uxoricide onstage was well placed in men's advances, women's weaknesses:

> Since Don Pedro Calderón crafted the air and decorum of the artistic Figures with such care, there has been no adultery that is not found to be the wife's fault, having been forced and tricked. And in his exquisite Comedia *The Painter of His Dishonour* he made the actor steal a married woman, without any guilt of the unfortunate lady, and she remained untouched when in his possession, and, that notwithstanding, because he doubts, the husband kills them both. For, what pen, no matter how severe it is, will say that married women will find more within reach here the desire to commit adultery, rather than the horror of the punishment, if they have been given to drink the one next to the other? (34)

In the strict confines of matrimony, the cathartic potential of such a situation could only be achieved by means of her death, a desirable punishment for adultery:

> And if they found it [the desire to commit adultery], it will be because of the evil in the eyes of the beholders, and not in the intrinsic malice of the object, for the entire discourse of the Comedia can be school of good spouses, and its goal, the terror of the bad ones. The curious one can now think where did that Father [the *moralistas*] found a single Comedia that ends as he says they all end, with a dishonest communication, a scandalous correspondence, an incest, or with an adultery. (34)

Honour, as a theatrical convention defined by a conflict between husband and wife that sprang from the male's suspicion that the female had adulterated the marriage, has been subject to intense scrutiny. Many fewer studies, on the other hand, have been devoted to the correspondence of what has been termed the 'code of honour' from Golden Age Spain with legal theories and practices of the time.[12] This is a surprising omission from literary and cultural history, given that in more ways than one such a code could be read as an arcane, primitive version of family law – given its links with the tragedy of the sexual family that Martha Fineman studies in twentieth-century law. In *El médico* the conflict intensifies as the wife is not able to dissipate her husband's doubts, and the play ends (as all the dramas that represented what Bances Candamo called the 'tragedias de la Venganza' do) inevitably with her death, performed almost by default in grand execution style.

The *casos de la honra* or honour plays (Lope's dictum economically fuses theatre with casuistry) grew to be extremely popular, since audiences and critics relished the suspense of the plot and the spectacle of vengeance.[13] Following Bances Candamo and Lope, most critics have focused on these points of artistic and political representation, and have developed a critical blind spot of this drama by virtue of the lack of visibility of the wife's subject. Her body, wrapped in taffeta, has become an emblem of the woman suspended in the point of tragedy, between life and death.[14] Shifting the reading gaze away from the wife's impotence and execution, and focusing on her lively recitation of the conflict between what the Law says she is supposed to be or do and what the law affords her to voice, readers can deploy the wife's litigious discourse as a tool to resist the mooring of the 'mysterious' union of man and woman.[15] With that, this subject stage represents wife, marriage, and honour in ways other than the ones demanded by the union as a potential primal scene of human violence.

In the cultural economy of early modern Spain honour translated into an obsession for men with *limpieza de sangre* (blood purity) and for women with the preservation (or appearance) of their own chastity, silence, and immobility; in this context, a wife's attempt to prove her innocence in a case of suspicion of adultery (and her husband's attempt to believe her) became a self-defeating enterprise.[16] This burden, stamped on the marital roles by Counter-Reformation design, represents what John Milton termed 'natural hatred,' that is to say, an evidentiary maze that drove spouses to distrust, hypocrisy, suspicion, and, in its extreme version, perennial silence and death (*Complete*

Works 3:332–498).[17] Readings of this play have tended not to question this premise, classifying the text as an archetypal honour drama and a traditional myth of the 'Hispanic character.' What has been sacrificed in this process is one of the central tenets of modern legal systems, the clarity of evidence needed to establish the burden of proof. However, it is possible to suggest a reading of these dramas in which men's compulsive obsession with their honour, women's inferiority and alleged imprudence, and even uxoricide are not, literally, the natural byproducts of a Spanish code of honour. Rather, *El médico* and other honour dramas can be interpreted as vehicles to articulate commentaries about the dramatic quality and great possibility for tragedy that such lack of burden of proof represented for both spouses. In this context, these dramas signal performances of marriage, violence, and the Law as critiques of certain disciplinary discourses that limited the power of agency of subjects willing to engage in marital relations.

As the title announces, this text performs the sign of violence most commonly under the rubric of honour, a precious and fragile commodity that contributed largely to the sustainability of violence in seventeenth-century Spain.[18] Indeed, copious textual evidence from this period shows that honour was a highly desirable currency that eventually became what in Golden Age studies has been coined a staple of Spain's baroque culture. On the other hand, the fact that not possessing honour translated into abuse, betrayal, fear, and death – especially for women, as María de Zayas's *Desengaños amorosos* painfully and repeatedly shows – has been interpreted most frequently in terms of a 'barbaric' cultural and political environment in seventeenth-century Spain. Only recently have critics begun to consider honour in relation to the specific economics of its representation in emerging social, political, and legal discourses and institutions.[19] The pervasive circulation of violence in this text, as well as the signs of resistance to it, have not been the central focus of its critical reception, being frequently dismissed in favour of a variety of other reading and writing agendas.[20] In ways prefigured by Gutierre's adulterated reading of the signs of his wife's alleged adultery – pun intended – critics have transmuted Calderón's complex fabrication into a work either in favour of or against an usually unspecified or highly encrypted code of honour. That honour is a prominent feature of *El médico*, and that it occupies the mind of every character appearing onstage is an evident fact – albeit not a self-evident one.

Despite the prominent place that honour occupies in the title and the language of the text, it cannot shoulder the burden of evidence by itself.

In relation to law, Kagan has argued that lawsuits pertaining to insults and defamation, a type of litigation substantially invested in the same preoccupation with honour that is central to the honour dramas, were related less to a 'peculiar sense of personal honor,' typical of many descriptions of Spanish national character, than to the rapid changes in the social and economic arenas (103). Honour, after all, is an unwritten Law, in the Justinian sense, agreed upon by the 'wise men' cited by the *Nueva Recopilación*, but without any clear boundaries of what is just or fair. Adultery was, in fact, illegal, clearly stated; but the methods to determine its occurrence – especially onstage, where the slightest reference to sexual acts or innuendos could translate into a closing of the theatre – engaged insufficient resources to establish proof, evidence, and much less certainty. Inscribing a fusion of languages and discourses in *El médico*, Calderón opens up a space where subjects negotiate, as characters arguing their cases in court, their own terms of reading and writing marriage and violence. Unfortunately, readings of *El médico* in dialogue with Spain's complex legal system have been obscured in part because the only 'cases' of law mentioned in relation to this play have been noted strictly as sources of the wife's execution scene, most commonly viewed as the centre stage of the drama. Cruickshank, for instance, proposes that citing actual cases of wife-murder in relation to *El médico* is an exercise in critical imprudence; scholars, he says, frequently refer to places and/or times other than seventeenth-century Spain and, as such, their examples are not representative of the baroque Spain Menéndez Pelayo and others evoke, one in which wife-killing was a common practice (*El médico* 28–9).

This critique notwithstanding, Cruickshank does not shift the focus of the representation of violence away from the moment of the killing, referring, as does McKendrick ('Honour'), to the bleeding of a suspected wife by accident narrated in 1530 in the *Libro de los siete sabios de Roma*, one of the heirs of the *Sendebar* tradition.[21] Hence, a reading that assesses how violence circulates in *El médico* beyond the climax of Doña Mencía's execution remains pending, so that readers can productively reread such an execution. As I have argued elsewhere, readers ought to take into account how Don Gutierre, Doña Mencía, Doña Leonor, Coquín, Don Arias, and Jacinta perform a variety of argumentative critiques of the closure imposed on marital relations by regulatory fictions ('The Burden of Evidence' 451). For Doña Mencía, the wife, all that is left is tragedy.

The Tragedy of Mencía

El médico speaks not only of the difficulty of managing the relations between men and women, and how marital regulations make these relations prone to abuse and lack of mutual trust, but also of the hardship that subjects face in order to sustain and prove their cases of marital disputation in court. The text represents early on a clear awareness of how the laws of men are inextricably bound to the presence and will of royalty, as the laws of nature have their own predetermined hierarchies. Thus Don Gutierre, in poetic rhyme 'ley / rey' (law / king), binds his duty to a still unsuspected Infante Don Enrique:

> Y pues sois rayo español,
> descansad aquí; que es ley
> hacer el palacio del rey
> también, si hace esfera el sol.   (90)

> (Since you are
> The sun's ray of your country, warm us here
> By resting longer. For a Prince can make
> A palace of his quarters by his presence,
> As surely as the bright sun makes a sphere.)   (12)

On the other hand, Doña Mencía, conscious of the importance of argumentation even in the face of royalty, attempts to resolve the mounting tension between the two men by telling Don Gutierre, on the one hand, that 'hay calidades de culpa / que no merecen castigo' (93) (there are kinds / Of guilt that do not merit punishment) (13). The Infante, on the other hand, refuted that 'ninguno es poderoso / en el ajeno albedrío' (93) (no person / Has power over another's will and judgment) (13). The Infante voices the limits of Doña Mencía's fair premise by exercising the hegemony of his royal will over those of wife and husband, and his pretended vows to continue to pursue her while ignoring their matrimonial bond:

> Guárdeos Dios,
> hermosísima Mencía;
> y porque veáis que estimo
> el consejo, buscaré

a esta dama, y della oiré
la disculpa.   (97)

(May God preserve you,
Most beautiful Mencía! And to show you
That I esteem your counsel, I shall seek
The lady out and hear her explanation.)   (15)

Doña Mencía's premature and yet visionary sense of the inevitable lethal conflict that she faces is recited by her in a pathetic and oft-quoted speech to her *esclava herrada* in which she voices her clear awareness of her subordinate condition:

Nací en Sevilla, y en ella
Me vio Enrique, festejó
mis desdenes, celebró
mi nombre, ¡felice estrella!
Fuese, y mi padre atropella
la libertad que hubo en mí
La mano a Gutierre di,
volvió Enrique, y en rigor,
tuve amor, y tengo honor:
esto es cuanto sé de mí.   (101)

(In Seville I was born, and there
Henry first saw me, and thawed my cold disdain
With loving praise – Oh happy Star! – and then
He went away on duty. When my father
Cut short the liberty I once enjoyed,
To put me in a convent, as I feared, –
I gave my hand to Don Gutierre. Then
Henry returned. I love him: yet my honour
Forbids. That's all I know about myself.)   (17)

As Doña Mencía ends her lament, the stage is readied for the first court scene (in the dual sense of palatial space and tribunal). The power play between theatre and politics in the court of Philip IV is tangible in the layout of the physical disposition of stages and audiences that Greer considers central to the making of court spectacles (*The Play* 82–3), as it is in Kagan's analysis of a woodcut representing a 'Sala de Chancillería' in Valladolid in the seventeenth century (9); comparing these judicial and courtly spaces can prove crucial to understanding the performative aspects of this scene, and how the king's historical label of 'El Justiciero' acquires great meaning by virtue of these verbal and spatial arrangements indicated in the text of El médico.[22]

The process of negotiation of this space for Doña Mencía mobilizes the *imago* that Eagleton proposes for tragedy, an image that is 'sublime in both humanist and psychoanalytical sense – pleasurable, majestic, awe-inspiring, suggestive of infinite capacity and immeasurable value, yet also punitive, intimidating, cutting us savagely down to size' (176). The discourse that Doña Mencía articulates from the very beginning of the play reflects her great sense of vision, underscored by the irony that her sight is blurred and does not allow her to see who the men approaching her husband's villa are, as she watches events unfold from the tower of her husband's villa. Nonetheless, her speech utters a number of vivid images that her eyesight has captured: a handsome gentleman, a light beast, a feathered plume, a sun, some stars, and even the field in spring bloom. Her sight is fine, until it is not, momentarily, the threshold to a moment of anagnorisis, the witnessing of 'a calamity'; as soon as she realizes who it is in her arms, she wishes it were a dream. It is the Infante Don Enrique, her old flame, and his presence in the country house where her husband keeps her from the ghosts of his past leads Doña Mencía to prophesy that in his being there, 'va mi honor en ello' (my honor is concerned in this) (81, 6). Faced with the conflict of the incompatibility of her past love lost and her present honour in a precarious position, she begs everyone for 'Silencio, / que importa mucho' (Hush! / Silence is imperative) (80, 6).

Her expressed desire to see that which is tragic in her life and to signify from among the ruins of such conflict (emblems, perhaps, of her own awareness of the ruin that tragedy represents as a vehicle to express her voice) is vehement, and she does not hesitate to acknowledge it when she is left alone with the audience and the Infante. Although her honourable position in society leads her to voice that 'soy quien soy' (I am who I am), she also says that such social status is

> Una cárcel de nieve, donde
> está aprisonado el fuego,
> que ya, resuelto en cenizas
> es ruina que está diciendo:
> '¡Aquí fue amor!'   (81)

('The silence and this prison, here, of snow,
Which is my breast! Its prisoner was once
A fire, which now has been reduced to cinders,
Whose ruined ash proclaims: 'This, once, was Love.')   (7)

The images of the prison, the snow, and the loss reveal what she sees in the pathetic state of her matrimony, her hubris, which eventually will lead to the nemesis that will try to cloak her and render her (in)visible. Before she dies, though, she will become visible, for as Evangelina Rodríguez Cuadros says, 'in the solitude that tragedy demands, the soliloquy of the woman there represented – as it does for the masculine character – has conquered the inner space, her only moment, paradoxically, of sentimental freedom' (*Calderón* 103).

Bearing this in mind one can understand that from such an early moment in the play Doña Mencía can recognize that death and silence are one and the same, and that faced with the sight of her old lover in her own house the inner fire of love only can lead her to recognize how dead she is in her present life, a thought she will resist throughout the entire play. Faced, again, with the old flame, this time he talks and makes advances to her; the unbearable weight of tragedy looms as the Infante, lying in a cot 'de un cuero turco y de flores' (of Turkish leather worked with flowers) (81, 6) that she has ordered for him, announces to the audience in an aside that 'presto de tantos favores / será desengaño el tiempo' (too soon these raptures will be dashed to earth) (85, 9). Don Arias enters and Don Gutierre senses his bewilderment, which he interprets in the context of the fall from the horse experienced by the Infante, 'acaso, sino agüero / de mi muerte' (but the most certain omen of my death) (87, 10).

Dismissing the possibility that he, one of royal blood, will be the one facing death, and asking him to be more discrete about the details of their household, Doña Mencía resists: 'Quien oyera a vuestra alteza / quejas, agravios, desprecios, / podrá formar de mi honor / presunciones y concetos / indignos de él' (Anyone, thus, to hear your Highness raging, / Accusing me, and cursing in this way, / Would form opinions and suspicions of / My honour, quite unworthy of it) (88, 10). To herself and the audience she confesses the overwhelming desire with which Don Enrique courted her. Since that did not yield a matrimonial union, however, she was led to honourably reject his advances toward her. All the same, her love for Don Enrique was so great that even in the present time she is willing to run the risk of dishonouring her husband's name in order to protect the Infante's health:

Si me casé, ¿de qué engaño
se queja, siendo sujeto
imposible a sus pasiones,
reservado a sus intentos,
pues soy para dama más,
lo que para esposa menos?
Y así, en esta parte ya
disculpara, en la que tengo
de mujer, a vuestros pies
humilde, señor, os ruego
no os ausentéis de esta casa,
poniendo a tan claro riesgo la salud.   (89)

(If I got married, how can you complain
That I deceived you, since I'm now an object
Impossible and unattainable
By your desires and passions? Would I be
The more a lady, if the less a wife?
So having now excused myself from blame
In what concerns my marriage, at your feet
I beg your Highness not to leave this house
At such great risk and peril to your health.)   (11)

The presence of royal blood in his house *fuori muri* blinds Don Gutierre as well and, without giving it a second thought, he offers the house and a horse to replace the fallen one to Don Enrique, while he later explains to Doña Mencía the violent paradox of honour: 'Y fuera de esto, ir sirviendo / al infante Enrique, entiendo / que es acción justa y debida, / ya que debí a su caída / el honor que hoy ha ganado / nuestra casa' (I ought to be attending on the Prince / Whose fall has brought such honour to our house) (97–8, 15).

She voices her opposition to his decision, expressing a proverbial wifely more: 'Oh qué tales sois los hombres! / Hoy olvido, ayer amor; / ayer gusto, y hoy rigor' (Al you men are thus. / One day it's love, the next day love's forgotten. / One day it's pleasure, and the next it's pain) (98, 16). The tragic plot thickens as it becomes more complex and beautiful when Doña Mencía confesses to Jacinta, the branded slave, what she knows about her own self, which stands in open contrast to the gentleman's short memory – another matrimonial flaw: 'La mano a Gutierre di, / volvió Enrique, y en rigor, / tuve amor, y tengo honor. Esto es cuanto sé de mí' (I gave my hand to Don Gutierre. Then / Henry returned. I love him: yet my honour / Forbids. That's all I know about myself) (101, 17). This critical anagnorisis (a character blinded who, by virtue of her own self-recognition, becomes a great source of catharsis) feeds her ironclad resistance to the 'love' intrusions of the Infante when Don Gutierre, by virtue of his short fuse, ends up in prison in the second act. When the husband reappears in the garden of the house, Doña Mencía strategically moves the Infante backstage to a 'pabellón / que en mi misma cuadra está' (summerhouse / Which joins my room, get in and hide yourself), to show him that despite his royal blood he occupies a second plane in her line of priorities (130, 33). As she bids him farewell, she articulates with brilliant insight the mooring into which she has signed up for life: '¿Ya, señor, no va una esclava? / Yo lo soy, y lo he de ser, / Jacinta, venme a ayudar' (My lord, a slave *is* going. I'm your slave: / I wish to be and must be. Come, Jacinta, / And help me to prepare it) (134, 35). The rejection is diffused by the presence of Don Enrique in the house, a point not lost in Doña Mencía's foresight of the end: 'Porque / si yo no se lo dijera / y Gutierre lo sintiera, / la presunción era clara, / pues no se desengañara / de que yo cómplice era' (If I had not said I had seen a man / And had my husband found him by himself / It would have made him certain of my guilt) (140, 38).

Don Gutierre, unconvinced when told about it, extends his arms to reveal the reach of his cloak, with which he envelops her next to the dagger. The husband's gorgeous and at once terrifying embrace fuses with astounding clarity and plasticity the referential palimpsest of the scene: the proxemic relation of the two actors makes them look like one, inscribing the theological principle of matrimony being a union where two subjects become one like Christ became one with the church; simultaneously, the self-referential level of the honour drama kicks in with the husband's use of his costume, for if this were really an audiovisual story about the husband, it would be a *comedia de capa y espada*. The tragic marital clasp, not funny but highly comic, signals also the negotiation of blindness and insight under way between the spouses. As she experiences the virtual squeeze of death, still in life, Doña Mencía whispers to Don Gutierre: 'Al verte ansí, presumía / que ya en mi sangre bañada / hoy moría desangrada' (To see you coming with that dagger thus, / I thought you were about to take my life / And that today I was to bleed to death / And bathe in my own blood. It was that dagger) (142, 39). This reads as an exact prophecy of her own execution, which reveals her uncanny capacity to foresee her future death, and her impotence before the crushing fate lying before her. Tragically, it is also by virtue of Don Gutierre's costume and muzzled scene in the garden that Doña Mencía's capable insight is confused and blinded.

Suspicions bloom and, in a highly stylized domino effect, they amount to what Doña Mencía shrewdly now sees, in an aside, as the ornaments of her house: 'Miedo, espanto, temor y horror tan fuerte, / parasismos han sido de mi muerte' (And horror mingles in his fiery breath / The pangs, the throes, the rattle of my death!) (171, 56). Despite the guilt implied by the signs of adultery, Doña Mencía finds herself innocent: 'Señor, detén la espada, / no me juzgues culpada. / El·cielo sabe que inocente muero. / ¿Qué fiera mano, qué sangriento acero / en mi pecho ejecutas? ¡Tente, tente! / Una mujer no mates inocente' (My lord, withhold your sword! I am not guilty. / The Heavens know that I die innocent! / What cruel hand, what bloody steel is this / With which you rip my breast? [Stop, stop! Do not kill an innocent woman]) (193, 69). The limbo between life and death, that horrendous sign of the surreal uncertainty that always forebodes the eruption of violence in marriage, reaches a sublime level of signification when Doña Mencía reads Don Gutierre's written supplement to her pretend message to the Infante: 'El amor te adora, el honor te aborrece; y / así el uno te mata, y el otro te avisa: / dos horas tienes de vida; cristiana eres, / salva el alma, que la vida es imposible' (Though Love adores you, Honour must / abhor you. / Though Honour slays you, Love would give you warning / And counsel. You have two more hours of life. / You are a Christian: save your soul, since, now, / It is impossible to save your life) (193, 69–70). Caged in her house with no one to hear her, the fictive domestic walls enshrine her new-found solitude, a terrifying stretch of time and space in which her sorrowful self floats, as she says, 'tropezando en la sombra de mi muerte' (stumbling in the shadow of my death) (194, 70).

After a brief ellipsis in which the king and Don Diego intervene with a group of musicians to alleviate the intensity of Doña Mencía's lethal confinement, Don Gutierre and Ludovico, the muzzled executioner, enter. Don Gutierre commands Ludovico to not be fearful as he joins the scene (despite the fact that he walks around with him holding a dagger against his chest) and, after threatening him with the verses cited at the beginning of this chapter, he brings him to the house. The elliptical trick has worked, and the symbolic wall behind which marriage violence hides has morphed into that other ritual wall that is the fourth wall of theatre. Doña Mencía has succumbed to the poison with which the fear in marital violence freezes the victims. Hence, when Ludovico gazes upon her chamber what he sees is not the woman full of life whom audiences have seen until then – a woman defending herself with an arsenal of arms of resistance to the dictatorship of matrimonial honour, generated by her own conscience of vulnerability and weakness. Instead of that eloquent and perceptive woman watched by the audience since the scene in the tower with which the play opens, Ludovico sees 'una imagen / de la muerte, un bulto, / que sobre una cama yace; / dos velas tiene a los lados, / y un crucifijo delante. / Quién es no puedo decir, que con unos tafetanes el rostro tiene cubierto' (an effigy of death, / A body lying on a bed, with two / Candles that burn on either side of it, / And, straight in front of it, a crucifix. / But who it is I cannot tell, because / A silken veil is draped over the face) (198, 72). Don Gutierre identifies the image of Doña Mencía wrapped in the banned cloth of silken taffeta with the lump that, in solidarity with his violence, many in the audience and readership have ignored from the critical map of the play: the woman who must bear in silence and alone the unsustainable scene of violence in marriage, a tableau vivant or live cadaver whom Ludovico begins to kill in this scene.

Once the voice and face of Doña Mencía disappear under the tragic effect of the taffeta, the bundle into which her figure has been turned is the only visual remains of her persona onstage. Then, the legendary sentence of the husband, quoted on the first page of this chapter, is uttered, fusing the labour of *poesis* with the horror of the climax of this tragedy of honour. The lethal blow against the wife remains, as always, 'behind the wall' as Tracy Chapman sang it in her heartbreaking *a capella* solo by that title. In *El médico*, the scene appears in all its baroque splendour: strength surrendered to the violence and loss of blood, which is code for unclean blood. The early modern version of gore freezes the executioner, commanded by the gentle man, to watch and gaze until the brief wound has allowed all breath of life out of her body (198; 72). Championing his well-deserved title of prince of pathetic, violent shadows of honour, Don Gutierre ponders the virtues of his decision: wounds cannot be hidden; perhaps this forebodes the complex relationship of psychoanalysis and other sciences with gender and marriage.

Also, he muses, the bleeding had to happen in order to cure her, perhaps the bandage of the bleeding got loose, or the bloodletter did not know who she was, if he was dressed to kill, for he was the surgeon of his honour, since 'todos / curan a cosa de sangre (bleeding's the best cure for Honour) (200, 73). Although the king pardons both the murderer and the lie – conveniently, as his own blood and the social order he represents depend on him keeping the secret – Doña Mencía's voice returns from beyond the grave through Ludovico's mouth to release her own tragic claim. Her last words rise, like a ghost in the legal machine, in the frame of the legal deposition of the executioner that the king, with the audience, sees and hears: 'No la vi el rostro, mas sólo / entre repetidos ayes / escuché: 'Inocente muero; / el cielo no te demande / mi muerte.' Esto dijo, y luego / expiró; y en este instante, / el hombre mató la luz, / y por los pasos que antes / entré salí' (I did not see her face, but only heard / Her voice, between repeated lamentations, / Sob softly: 'May Heaven not require my death: / For I die innocent.' Having said this, / She then expired. The man put out the lights, / And I retraced the selfsame steps by which / I entered) (203, 75).

Silence

Evangelina Rodríguez Cuadros has seen Mencía very clearly, for as she says, the emotional dimension of anagnorisis travels a singular path from the written page to the actors and producers of the scene, to the audience putting together the cathartic gaze; such gaze is a 'recognized truth, while the characters may remain blind in a scenario that has denounced how the law of honor – mythical symbol of a system founded upon a fanatic intolerance – taken to its extreme consequences can be transformed in a space of extermination in which freedom (or perhaps simply compassion) have been expelled' (*Calderón* 106). On that note, and to conclude this terrible chapter, I beg for a minute of silence. The silence that Doña Mencía herself and her husband demand from the blindness of their scene is analogous to what David Eng says about silence, 'not the opposite of speech but, indeed, its very condition of possibility, the precondition of knowing and meaning' (86). With that, adds Eng, those who have disappeared by virtue of nationalisms and state-sanctioned acts of violence (as happened in Argentina between 1976 and 1983 as well as in many households today with events of domestic violence) can be restored, from death to life and be found in the 'bodily remains of the bodies or, more accurately, the lack of such material evidence' that follow these figures (85).

To deny Doña Mencía's cadaver the negotiation of her own tragedy is to deny her violent death by sublimation, as well as the lump of her remains, an absence of the dead body that, Eng rightfully argues, 'makes the work of mourning especially difficult, often leaving it in permanent suspension and denying possibilities for closure' without which there is neither catharsis nor healing (85). After that moment of silence, in which the loss of Mencía can be recognized as the tragedy that it is, other possibilities open up to help us further understand and change the tragic primal scene of violence between spouses. While en route in her own journey to tragedy Doña Mencía, like the *lacrimosa* in Chapman's song after she has been abandoned by everyone else who were prompted by the police to do so, asks the audience members not to fall asleep in their comfy chairs, and instead to continue to read. That way, perhaps, at some point in time the image of her eloquent cadaver could morph into the image of a woman made of hauntingly beautiful flesh and blood.

5 Punishing Illicit Desire

O marvel! A garden amidst flames. My heart has become capable of every form: it is a pasture for gazelles and a convent for Christian monks, and a temple for idols and the pilgrim's Ka'ba and the tables of the Tora and the book of the Koran. I follow the religion of Love; whatever way Love's camels take, that is my religion and my faith.

> Muhyiddin Ibn 'Arabi, 'Poem 11' of the *Tarjuman al-Ashwaq*
> (Interpreter of Desires)

The drama of honour unfolded as the theatrical convention par excellence to stage the crime and punishment of the wife's adultery and permit the husband, brother, or male guardian of her honour to defend the family's blood and name. A different, albeit related, dramatic conflict found its way onto the early modern Spanish stages and eventually became another great theatrical convention: the one experienced by subjects from different *estamentos* (social strata), a condition of separation by birth, lineage, or social standing that made illicit the expression of desire between such subjects and their potential marital bond. As Edda Samudio Aizpúrua argues, the case of María Dolores Balza, a woman of *calidad parda* (dark brown quality or race), born in the Venezuelan township of Mérida, and Don Pedro María Maldonado, white, born in Pamplona and residing in Mérida as a student of the Real Seminario de San Buenaventura, illustrates the broad impact of the *Estatutos de limpieza de sangre* (statutes of blood cleanliness) in the Hispanic world.[1]

Although the historical specificity of marriage laws, in theory and practice, as well as of the *estatutos*, varies significantly between Spain and the Americas, and between the 1500s and the early 1880s when the case of Balza and Maldonado takes place, the legal codes invoked to prosecute them were the same ones that bound subjects to the institution of marriage in the metropolis during the renaissance and baroque periods. Balza, not only *parda* but also a seamstress, felt overwhelmed by what Samudio aptly terms 'the obstacles of their ethnic and socioeconomic inequality' (n. p.). Despite this bleak circumstance, which might surely have eliminated any subject's desire to marry, Balza agonized over her dilemma: should she live in dishonour, or should she and Maldonado opt for a clandestine marriage? Consequently, she and the student of the Royal Seminary chose to trick the marriage institution, and in a brilliant stroke of comedy they declared themselves husband and wife as the priest, Father Francisco Antonio Martos Carrillo, said mass on 8 July 1809. A few subjects who performed as witnesses in the pretend ceremony tattled to Martos, the church representative, and a civil suit ensued.

Balza, twenty-two years of age, and Maldonado, twenty-five, acknowledged having rewritten the Tametsi script. Interestingly, though, they swore at the same time that they were unaware of the fact that such an act was a threat to civil authority – they thought they were defying a religious law. However, the solution they chose to solve their predicament was not merely regulated by theological principles; it had become part of the civil code as a crime punished by civil and ecclesiastical authorities. Samudio economically describes the impact of the Tamtesi on this matter:

> It granted ecclesiastical authorities the faculty to punish and to annul that practice that was considered harmful to society. Moreover, it established rigorous sanctions for those who committed the crime of clandestine marriage. The *Novísima Recopilación* imposed as sentencing the disowning of the spouses, the confiscation of their assets, and exile, according to the case. (n. p.)

When they initiated their relationship, the lovers had asked for permission to be married, but the groom's father, Don Gregorio Maldonado, denied their request. As soon as he was briefed about the details of the case, Bishop Santiago Hernández Milanés demanded that Don Pedro María be denied the *hábito* (livery) he was seeking in Mérida. This was undoubtedly a disastrous outcome for the honourable Maldonado family, who as Samudio rightly annotates, by virtue of their distinguished standing in Pamplona, 'must have had very clear their *pureza de sangre*, free of contamination of bad blood' (n. p.), a factor that no doubt helped Don Pedro María to become a member of the Royal Seminary in the first place.[2]

The unlawful conduct that Balza and Maldonado engaged in when they chose to perform their union as a clandestine marriage was provoked by their deep desire to participate in a ritual ceremony made impossible by their socio-racial difference. The honourable family they planned to build never came to be: once convicted, their 'clandestine act' was declared 'without effect' and they were first imprisoned and then forced to attend mass 'kneeling in the last step of the presbytery, with candles in their hands, which would remain as gifts for the church' (Samudio n. p.). Maldonado was also coerced to fast for a month 'four days a week, two of those with bread and water' (n. p.); Balza also fasted, but with a less severe diet. Maldonado returned to the shackle where he had been placed before the trial, and Balza was forced to pay 'for all the costs of the legal cause' (n. p.). After their punishment was complete, he was exiled and she, like Oriana in that pretend naval battle performed for Anna of Austria, was erased from the legal system and banished from the town.

The Balza-Maldonado case illustrates how subjects imagined and devised scenes that played with the impact of social segregation upon the institution of marriage.[3] In the theatre, *comediantes* produced the generic frame of the *comedia palatina* (palatine play), in which a gentleman agonized over his love for a common woman and resolved the conflict by finding a way to move her to a higher social stratum.[4] These *comedias* capitalized like no other artistic form on the dramatic conflict represented by the illicit desire and will to wed between subjects of different social standing.[5] Onstage, the conflict was resolved by finding a legal way to make her his wife, a feat of social acrobatics viable with the purchase of a title of nobility or another strategic repositioning of the commoner. However, as this chapter notes, ideologies and legislation of *limpieza de sangre* severely limited the capacity of a person to engage in marital negotiations with a partner from a different social stratum, on the grounds that the two were incapacitated by the complicities of the Tametsi and the *Estatutos*, and told not to engage in such illicit desire.

El perro del hortelano (The Dog in the Manger) by Félix Lope de Vega stages the case of a noblewoman, Doña Diana de Belflor, who desires and treats her secretary, Teodoro, sadistically; her motives to do so, though, are clearly masochistic. He responds to her, in turn, with ample masochism of his own, thus subverting the generic frame of the *palatina* by placing at centre stage a relentless attraction that, by virtue of the secretary's unclean blood, constitutes an illicit desire.[6] To compose this critical image of marriage and the impact exercised upon it by the *Estatutos*, the dramatic text of *El perro* deploys elements of audiovisual language such as a sequence of slaps to the secretary's face, his bleeding, and a grand metatheatrical scheme. These theatrical strategies release comic energies as they represent the overwhelming context of *limpieza de sangre*. The farcical routines that lie at the base of these comic gestures are supported by the powerful artistic impact of a theatrical mechanism called the *bofetón* (about-face machine), designed to move objects and actors with the physical action of a slap (fig. 2). The cathartic result, vividly staged in the 'unclean' blood that spills from the secretary's face as a result of the slaps he receives from his lady leads, in turn, to the production of a *lienzo* (napkin, canvas) that by virtue of the magic of theatre wipes away Teodoro's unclean blood, just as the clandestine ceremony of Balza and Maldonado would do in Mérida almost two centuries later, and paints a scene of illicit desire that makes the spectators question the alleged power of the *Estatutos*.[7] In the end, the masochistic slapstick pays off, and a legally acceptable husband is produced, in the economic language of theatre, to capitalize on a newly granted legal capacity for action in the marital situation and its product, blood or lineage.[8] This chapter explores how the subject stage of the born-again husband-and-wife plays, with their troubled genealogies and masochistic desires to contest marital legislation, turned the public theatre into the magical locus of production of libidinal economies and redefined marital negotiations of property, propriety, and desire.

Two of Lope's most cherished plays – *La dama boba* and *El perro del hortelano* – engage the production of libidinal economies in the space of the theatre. Given that the core of concern for the *moralistas* (moralists) was that the body movement and flirting of women in the theatre were responsible for the disease of the Republic, it is telling that both texts explore the ways in which women redefine the very marital prescriptions and negotiations that designate them as submissive, passive subjects in the receiving end of the marital game; in metatheatrical and/or feminist readings of these texts, Doña Finea and Doña Diana play in an unthinkably precise manner the role of director of the show.[9] For Edward Friedman, these two dramatic texts develop what he aptly calls 'sign language,' two distinct referential networks with which the plays give new meaning to love and desire of the illicit kind. In *El perro*, the difference in class that separates Doña Diana, Condesa de Belflor, from

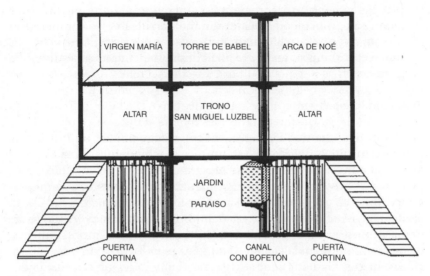

Figure 2 *Fachada con canal con bofetón* (Stage façade with lift/about-face machine). Adapted from José Ruano María de la Haza '"Teatro" para *La Creación del mundo*, de Lope.' Drawing, 10.2 cm x 7.6 cm (Ruano and Allen, *Los teatros comerciales*, 550).

Teodoro, her secretary, is very rigid and, as Friedman notes, the promises of matrimony uttered in the final scene may represent 'feigned emotions' and not genuine feelings of love between a *mujer principal* (noble lady) and her staff member (4). For Friedman this play is a sustained, artful act of deconstruction marked by rhetorical instances of deferral that make the textual inscription of love tantamount to a relentless preamble to sex, what some may call in plain English an insufferable foreplay.

However, Lope's *El perro* stages a much more complex affair than mere foreplay, and this complexity constitutes the object of my criticism. My aim is to dwell in the dangerous poetic and linguistic liaison that Doña Diana and Teodoro mobilize by their generation and expression of desire, which is frequently interrupted by Doña Diana herself as well as by other characters of *El perro*. This series of games they all play can be best understood as relations of the masochistic kind.[10] Although medical and social discourses consider masochism a 'perversion' and perhaps even a 'disease,' it is not my intention to apply a discursive ointment to

El perro, but rather to insist on the point that the play's fabrication of love constitutes a *pharmakon* (medicine) – in the Derridean sense of rhetorical enveloping love and toiling with audiovisual, theatrical language – to counteract the punishment of the illicit desire that Balza and Maldonado endured and suffered as a result of their marital play.[11]

Slapstick Masochism

My analysis of the ways in which Lope writes sexuality in this text is designed to initiate a dialogue concerning the circulation of masochism, theatrical games, and *limpieza de sangre*. Centuries before philosophy, psychology, medicine, or erotology theorized masochism, Lope represented this type of sexual dynamics in *El perro* to unleash ludic and libidinal economies that interrogate and even have the potential to refigure a most sacred premise in a caste society: the impossibility of members of different social strata to engage in love, sexual, or marital affairs. In this chapter, I concur with Friedman in seeing class and honour satirized in *El perro*, but my concern focuses on the theatrical strategies tangibly present onstage in the usage of the terms *bofetones* (slaps in the face, stage machines), *lienzo* (handkerchief, canvas), and *sangre* (blood), and on a masochistic primal scene by means of which Lope creates a 'religion of love' like the one represented in 'Poem 11' of Ibn 'Arabi's *The Interpreter of Desires*, an example of love poetry from the classical Arabic tradition that, following the exclusionary politics of the *Estatutos* and other programs of *limpieza de sangre*, would be equivalent to the presence of *sangre impura* in the text.[12] In staging illicit desires in a theatrical space heavily regulated and policed by the crown, and by playing creative games about such desires with a flair that the nineteenth-century psychoanalytic revolution did not even imagine, Lope's *El perro* plants the seed for a collective imaginary in which the theatrical building of slapstick masochism could be used by audiences to free themselves from social bonds and the dictates of the caste system mandated by *limpieza de sangre* programs and ideologies.

This is closely tied to how Renaissance stage practices in Spain and Italy, as William Egginton's title suggests, became critical steps in the process of 'how the world became a stage.' Combining psychoanalytic and performance theories, Egginton notes that spectatorial subjects 'are not transfixed by what they see on the stage, but rather by what they fail to see anyway; in other words, they are transfixed by what is concealed' (111). In developing the most effective stage, says Egginton, the

Comedia 'tried to oblige precisely that desire by making the screen multi-leveled, and opening the rear curtain or trap door in order to effect "discoveries" that, more often than not, represented the fullest, most substantial possible entities: cadavers or mutilated bodies' (111). In *El perro* the drawing of blood from the secretary's body is a critical act that mobilizes what José María Ruano de la Haza calls 'the feast of the senses' ('Hacia una metodología' 82), in order to interpellate the sustainability of the *sociedad estamental*. The fact that this play was written when the expulsion of the last Muslims of Spain was taking place makes the theatrical games Doña Diana and Teodoro play timely and poignant, because the memory of Arabic poetry could be read as a collective impossible love flickering in the comic screen.

Their masochism, not exactly fitting the mould of a perversion, could perhaps be read as the sublimation of a racialized and sexualized pleasure unthinkable at the time, a difference that theatre could imagine by changing the level and orientation of the actors by mechanical devices such as the *canal* (lift) or the *bofetón* (about-face machine).[13] The subject stages of *El perro* unfold with a spirit familiar to Ibn 'Arabi, a heart (as the above epigraph says) 'capable of every form.' As we shall see in *El perro*, the feeling and meaning of the poetic form are highlighted by the space of the theatre and spectacular machinery. Although *El perro* does not call for the specific machine of the *bofetón* as other plays do – like Ana Caro's *El Conde Partinuplés*, for instance – the spectators' awareness of the existence of such machinery propelled the farcical movement of bodies to different levels of meaning. In other words, the link between Doña Diana, Teodoro, Marcela, and Tristán, their masochistic acts, and their rising above the limitations of the *Estatutos* and marital regulations rests on the powerful development of theatre as a medium and a space in which a subject could be moved out of his/her social inferiority by means of a *bofetón*, the slap that, by extension, conveyed to audiences the capacity that the about-face machine conferred upon a character to flip him or herself into another identity.

The theatrical map of masochistic perversion is contained in the poetic blueprint of nine sonnets that span three acts, recited by Doña Diana, Teodoro, and Marcela – the third leg of what some would call today a *ménage à trois*.[14] The first level of perversion is that of the sonnet form, ostensibly designed after Petrarch's *Rime Sparse* to lure readers into the realm of incantation of an adored, assumedly female 'you' figure whom the assumedly male poet yearns for and approaches with his poetic voice.[15] In open contrast with the portrait tradition that informed the sonnet and yielded splendid female figures for readers to see and likewise desire, the nine sonnets in *El perro* offer a virtually non-negotiable landscape of impossible love. In fact, readers find in them future subjunctive tenses that frame words of envy, lamentation, jealousy, voyeurism, alienation, disbelief, disdain, deception, impatience, more envy, lamentation, and disbelief. In the last three sonnets located in the third act, Teodoro utters his irrevocable dismissal of his affair with Marcela. She, in turn, banished by Doña Diana from Teodoro's side, closes the series with a desperate lament to reinvent love. The ghostly memory of Ibn 'Arabi's plea to interpret desires, as the above epigraph reads, by the power conferred upon a subject by a religion of love and faith is breathed into the closing sonnet by the dismissed Marcela:

> ¿Qué intentan imposibles mis sentidos,
> contra tanto poder determinados?
> Que celos poderosos declarados
> harán un desatino, resistidos.
> Volved, volved atrás, pasos perdidos,
> que corréis a mi fin precipitados;
> árboles son amores desdichados,
> a quien el hielo marchitó floridos.
> Alegraron el alma las colores
> que el tirano poder cubrió de luto;
> que hiela ajeno amor muchos amores.
> Y cuando de esperar daba tributo,
> ¿qué importa la hermosura de las flores,
> si se perdieron esperando el fruto?   (194–5)

(Why set my heart on what can never be
opposing so much might with vain persistence,
when jealousy with power, it's plain to see,
will stop at nothing if it meets resistance?
Retrace your steps, my feet, lest we be lost;
you hurry me too quickly to my doom,
for star-crossed lovers are like trees that frost
blights in the fullest beauty of their bloom.
The brightness of that bloom was a delight
that her vindictive power has now brought low;
for many a love another love will blight,
withering the hopes that had begun to grow.

What matter then the beauty of the flower,
    if flower and fruit are blighted in an hour?)   (D 97)

Her voice presents audiences with a variety of literal adulterous scenes
of marriage – suspicion, rumination, surveillance, revenge, and other
prime catalysts for high drama. Mysteriously, it evokes medieval songs
and tales, which, as María Rosa Menocal has argued, adulterated the
poetics and politics of marital negotiations, both at a private, domestic
level, and in public, protonational arenas (*The Arabic Role* 103). As the
following pages will make evident, the dramatic craft of *El perro* sought
to perform precisely this mix of poetics and politics, licit and illicit,
remembrance and oblivion, vulgar and sublime.

Courtly Love, or the Art of Masochism

The primary text in the formation of courtly love mores is *De arte hon-
este amandi* (The Art of Courtly Love) by Andreas Capellanus, André
the Chaplain, who established the proper forms of the art of loving
since the times of Ovid in ancient Rome. For Capellanus, love is literally
caused by two acts of imagining beautiful forms, which lead the lover
to be subjected to the chains of desire.[16] As a result of his inflamed imagination the lover falls prey to the state of suffering with a kind of illicit and sensuous desire directly correlated with the production of a
spectacle.[17] This cultural scheme, dating from the twelfth century, had a
lasting impact on the evolution of the arts throughout Europe. Buried
by the rhetorical excesses of genocide, world wars, virtuality, globaliza-
tion, and other modern and post-modern conditions, the art of courtly
love seems to have all but disappeared, becoming, at best, a distant
memory. In the last decade of the twentieth century, an unlikely character picked up this question. In a series of essays on what he terms 'the
metastases of enjoyment,' the Slovenian philosopher Slavoj Zizek explores six aspects of 'woman and casualty,' with courtly love as one of
them. His analytical piece 'Woman as Thing' begins with the rhetorical
question, 'Why talk about courtly love [*l'amour courtois*] today, in an age
of permissiveness when the sexual encounter is often nothing more
than a 'quickie' in some dark corner of an office?' (89).

Zizek's brilliant essay proves that the libidinal economy of courtly
love visibly transcends its original time-period, and also reasserts the
spectacular nature of this engagement by arguing that in the art of
courtly love, a male victim stages – eerily like both Diana and Teodoro

in *El perro* – his own servitude. To articulate his love, the troubadour writes a script of submission to a female Master in which 'violence is for the most part feigned, and even when it is "real," it functions as a component of a scene, as part of a theatrical performance' (92). In this rehearsed world of displacement of desire and formulation of a tortured spectacle, the world beyond the lover and his Thing, Woman, seems not to be of any significance. However, Zizek points out that the victim never gives in to the rules of the game, returning to his socially acceptable persona once the session is over. The game of courtly love is nothing but a 'surrealistic passionate masochistic game, which suspends social reality, none the less fits easily into that everyday reality' (92). The blind spot of this meteoric history of courtly love is how it considers sex the only thing that matters, and how it fails to consider gender role-playing a central character in this kind of primal scene. Capellanus, in fact, speaks of the *formae alterious sex* (the beauty of the other sex); Zizek does not. I am not interested, however, in entering a masculinist scenario to prove that Woman resists, or doesn't resist, symbolization – how could I possibly comment on that?

Instead, I see a theatre in which women speak by making spectacles of their desires – not to consume the figure of the lady, but to consummate a critique of the rules of gender that annihilate women. With it, I follow another thread from Hokenson's idea of comedy: 'Woman is the allegorical post-Man of desire, still within the socializing circuit yet thereby still unknowable – except allusively through the joking transaction' (213). The abstraction of Woman into an allegorical unknowable only accessible 'allusively through the joking transaction' may represent a kind of death of desire – perhaps a possible unintended consequence of 'the Woman as Thing.' Be that as it may, her post-Man does not necessarily mean that the social components of desire are dead, but that the divide that separates men and women may collapse if comedy is *not* taken into account. Jerry Aline Flieger argues rather that 'through Freud and Lacan the postmodern social text may be read instead as a comic allegory of human desire initiating a process of circulation and exchange, whereby all space, even the interior space of the psyche, may be considered public space, a scene of agonistic intersubjective interaction' (121). The fractured mimesis of *El perro* punishes illicit desire as it allows it to circulate; the postmodern social text ensues, between the spectators who see Doña Diana and Teodoro onstage, remembering themselves in the dramatic page, between them and their memory of the actors who played those parts. To this text also contribute the *alguaciles* who watched over their words and actions, and the members of the audience; and readers then, and now; and Zizek, and Woman.

In this tale, closer to Judith Butler's gender trouble than to a dutiful history of courtly love, a woman's voice articulates a critique of gender policing, yielding not only a new place and visibility for her subject in artistic arenas, but also the possibility of rereading various libidinal economies.[18] According to this tale, moreover, the art of troubadours inscribed in Diana and Teodoro's slapstick masochism in *El perro* is not designed strictly within the self-consuming parameters of a heterosexist matrix. Rather, their art interpellates various modes of institutional control of the sexes, among them the public transcript of marriage, the 'Real' domination of man over woman, and the homogeneity (in class, race, or gender) of one lover over the other. In this cultural space the *comediantes* claim the power to decide which way and to what extent to lay with the dominant fantasy of *limpieza de sangre*, determining when, how, and why they expose themselves to the slaps and the masochism required by the parameters of the *sociedad estamental*. In the space of slapstick masochism, desire is unleashed, and the vehicle of communication is primordially spectacular, not narrative, legal, or political, and not predetermined (although definitely determined) by anxieties of historicity.

The poetic chain of the sonnets and the progression of the games that Doña Diana, Teodoro, and Marcela play with each other in *El perro* as well as with a chorus of other characters (Tristán, Anarda, Otavio, Fabio, Don Federico, and Don Ludovico, among others) clearly engage *avant la lettre* the consummate theory of sadism and masochism laid by Freud in the *Three Essays on the Theory of Sexuality* he first wrote in 1905 and then rewrote through 1923. In the first of these essays Freud defined these two concepts as 'the most common and the most significant of all the perversions – the desire to inflict pain upon the sexual object, and its reverse' ('The Economic Problem' 23). In Freud's psychoanalytic scheme the two terms 'bring into prominence the pleasure in any form of humiliation or subjection' ('The Economic Problem' 24). Favouring pleasure, said Freud, stands sadomasochism (S/M) in frank opposition to *algolagnia*, the term preferred since 1899 by Schrenck-Notzing to highlight the cruelty of the sexual perversion or the pleasure derived by the subject in the pain of its sexual object. The biological call of sadism, which Freud associated with males and their aggressiveness or desire to subjugate, is due to 'the need for overcoming the resistance of the sexual object by means other than the process of wooing' ('The Economic Problem' 24). That leads to a usurped leading position in sex; at once, masochism 'comprises any passive attitude towards sexual life and the sexual object, the extreme instance of which appears to be that in which satisfaction is conditional upon suffering physical or mental pain at the hands of the sexual object' ('The Economic Problem' 24).

Readers familiar with *El perro* surely have already gathered that this gendered division of labour in S/M is not rigidly followed in this *comedia*, since Doña Diana, the *dama principal*, is the executor of the aggressiveness characteristic of the leading sexual position, while the object of her sadistic schemes is the masochist Teodoro; to borrow Mercedes Maroto Camino's apt words, 'the secretary's work and body are thus feminized in that they are under the control of the master, normally a man, and are also to be controlled by him' (19); as a result he is associated with objects (props) that belong with women, such as doors, closets, or locks. At the same time, in *El perro* Doña Diana also allows herself – albeit fleetingly – to be dominated by Teodoro, a turn of the masochistic screw that makes him (and perhaps some members of the audience) harbour the illusion that he is on top, which again associates him with a tradition of 'women on top.'[19] The *bofetón* does not put Doña Diana on top all the time in a staticized S/M scheme (where's the play in that?). Instead, Lope triggers the inversion, subversion, and perversion of S/M sexual roles in his text. With it, *El perro* mobilizes a parodic engagement of the issues of *limpieza de sangre*, given that the respective *estamento* that these two characters occupy is what determines the boundaries of their behaviour.

Freud himself argued that the S/M gendered division he observed was not as clear as he theorized it. As he himself noted toward the end of his essay:

> The most remarkable feature of this perversion is that its active and passive forms are habitually found to occur together in the same individual. A person who feels pleasure in a sexual relationship is also capable of enjoying as pleasure any pain which he may himself derive from sexual relations. A sadist is always at the same time a masochist. ('The Economic Problem' 25)

The ambiguity in the performance of these power games and the confusion in the role-playing of domination and submission noted in the *Three Essays* constitutes in *El perro* a stunning reversal of the axis of male aggressiveness that Freud first identified with the exercise of sadism.[20]

Punishing Illicit Desire

El perro opens with a meteoric exchange of two fugitives on the public side of the curtain. Tristán and Teodoro wonder if their identities have been compromised in their unruly amorous stint in palatial grounds. As they flee the scene, the countess storms onstage and begs the gentleman to stay:

¡Ah, gentilhombre, esperad!
¡Teneos, oíd! ¿Qué digo?
¿Esto se ha de usar conmigo?
Volved, mirad, escuchad! (77)

(Wait, sir
Sir, stay! Remain! Hear what I say!
This is an outrage,sir. Come back! Look, listen!) (D 43)

The lady subsequently asks the audience to identify a servant, or a man who can validate what she has seen, thus protecting her estate:

¡Hola! ¿No hay aquí un criado?
¡Hola! ¿No hay un hombre aquí?
Pues no es sombra lo que vi,
ni sueño que me ha burlado.
¡Hola! ¿Todos duermen ya? (77)

(Hello! Where are those servants? Hello! No one?
It was no ghost, I know; I wasn't dreaming
Hello! Are you all asleep?) (D 43)

The urgency in her voice and the force with which she charges around the palace seeking the intruder wakes everyone in her way, as she searches for both the fugitive who is putting her estate at risk and the guard who should have been policing the premises. In uncanny remembrance of Penelope's framed odyssey, the countess spins a web of what Nancy Miller once termed 'arachnologies,' and stages the double bind of rejecting possible suitors from her household while at the same time acknowledging the need to have men in the house to help her eschew the perils of publicity, which would be tantamount to her dishonour. Her claim that she has noticed the presence of strangers while her

ranks slept through it – a note of scriptural typology – clearly interpellates the gender divisions stipulated by Law:

> Andan hombres en mi casa
> a tal hora, y aún los siento
> casi en mi propio aposento;
> (que no sé yo dónde pasa
> tan grande insolencia, Otavio)
> y vos, muy a lo escudero,
> cuando yo me desespero,
> ¿Ansí remediáis mi agravio?   (77)

> (I find men roaming around my house, at this hour,
> and almost in my chamber – such effrontery –
> and when I'm in despair, this is the way
> my trusty servants speed to my assistance?)   (D 41–2)

The position in which Doña Diana finds herself is denotative of the
contradiction in terms upon which her dramatic character (and, by extension, this play) rests. As McKendrick points out, characterization in
the *comedias* was typically constituted by a mixture of various types:
'"complicating" characters: figures of authority such as fathers, husbands or brothers, or figures of subversion such as rivals, jealous suitors, enemies, even the Devil. Often there are representatives of law and
order – dukes, princes, kings – who contribute in some way to the solution at the end' (*Theatre* 73). In *El perro*, Lope builds meaning from characters who desire to be, or to be with, someone else whose presence is
precluded by virtue of the narrow views on gender policing stipulated
by the same laws that the countess is supposed to represent – if she
were a man.

Hence, Doña Diana is left either to desire to be a man (so she does not
need one to protect her estate and her honour), or to have the man that
she wants by her side, who happens to be Teodoro, the man whom
Marcela desires. Teodoro desires Marcela, then Doña Diana, then to be
noble, and then Marcela again when Doña Diana rejects him, and so
forth and so on. The play, as a result, unfolds as a series of strategies
designed ultimately to subvert the notion of gender in itself as a social
organizing principle. This yields a complex comedy of errors, at the end
of which Doña Diana not only manages to preserve her life, material
and immaterial, but also gets to subvert the gendered plot that would

have her, a priori, paralyzed, silenced, and imprisoned, guilty only of the crime of being a woman whose husband is dead. In no small part because of that fact, Lope's poetic and dramatic production of *El perro* (nine memorable sonnets, a *comedia palatina*, and one of his best comic texts), serves as a significant negotiator of rank and space in the public theatres, where the unmovable differences in sociopolitical standing were tightly controlled and clearly divided by spatial boundaries.[21]

Doña Diana's question '¿No hay hombre aquí?' (Hello! No one?) poignantly resonates within textual and spatial boundaries, setting in motion a key question for the play: is there a guard to the estate of Belflor who is not asleep? Is there a man, a stranger, in the house who is threatening the estate's welfare? Is there a father who can pose as an authority figure so I do not have to? A brother? A suitable suitor? The first scene figuratively wraps her in the need to find and mobilize help, creating a semantic field of movement and action that seeks to neutralize the threat of the unknown men who have penetrated her space and property, which could be read as code for unclean blood finding its way inside her clean, noble lineage. However, and more important, the forceful performance of her loud interrogation interpellates a wider audience with a different set of questions: is there a *galán* (lead male actor) in this play who will inspire audiences to be back to the theatre? Is there a desire to continue with this charade of the theatre? Is there an *alguacil* (police) or an *alcalde* (local or municipal official) watching over the traffic of gender on- and offstage? Is there a king reigning over the country watching for the interests of his subjects?

After much deliberation, acting, and deception through the play, the defeated secretary voices his desire to leave the palace of Belflor and Naples; exile, and not *engaño* (deceit) or murder, appears to be the only path he can follow. Teodoro's sonnet, a brilliant poetic exploration of loss and melancholia before the fact, expresses the idea that the unfeasibility of this love (for Doña Diana, for the theatre, for the court) is, for him, tantamount to death:

Bien al contrario pienso yo dar medio
a tanto mal, pues el Amor bien sabe
que no tiene enemigo que le acabe
con más facilidad que tierra en medio.
Tierra quiero poner, pues que remedio,
con ausentarme, Amor, rigor tan grave,
pues no hay rayo tan fuerte que se alabe

que entró en la tierra, de tu ardor remedio.
Todos los que llegaron a este punto,
poniendo tierra en medio te olvidaron;
que en tierra al fin le resolvieron junto.
Y la razón que de olvidar hallaron
es que amor se confiesa por difunto,
pues que con tierra en medio te enterraron.   (188)

(For love's unending tortures I intend
to find a very different cure, for Venus
knows all too well, no power on earth can end
her hold on us so well as earth between us.
If I put earth between us – go away –
I too may cool the ardour of desire,
for flaming thunderbolts can never say
they pierce the earth; the earth contains their fire.
And many have learned, who needed to deny
their love, as I do now, that lovers must
put earth between, to let its memory die,
and so turn earth to earth, and dust to dust;
the fact their love has died was only
when once they'd buried it with earth between.)   (D 94)

Exile, the path imposed on Jews and Muslims in the peninsula since 1492, is for the lovers the only thing that will cure their 'tanto mal' (unending tortures), since 'el amor bien sabe / que no tiene enemigo que le acabe / con más facilidad que tierra en medio' (Venus / knows all too well, no power can end / her hold on us so well as earth between us).

This strategic move by Teodoro, rendered literally in the most beautiful literary form – the sonnet – unleashes a most erotic scene between him and Doña Diana. Against all odds, and in a symbolic slap in the face to the *Estatutos* and the control of interfaith, interclass marriage, the intense desire of the lovers to consummate and publish their attraction moves them so close as to play with the Law, while the words of the poetry, in grand masochistic fashion, force them to be apart. As they foresee this separation, they imagine themselves as close as they can be onstage:

TEODORO: Haré tus contrarios mudos
con mi ausencia. Dame el pie.

DIANA: Anda, Teodoro. No más.
Déjame; que soy mujer.   (190)

(TEODORO: Your enemies will be silenced if I go.
I kiss your feet.
DIANA: Teodoro, stop, no more.
Please, please, leave me; I'm a woman, after all.)   (D 95)

The blood spilled in the primal scenes of uxoricide seen in the previous chapter is redefined by Lope with a *comedia* mirror – how could it be otherwise?[22] In *El perro*, the looking-glass of exile and impossible love presents audiences and readers with a series of *bofetones* with which Doña Diana punishes the obscure object of her illicit desire, Teodoro, thus punishing herself. This scene is a climax for the wishful thinking and feeling of the members of the audience, in no small part due to the pendular masochistic games played by the lady and her secretary with which they drag everyone into the theatrics of their masochistic mud. Marcela, Anarda, Tristán, members of the audience, and any other characters whose flights of poetic and slapstick imagination can fly that high will be reminded of the acrobatic games of *volatineros* common in public squares and performances since the previous century.

These games also prefigure the metatheatrical scene that Tristán will concoct to end the rule of *limpieza de sangre* and control of the desired marital union between Doña Diana and Teodoro. The pretence arrives right on time, for in Sonnet 6 Diana shows her impatience, a sign that she may, like Balza and Maldonado after her, make a terribly wrong choice:

¿Qué me quieres, amor? ¿Ya no tenía
olvidado a Teodoro? ¿Qué me quieres?
Pero responderás que tú no eres,
sino tu sombra, que detrás venía.
¡Oh celos! ¿Qué no hará vuestra porfía?
Malos letrados sois con las mujeres,
pues jamás os pidieron pareceres
que pudiese el honor guardarse un día.
Yo quiero a un hombre bien, mas se me acuerda
Que yo soy mar y que es humilde barco,
y que es contra razón que el mar se pierda.
En gran peligro, amor, el alma embarco,

mas si tanto el honor tira la cuerda,
por Dios, que temo que se rompa el arco.   (165)

(Oh, Love, what do you want from me? When I
think I've forgotten him, he haunts my mind.
What do you want from me? But you'll reply:
'Not I, my shadow, following behind.'
Oh jealousy, you will not be denied.
Like advocates, you lead, but lead astray.
Were she to heed the counsels you provide,
a woman's honour would not last a day.
I love a man, my fearful heart's afloat
in dangerous seas; but how can I forget
that I'm an ocean, he a humble boat?
How can it be the sea that's overset?
Yet now Love's bow's so stretched, I fear it might
be split apart, if honour pulls too tight.)   (D 83)

Desire responds under the guise of Teodoro's explicit declaration of love:

Y así, a decir me resuelvo
que te quiero, y que es disculpa
que con respeto te quiero.   (167)

(And therefore I've decided to declare
I love you – though of course with great respect –
I love you – please forgive my being so nervous.)   (D 84)

Countess Diana slaps him with a *bofetón*, her mechanical act pregnant
with sarcasm that, ironically, as it elevates the secretary to a higher,
more visible level, reminds him of the place he is to occupy:

¿Por qué no me has de querer
si soy tu señora y tengo
tu voluntad obligada,
pues te estimo y favorezco
más que a los otros criados?   (167)

(Why indeed
should you not love me, since I'm your employer

and have deserved your love by having prized you
and favoured you above my other servants?)   (D 84)

Teodoro, in total disbelief, responds to this gesture with which Diana eschews his love by telling her that the sadist language she is using is incomprehensible to him.

As the *condesa* acts on the proverb that gives the play its title, being *el perro del hortelano que no come ni deja comer* (the dog in the manger, which neither eats nor lets anyone else eat), she does not deliver herself to Teodoro. How could she possibly do that without betraying the honour of the House of Belflor? At once, she bans him from delivering himself to Marcela; Teodoro characterizes the love he has for Marcela, and she for him, as 'honesto' (decent, licit) a concept that moves Doña Diana to physical abuse. Teodoro, panicked, asks '¿Qué hace vuseñoría?' (What's this, / your ladyship?) (169, D 85), to which Doña Diana replies: 'Daros, por sucio y grosero, / estos bofetones' (The beating you deserve / for such indecency, such boorishness) (169, D 85). Teodoro bleeds, while Doña Diana leaves the scene, only to return shortly thereafter to express her concern for him. The secretary's reply clearly articulates the conundrum:

> Tan poco
> que te siento y no te entiendo,
> pues no entiendo tus palabras,
> y tus bofetones siento;
> si no te quiero te enfadas,
> y enójaste si te quiero;
> escríbesme si me olvido,
> y si me acuerdo te ofendo;
> pretendes que yo te entienda,
> y si te entiendo soy necio.
> Mátame o dame la vida;
> da un medio a tantos extremos.   (174)

> (Yes indeed, so little
> that though I feel, I cannot comprehend.
> I feel your blows, can comprehend your words.
> You're angry if I love you, or I don't.
> If I forget, you write; if I remember,
> you say I'm wrong; you'd have me understand you,

and if I understand you, I'm a fool.
So give me life, or death; give me some quarter,
Some happy mean between these wild extremes.)   (D 88)

His words lead Doña Diana to ask a critical question: '¿Hícete sangre?'
(Did I perhaps draw blood?) (174, D 88). His unclean blood, spilled
over the white cloth, is the catalyst for desire to cascade out of the lips
of the lady; after she asks the secretary for his *lienzo* he wonders why,
and she utters: 'Para que esta sangre quiero' (I want this blood) (174,
D 88). The material of the *lienzo* is in plain sight, like the unclean blood
of the secretary resulting from the lady's blows to his face. All at once,
Lope seems to paint a scene with the *caligram pas un mouchoir* – Magritte
and his treacherous images again – showing not just a handkerchief
but a little canvas on which a new scene of masochism is painted: in exchange for the stained *lienzo*, Doña Diana gives Teodoro two thousand
ducats 'para hacer lienzos' (For handkerchiefs, she said) (175, D 88).[23]

   Doña Diana wraps the sequence of masochism, *limpieza de sangre*,
and gaming by ordering Otavio to finance a rich operation designed to
reproduce Teodoro's blood metonymically, by replicating the *lienzo*.
Tristán, taking notes from Doña Diana, capitalizes on Teodoro's potential to benefit from his own *limpieza de sangre*, and advises him that 'Bien
puedes tomar al precio / otros cuatro bofetones' (You wouldn't mind
a dozen blows at that price) (175, D 88). He also summarizes Freud's
S/M gender-bender rather economically when he tells Teodoro, who
wonders why Doña Diana took his bloody *lienzo* away, that she 'pagó la
sangre y te ha hecho doncella por las narices' (*Droit de seigneur*, it's
called. 'Cause she's deflowered you, and made you bleed, she's paid
you – through the nose) (175, D 88). The blood, which for Tristán signals
the effeminization of the secretary's subject and a symbolic deflowering
(collapsing the nose with the female genitalia), is a sign that would not
be lost on the audiences of the times who were familiar with the myth
of the menstruating Jew.[24]

   The *gracioso* (Fool), in fact, told the secretary earlier in the play that
love can only lead to hurt, and that feigning of the kind that Balza and
Maldonado performed is the only way out – after all, 'Con arte se
vence todo' (Art conquers all) (91, D 48). With these words Tristán
forewarns the secretary about the direction in which the *sangre*, the
lienzo, and the *bofetones* are leading him. He recounts his own memory
of a broken heart, a landscape reminiscent of love poems from Arabic
traditions such as Ibn 'Arabi's 'Poem 11' cited in the epigraph, which

portray gardens in which the lovers would meet that later melt into deserts and sarcasm:

> Y en queriéndola olvidar
> —que debió de convenirme —
> dio la memoria en decirme
> que pensase en blanco azar,
> en azucena y jazmín,
> en marfil, en plata, en nieve,
> y en la <u>cortina</u>, que debe
> de llamarse faldellín,
> con que yo me deshacía,
> mas tome más cuerdo acuerdo,
> y di en pensar, como cuerdo,
> lo que más le parecía:
> cestos de calabazones,
> baúles viejos, maletas
> de cartas para estafetas,
> almofrejes y jergones;
> con que se trocó en desdén
> el amor y la esperanza,
> y olvidé la dicha panza
> por siempre jamás amen;
> que era tal, que en los dobleces
> (y no es mucho encarecer)
> se pudieran esconder
> cuatro manos de almireces.   (95)

> (I wanted, with good reason, to forget her;
> but memory prompted me to think of jasmines,
> white-orange blossom and Madonna lilies,
> of gauzy veils and pretty petticoats.
> But then, more sensibly, I thought to think of
> those things which I thought most resembled her:
> baskets of pumpkins, ancient trunks and mailbags
> stuffed with old letters, mattresses and bolsters.
> so love and hope were turned to disregard,
> and I forgot said paunch for evermore
> —which was so huge (without exaggeration)
> you could have hid four pestles in its folds.)   (D 49–50)[25]

In the end, Countess Diana's *bofetones* to Teodoro leave the mark of masochism on the audience, who by seeing and experiencing Teodoro's beaten body and loss of blood can figure out meanings for their own memories of illicit desires. The possible cascades of catharsis, agency, and action will always face the barrier of *limpieza de sangre*, forever inscribed in the text and its context, which hinders the marital 'The End' desired by the main characters in the play and, perhaps, by some members of the audience. The relentless encounter between the two lovers, one submitting to the other's aggressiveness to sublimate wooing, is bound for the disaster of nothingness.

But in Lope's comic world of slapstick masochism, the nothingness of an excluded subject position inspires the Byzantine fable concocted by Tristán to grant Teodoro the *limpieza de sangre* he needs in order to be able to earn Doña Diana's hand in matrimony. The fable, like the *bofetones*, is not wrapped in the taffeta that dressed honour dramas, but in other fabrics worthy of theatrical quality. For the *gracioso* is dressed in oriental garb, made with rich fabrics equivalent in weight and symbolic capital to those traded for theatrical costume. And even though editors do not agree on the specific manner of this costume, they all approximate a Mediterranean image that would without a doubt play off of the appearance of subjects such as those called *moriscos* (converted Muslims) and the ghostly scent of Arabic poetry surfacing time and again throughout the play.

The citation by editor David Kossoff of the stage quotation in which Tristán's costume is described follows primarily from the two editions from 1618 (the Madrid *Onzena Parte* and the Barcelona *Doze Comedias* collections); it reads: Tristán enters, 'vestido de Armenio con un turbante graciosamente' (comically attired as an Armenian, in a turban) (196, D 98). The edition prepared by Vern Williamsen for the ACHT website – which cites both Kossoff's 1970 Castalia edition and Victor Dixon's critical edition published in London by Tamesis in 1981 – refers to a later editorial garb, recorded in Zerolo's 1886 Parisian edition of the play (but curiously rejected by both Kossoff and Dixon), in which Tristán and Furio appear 'con traje griego' (dressed as Greeks) (n. p., B 162). This illustrates what Dixon rightfully notes in his critical edition in Spanish: that 'Lope alternates *griego* and *armenio* with blithe insouciance' (*El perro* 213). Kossoff cogently argues that confusing these two ethnic costumes was not uncommon, 'since both peoples had been for a long time Christian subjects of the Turk, and of the same faith, the Oriental Church;

besides, both peoples were devoted to the trade of carpets and fabrics of Persia' (196). It is precisely this ambiguity with which people from Eastern origins were forged as constructs that Tristán's Byzantine fable becomes such a great feat of political theatrics, a cultural, political and social set of dynamics seen by Barbara Fuchs as a performance of 'virtual Spaniards.'[26] Moreover, this referential ambiguity deployed by Lope, another turn of the slapstick screw, prefigures important poses in nineteenth-century European portraiture of masculinity; for example, see Oscar Wilde's fabulous Greek costume (fig. 3) which he immortalized in his 'Woman's Dress' published in *The Pall Mall Gazette* on 14 October 1884, in which he praised the virtues of such costume.

Wilde, like Jean-Jacques Rousseau did before him with the folds of Armenian and Greek costuming, dwelled in the cover that such fabrics afforded him. Before them, Tristán found a likewise far-fetched dress, one whose very image, ironically, should raise doubts about his subject and the stage in which he dwells. However, the Armenian /Greek costume in the hands and body of the *gracioso* is paradoxically designed to kill the irrevocable condition of *limpieza de sangre* that leads Teodoro and Countess Diana to engage in masochism. Tristán's words, again, show the broad slap-and-lift that comes with a fully developed theatrical consciousness, as he sprinkles his tale with high drama and great flair for rich fabrics and costuming:

> De Constantinopla vine
> a Chipre, y de ella a Venecia
> con una nave cargada
> de ricas telas de Persia.
> Acordéme de una historia
> que algunos pasos me cuesta;
> y con deseos de ver
> a Nápoles, ciudad bella,
> mientras allá mis crïados
> van despachando las telas,
> vine, como veis, aquí,
> donde mis ojos confiesan
> su grandeza y hermosura.   (196)

> (I sailed from Cyprus to Constantinople,
> and thence to Venice, in a ship well laden

Figure 3 Oscar Wilde in traditional Greek costume. Black-and-white photograph (London: British Library. Eccles Collection, Additional MS 81783A, fol. 3).

with Persian cloths and carpets of great price.
Recalling, though, a story which has caused me
no mean concern, and keen to visit Naples,
I left my minions there, unloading fabrics,
and as you see have journeyed here myself
to gaze upon this fair and mighty city.)   (D 98)

To convince Don Ludovico and the audience that Teodoro is his long-
lost son, the *lacayo* (lackey) no doubt puts on one of the most memorable metatheatrical shows of the long century. Desiring that Teodoro
further his own desire, the Armenian or Greek takes a page from Doña
Diana's book. Like her, Tristán pretends, manipulates, and controls the
labours of love around the *mujer principal* (noble woman) that she is to
produce and reproduce, in rather queer fashion, the *sangre* that, by virtue of the dictates of the *sociedad estamental*, is inappropriate to be mixed
with hers, the countess of Belflor. Their fabrication of a *lienzo*, composed
with slapstick masochism, reframes Diana's subjectivity and the love of
women that others around her feel. This parody of the punishment of
illicit desire, differing vastly from the story of Balza and Maldonado
with which this chapter began, brings to mind another tale: the actress
immortalized by Juan de Zabaleta in his 1660 *El día de fiesta por la tarde*,
was a *dama* who inscribed the seriousness of her theatrics in the materiality of a piece of fabric that superseded, in monetary value, the payment for her histrionic work:

> I saw a very famous *comedianta* (actress) (who has recently passed away)
> who, in representing a rage scene, finding herself … perhaps with the
> *lienzo* in her hand, shredded it into a thousand pieces to express the affect
> she was feeling; sadly, the *lienzo* was worth twice the salary she was going
> to earn. But she still went further, for since she thought that was a great
> thing to do, she shredded one *lienzo* every day for the entire duration of
> the show. (*El dia de fiesta* 312–23)

A historicized reading of these games of masochism played by
Countess Diana, Teodoro, Marcela, and Tristán may seem to some a
revival of courtly love mores, or a reduction of Doña Diana to Woman
as Thing, when she marries Teodoro in the end. By looking carefully
into *El perro del hortelano*, we can see how the suffering that Capellanus
deployed to characterize love prefigured Freud's understanding
of masochism, playing with sexualities to imagine, or perhaps to

remember, the intensity of Andalusí love poetry such as Ibn 'Arabi's 'Poem 11.' Despite their difference in class, behaviour, and standing in life, there is no doubt that the slapstick masochism, camels and all, guided Diana and Teodoro through their impossible journey through desire and blood.

6 Woman in Breeches

Yo no vivo
sino sólo de mi hacienda;
ni paje en mi vida fuí;
vengo a pretender aquí
un hábito de encomienda

(I do not live
but from my own resources;
and I never was a page;
I have come here to pretend/seek
the investment of a livery)
                    Gabriel Téllez (Tirso de Molina), *Don Gil de las calzas verdes*[1]

From the onset of his dramatic life Don Gil de las Calzas Verdes finds obstacle after obstacle to exercise his capacity for self-fashion, in no small part because his interlocutors express doubts about his manliness, which puts him in an untenable position when the time comes to hire the services of Caramanchel, a lackey.[2] Abused at the hands of four masters who include a 'pelón' (poor, troubled person or man who lives off the labour of a prostitute) and a 'moscatel' (dumb, obnoxious person), the rogue seeks relief for his hunger and poverty but finds the idea of becoming the lackey of a 'paje' (page) or half-man untenable (100–123, M 63–73, BM 206–11).[3] As the exchange between the two men takes place Don Gil speaks of his resourcefulness, his past, and his intentions to obtain the investment of a made-to-order suit in Madrid.[4] Caramanchel, throughout the whole play suspicious of Don Gil's capacity to manage his services, interprets Don Gil's offer as a '!Lenguaje nuevo!' (New foreign tongue!) (123, M 73); and only at the very end of the play will he begin to understand such rarity.[5] The colour of his interlocutor's breeches and his name (or, rather, his lack of a proper last name) support the swindler's doubt; don Gil lacks the *gravitas* expected in a master, for as Sebastián de Covarrubias stated the *Tesoro*, 'Gil' was the name for 'zagales y pastores en la poesía' (young men and sheperds in poetry), and 'being green' meant 'no dejar la lozanía de mozo habiendo entrado en edad' (not having left behind the youthfulness of adolescence despite being of age) (589, 959).[6] Don Gil defends himself with his fabulous garb, the fabrication of which has turned doña Juana Solís 'de damisela en varón' (a damsel into a man) (80).[7]

Don Gil's tale of self-serving fashioning it not completely inaccurate: he is in possession of sufficient material and entrepreneurial resources to manage a lackey, he has been neither servant nor page, and he has arrived in Madrid with a shrewd plan to seek, by means of pretences, a remarkable suit.[8] What his poetic speech also reveals (even if Caramanchel does not understand this dimension of his master's 'pretender') is that the estate belongs to his father, that 'he' is a 'she' and henceforth never initiated into manhood rituals such as being a page, and that the livery he seeks is one defined by material clothing designed and worn critically with respect to the marriage institution: the unofficial, transgressive, gender-unaligned garb of the transvestite.[9] According to Covarrubias, 'hábito' (costume) is the clothing known as everyone's dress or suit; hence the proverb, 'The habit the monk doth not make' (618). Be that as it may, the transvestite's breeches in *Don Gil* question this proverbial truth as they compose a critical clothing matter that produces, as we shall see, endless sartorial expressions that define a symphony of dramatic *personae*; the transvestite habit the manly woman doth make. With her clothes and acting, the transvestite articulates a sustained conflict between sumptuary objects, laws, and the subjects that own them and wear them, subjects that such laws seek to define within and without marriage.[10] Despite the sexual binarisms and clothing polarization publicized throughout the sixteenth and seventeenth centuries as the law of the land in Spain, the sensational performative essay of *Don Gil* shows how a transvestite, or breeched woman, was able to forge a stage presence unaligned with either one of the matrimonial roles stipulated by the regulatory fictions of that age, but rather in frank semantic solidarity with the fabric of the actor (fig. 4).[11]

Figure 4 Diego Velázquez, *Pablo de Valladolid* (The Buffoon), c. 1635. Oil painting, 209 cm x 123 cm (Madrid: Museo del Prado).

In playing Don Gil the leading lady does not seek a bridal gown, the appropriate clothing for her biological equipment, nor the scene of multiple weddings that was common at 'The End' of the *comedias de enredo*, of which *Don Gil* is quite the exemplar; neither does she aspire to be literally invested with the livery of a *comendador* or a gentleman, breeches designated legally and decorously to mean the man whom she pretends to be.[12] Although important for the development of the political theatrics deployed by Don Gil, these two costumes are not the central objective of the play and its title figure, for they represent characters that in the marital scheme of the Catholic Universal Monarchy were meant to be united in unequal terms. Aspiring to perform one of those two roles – wife or *comendador* – would represent a lamentable waste of Don Gil's life, a premise cynically uttered by the *gracioso*: '¿A pretender / entráis mozo? Saldréis viejo' (You enter this stage of pretence as a youth? You'll leave it an old man) (124). Reading Don Gil as a subject who merely aspires to wear an institutionalized bridal gown – or to put on a *comendador* or gentlemanly gown with the sole purpose of gaining the bride's garb – entails a limited interpretive scope for this play, since it grants the sole authority on meaning to the Tridentine marital sign, which will determine in rather constraining terms the possibilities of human reproduction and growth that the play suggests. This metonymical interpretation of the text, in turn, would eliminate the generative capacity of *Don Gil* as theatre, a foundational unit of performance that Richard Schechner has termed 'schismogenesis' or power to create something with and from the ruins of a dramatic conflict.[13]

The goal of this chapter is to further understand how the industrious performance of the transvestite unfolds in *Don Gil* by virtue of the polemic object of her green breeches, with which s/he negotiates an economy of marriage that plays with the fluctuating values of blood, luxury, money, and beauty in the matrimonial markets of seventeenth-century Spain.[14] The miracle of performance takes place when the raw material or fabric of the green breeches transforms both the title character, the leading actor, and the dramatic text into a bundle of critical matter that mobilizes that great form of evasion and consumption that was the first professional theatre of Spain, in which many a subject participated to create critical scenes of marriage and, in this case, its relation to the sumptuary laws that sought to control their sexuality. Doña Juana's utterance 'vengo a pretender aquí' (I come here to seek with and by pretence) invites spectators to think like *comediantes* so they can visualize and interpret her dramatic persona otherwise. As Covarrubias also said, *pretender* is 'to procure the achievement of something,' an *encomienda* that in theatre is tantamount to living in a relentless process of self-making, rather like haute couture, where suits are tailored to the body and not simply cut to accommodate an anonymous, generic body with clothing designed and cut for purposes of merely consuming its fabric (834).[15] As the last line of the play says, Don Gil the transvestite is one and the same with the 'comedia con calzas' (the breeched play) that calls for the curtain to be drawn when Caramanchel recognizes, in a spectacular scene of anagnorisis, the very figure of Don Gil whom he has not been able to read clearly during his dramatic life. Catharsis, that libidinous juice of theatre, is unleashed by and with the breeched woman, thus leading Caramanchel and hopefully other members of the audience to open themselves to new economic and affective horizons (306).

In this interpretive frame the uncanny materiality of theatrical costume in *Don Gil* represents a *mise en abîme* of the sumptuary laws of that period and their relation to sexual normativity, a costume design that adds something novel – as Freud had it – to an original and strangely familiar image that excites simultaneous feelings of awe and fear (123). Don Gil (the one pretended/sought by Doña Juana, that is) reveals his consciousness of this artistic process when he puts on the virtual womanly costume of Doña Elvira. Upon seeing the strange figure of Don Gil sport a feminine gown that is not that of Doña Juana, her original persona, Quintana, her true servant, inquires, '¿para qué tanto ardid?' (why weave such a tangled web?) – to which the twice-removed impostor responds: 'que he de perseguir si puedo, / Quintana, a mi engañador / con uno y con otro enredo / hasta que cure su amor / con mi industria o con su miedo' (Because, Quintana, if I can, / I'll hunt my cruel deceiver down / With all the tricks at my command / Until his lovesick fever's cured / Through his great fear or my shrewd plan) (244, M 187).[16] The breeched woman thus composes a fantasmatic presence that at once elicits fear, awe, and desire to cure the libidos and fashion senses wounded by limiting marital prescriptions.

Woman in Breeches

The theatrical sign of the green breeches projects a figure that interpellates and destabilizes afflicted, repressed love. It is a critique of that archaeology of sexual knowledge which, with its prescription of a dominant male/husband and a submissive female/wife, had fabricated a clearing house of marital legal ideologies designed to control and contain sexual, artistic, cultural, and economic relations of the time. With her transvestite garb and moves Don Gil mobilizes the sacred premise of theatrical costume, which José Ruano de la Haza says was the key to convert dress and its social codes into a new system of meaning in the *Comedia* (*Los teatros comerciales* 295–321).[17] The clothed bundle of tears and laughter called the transvestite thus generates new ways of wearing costumes and imagining sexuality.[18] With his metatheatrics Don Gil negotiates two opposite poles: on the one hand, Lope de Vega's acknowledgment that the 'disfraz varonil' (manly / virile / masculine costume) was the obscure object of the *vulgo*'s desire, and on the other, the fact that such a transvestite was evidence to judge theatre as an illicit practice.[19] *Don Gil*, to be sure, ends in a multiple wedding scene that achieves one aspect of doña Juana's *encomienda* of pretension. At the same time, his garb harbours the possibility of activating in the spectators something more original and encompassing: a memory of that familiar scene of the wedding ceremony informed by the truth and dare of the comic actors as they faced, and critiqued, a sexual order that in turn was presented, invested as an ideological pretence, as natural law and philosophy by the legal marital tables of ecclesiastical and civil laws.[20]

As with every baroque objet d'art this breeched woman, in 'The End,' stands as a highly contradictory and ambiguous sign, pregnant with endless meanings – in more ways than one a most appropriate garb for a transvestite.[21] After an exciting life of adventure Don Gil and his followers enter a state of matrimony both desired and desirable, not merely because of their compliance with the primary scene of heteronormative genesis and domesticity, that epicentre of the reproduction of the ideologies of blood purity in imperial Spain, but precisely because they have learned to play with it artistically and spectacularly. Doña Juana, Don Martín, Doña Inés, Don Juan, Doña Clara, and Don Antonio join the 1570 Burgos *comediantes*, Countess Diana de Belfor and Teodoro, Doña Mencía and Don Gutierre, and many other actors in representing that great theatre of the world, the wedding ceremony that in its liturgical dimension was supposed to cite poetically the promise of marriage. The three weddings at 'The End' of *Don Gil* restore a sense of order in which men seemingly resume their lost lead, and women seem to serve a procreative purpose, as if their bodies were merely significant by virtue of their capacity to produce the heirs of great fortunes of the families from whence they come.

All at once, this splendid closing ceremony of the dramatic games also signals other meanings for both 'bride-and-groom,' key signs of the theatrical process emblematized by the fabrication of the breeches with which the industrious craft of the transvestite realizes his economic critical matter.[22] After all, Doña Juana and Don Martín marry in 'The End' 'vestida de hombre' (she, dressed as a man) and 'calzado de verde' (he, dressed in green), a pretend wedding ceremony that signals the desire of both spouses-to-be for the transvestite fabric and garb. That is the spirit and the law of this *comedia*, because it fuses subjects and objects in an unpredictable, dynamic relation of desire that internalizes the very power and authority strategies that their own effigies question (301, M 239, BM 286).[23] The satellite gaze of the crown's panopticon, Caramanchel, interrogates the breeched woman, asking the question with which marital ideologies interpellated every subject stage: '¿Y sóis hombre o sóis mujer?' (And are you a man or are you a woman?) – to which she responds with a visible, legal 'mujer soy' (Woman, I am) from her well-clad position, also visible and valuable, albeit not so legal, since her *'vestida de hombre'* defies the *Reglamentos* (quoted in Varey and Shergold, *Teatros* 305).

This green-breeched woman no doubt would bring to many a spectator's mind Catalina de Erauso, who managed to convince all those who surrounded her of the possibility that a woman with *industria* was able and willing to occupy the physical and symbolic space of a man by virtue of her material façade, that is to say, by making herself up in men's fashion to fabricate an uncanny, unpredictable subject stage. Erauso (1592–1650), born in San Sebastián de Gipúzcoa, Spain, travelled to Chile and Tipoán, where she was a soldier; in 1626 King Felipe IV's council granted him 'una pensión de encomienda de quinientos pesos de a ocho reales' (an *encomienda* pension of five-hundred eight *reales* pesos) with which, according to Munárriz in his edition of the *Historia de la monja alférez escrita por ella misma* (History of the Lieutenant Nun, Written by Herself), she settled in México where s/he worked as a merchant under the name of Antonio de Erauso (6). Pérez de Montalbán wrote a *comedia famosa* about her, and her *Historia* was translated into French and adapted loosely into English. Her story has been adapted to various mass media, particularly film, a dissemination of her persona that has contributed to what Sherry Velasco has termed the 'fama y escándalo' (fame and scandal) of the Erauso case. In the transvestite's own words, 'allí me crié; que tomé el hábito; que tuve noviciado; que estando para profesar, por tal ocasión me salí; que me fui a tal parte, me desnudé, me vestí, me corté el cabello; partí allí, i acullá, me embarqué, aporté, trahiné, maté, herí, maleé, correteé' (I was raised there;

I received livery; I was a novice in a nunnery; when I was about to take the vows, for that reason I got out; I went to a place, undressed myself, dressed myself, cut my hair; I left to go here, and there, I embarked, gave, took what was not mine, I killed, I hurt others, I did wrongful things, and I wandered) (cited in Velasco, *The Lieutenant Nun* 177).[24] Don Gil, like the lieutenant nun, lived for and by means of her becoming a transvestite, which did not merely mean becoming a man. Hence, it is imperative to focus the reading gaze on the process as much as on the result of her metamorphosis.

The transformation of her character and persona in the lieutenant nun, fabrication and industry on which her life came to depend, worked by virtue of a well-designed process of translation of her clothing into signs of identity. As it happened with Don Gil, such translation and not a simulated manly ideal is what opens up the possibilities for a new, more encompassing life than the marital script of a submissive wife; hence, one can conclude that Catalina de Erauso, like Doña Juana de Solís, *pretende* (seeks with pretension) a costume not defined a priori, a set of breeches fabricated by an *encomienda* of imagination – that of the transvestite. Erauso's *Historia*, in that sense, can be read as a supplement of the story of the green-breeched woman:

> Allí acogíme y estuve tres días trazando, acomodando y cortando de vestir. Híceme, de una basquiña de paño azul con que me hallaba, unos calzones, y de un faldellín verde de perpetuán que traía debajo, una ropilla y polainas: el hábito me lo dejé por allí, por no saber qué hacer con él. Cortéme el pelo, que tiré, y a la tercera noche, deseando alejarme, partí no sé por dónde. (12)

> (I took refuge there and spent three days designing, putting together, and cutting my clothes. With a blue cloth long overskirt I was wearing I made myself a pair of pants, and from the green underskirt made of *perpetuán* I had under that one, I made myself underwear and tights; I left the old garb there, not knowing what to do with it. I cut my hair, which I threw away, and the third night, wishing only to get away, I left not knowing where I was going.)

Don Gil, like the impostor figure of the lieutenant, designed and traced with great *industria* her breeches, inscribing in her clothing a wealth of material and cultural signs that mobilized a new economy of sex, gender, and costuming. The transvestite, to be sure, showed how to trace, adjust, and cut 'de vestir' (to dress), and how to leave the old costume 'por allí, por no saber qué hacer con él' (back there, not knowing what to do with it).

The lieutenant nun and the green-breeched bride also cite all those other women who applied for and were granted *hábitos* (livery) from the military orders. These *hábitos* conferred a high degree of visibility and privilege on the subjects who possessed them. In no small part this was due to the institutional lineage of the orders which, as Elena Postigo Castellanos has documented, in the case of their *Consejo* (Council) translated into a rather powerful claim in political and cultural authority in early modern Spain. The *Consejo de las Órdenes Militares* called themselves 'a Tribunal of Honour and Privilege,' a space of cultural war in the name of the foundation of nobility: 'In this Council we battle for honor, the most valuable jewel in life, we battle for life itself, for there is none without honor, and between honor and life we battle for resources, for in such mission those are not to be despised' (13).[25] As Postigo adds, members of this *Consejo* inherited the foundational privileges granted to their institution, originally instituted 'as monastic bodies, obtaining from the popes the necessary authority to live with the independence corresponding to their nature, but also as political-military bodies, thus receiving donations of land and juridical concessions from the kings, and in this fashion and with this power they reached incorporation' (13). As members of a corporate body, subjects receiving these *hábitos* were invested with the power that the orders and the tribunal entailed, even if they did not serve as members of the *Consejo*.

By the time the *Consejo* attained incorporation it managed the advisory, administrative, and judicial capacities of the invested knights of the military orders of Santiago, Calatrava, and Alcántara as a group (14–15). As Postigo adds, in the seventeenth century the council had the means and authority to engage significantly in processes of social definition, and given their mission to preserve honour and nobility the council saw petitions from nobles and dealt with them (by the rules of the orders or following dictates from common law as necessary) always with the goal of preserving the prestige of the gowns (16). Evidence published by María A. Pérez Castañeda and María Dolores Couto de León has shown that women wanting to become nuns in the religious orders of Santiago, Calatrava, and Alcántara were required to prove their *hidalguía* and blood purity, which made the process of their becoming members of this order the same as that required from the men seeking military livery in these organization – if that did not mean that the privileges granted to the knights of the military orders and the nuns in these religious orders were equal.[26]

However, the archive collections of the Santiago order document the granting of some military livery to a few women, some of them because 'they were ordained in old times' and others, by virtue of their marriage (OOMM Orden de Santiago Casamientos Lib. 10 cajón 119, fol. 2).[27] These women, like the lieutenant nun and the woman in breeches, got the livery they sought by crafting a strategic design; in the case of the female members of the Santiago order, they learned to navigate forensic protocols that, different from the dramatic breeches of don Gil, granted them the power that came with the livery of the military orders. The fact that their names made history by being registered in the 'Index' shows that these women understood that if they designed and fabricated their clothing with *industria*, they could achieve a social presence in their lives that otherwise they could not afford, obtain, or manage. Other women understood this premise, and resisted their fate as mere *loci* of biological reproduction with numerous sumptuary productions that brought as a result spectacular womanly figures.

Worn Worlds

As Pilar Ríos Izquierdo has noted, such was the case of Queen Mariana de Austria, who set the trend for the *guardainfante* or 'amplísima armadura formada por arcos de hierro, cuerdas, ballenas, paja, pelo, estera y otras cosas' (very large armature made of iron arches, ropes, underwire, straw, hair, wicker, and other materials) despite the acrimonious opposition that she faced for that (96). The queen incurred monumental material and economic expenses, and was the author of flagrant legal and moral transgressions with the fabrication of her *guardainfante*, which according to Juan Comba was simply 'atraerse más al rey, que era de los más partidarios de estas grotescas invenciones, porque sus galanteos le proporcionaban la sorpresa de lo desconocido' (to attract the king, who was the biggest fan of those grotesque inventions, because with his womanizing he experienced the surprise of the unknown) (6). Ironically, Comba framed his masculinist interpretation within the contentious walls of the marital institution, failing to appreciate how fabricated 'grotesque inventions' such as the queenly *guardainfante* fostered the circulation of 'the surprise of the unknown' out of palatial bounds and the monarchic matrimonial bed. In this sumptuary hall, historical *pasarelle* waiting to be fully disclosed, many a woman in breeches, *guardainfantes*, or military livery, like Don Gil, generated copious (in)vested interests that further the development of the marital institution outside of the legal bounds.

This type of economics in which clothing was a powerful currency for men and women was not a phenomenon exclusive to baroque Spain. As Peter Stallybrass has argued, in the 'worn worlds' of sixteenth-century England livery reached a higher value than income, which in turn lead to clothing's life of its own ('Worn World' 291). Encarnación Juárez Almendros summarizes this pan-European trend in which costume transformed the body into a key figure to build identities in Golden Age Spain; a society like this, says Juárez Almendros, 'is a society in which clothing works as value and merchandising and as a way of social incorporation. Clothing established social networks by virtue of its ability to penetrate and transform both the producer and the one who wears it, for its durability and its powerful association with memory' (36). *Don Gil* composes a referential universe in which costume, the fabrication of cloth and the utterance of an industrious clothing lexicon, transforms its characters and audiences. The richly dressed catharsis generated by Don Gil, a very different reproductive event than the physiological script with which Trent charged women in marriage, cannot be fully experienced without first recognizing the interactive game of the materiality of the breeches and the legal and political theatrics of matrimony posed by the breeched woman in this play.

Alan Hunt has observed that as the evolution of fashion and sumptuary laws in sixteenth-century Europe marked progress toward modernity, breeches came to be designed so richly that they represented the high social and economic status of the breeched subject – a datum that no doubt feeds in part Don Gil's transvestite figure.[28] In the case of sixteenth-century Spain Carmen Bernis considers that this piece of clothing belonged to the category of 'ropa de vestir a cuerpo' (clothes closer to the body, to be worn below the overcoats) among which one finds 'medias, calzones y braguetas' (socks/stockings, shorts, and flies) with which gentlemen decorously clad, like Don Gil, covered their abdomen and completed the cover of their torsos, usually with a matching 'jubón' (bodice or doublet) (14). As a result, as the century advanced breeches were considered more and more frequently a luxury item, and their design and confection displayed enormous imagination, with a great diversity of colours, textures, and designs that achieved great visual impact – despite the fact that they always remained an essential and functional garment (152).[29] By the beginning of the seventeenth century, breeches were a rather voluminous garment that, according to Bernis 'was made of *cuchilladas* or *fajas* (vertical stripes of cloth), *entretelas* or lining, and stuffing material to give them volume' (152).

In that period, as a matter of fact, breeches were such a luxury item that the state took notice and sought to control them by means of *pragmáticas* or edicts:

> Breeches can be worn of any kind of silk and on the side every stripe can have a trim of velvet or some other kind of silk, with its backstitch and a rim on each side of the *faja*, but not anyplace else; and if the *faja* is wide, it can have a trim on each side, rim and backstitch, and the stripes can be covered with taffeta; and such breeches can be made of any kind of trim, or of embroidered silks, and the trims must have neither piping nor ridge, nor any edging made of satin or taffeta. (*Premática y nueva orden* 242)

These cited and banned luxury items reiterated the attempts of the crown to control what José Damián González Arce calls 'apariencia y poder' (appearance and power) negotiated in the peninsula since the thirteenth century in various waves of sumptuary laws, with the goal of 'preservar determinados símbolos externos para ciertas categorías sociales, en función de un lenguaje estético, trasunto de una jerarquía ética' (preserving specific external symbols designated to represent certain social categories, by virtue of an aesthetic language that corresponded with an ethical hierarchy) (24).

As González Arce cogently argues, critics usually pay little or no attention to sumptuary laws when studying a particular text or context related to clothing, because the frequent reiteration of these laws seems to have no social impact. Be that as it may, he says, such laws represent legislature's intent, which assumes an ideal society 'expresada de manera directa a través del carácter imperativo de las leyes; así como de manera indirecta a través del rico mundo simbólico, de códigos éticos y estéticos en que se sustentaban éstas' (expressed in direct manner through the imperative character of those laws; likewise, indirectly through a rich symbolic world of ethic and aesthetic codes that support them) (24). To fully grasp how *Don Gil* inscribes this correspondence between appearance and power one must read the specific materiality of the breeches, since that constitutes the base of the rich meaning of the green suit so skillfully woven by the transvestite.[30]

The King and Her

Breeches evolved from a simple piece of cloth commonly used during the Middle Ages to cover the legs, which, as Carmen Bernis notes, was divided in two parts – one for the thighs, which continued to be called breeches, and the other, to cover from the knees down to the feet, which came to be known as socks or stockings (152). As Bernis also points out, historical evidence shows that in the first half of the sixteenth century the design and couture of breeches favoured their function and the colour black (fig. 5).[31] With the promulgation of a series of royal edicts King Felipe II dressed his court with a restraint that became fashionable in Europe, especially in the second half of the century. In 1537 Valladolid, for instance, four *Real Cédulas* were published dictating the parameters to produce, traffic, and wear 'dresses and silks,' 'dresses and suits of servants,' 'moderation in dresses,' and 'moderation in dresses and silks' (quoted in Moreno y Garbayo, numbers 39, 40, 41, and 43). In 1563 an 'Edict of suits and customs; promulgated by the King our Lord' was published in Monzón de Aragón, and in 1565 an 'Edict, in which the order of what to wear during mourning in these Kingdoms' was published in Madrid (quoted in Moreno y Garbayo, numbers 76 and 77).

The resulting style of masculine fashion, as Bernis says, was defined 'at the service of an ideal that sought to reduce to a minimum all possible movement, to give the figure peace, rigidity, and stuffiness ... Rigidity and loftiness went hand in hand with urbanity and courtesy' (203).[32] Despite all this, the Prudent King did not hesitate to dress up his figure with great sumptuary diversity, most pointedly as he donned a great costume with codpiece to sit for a portrait his father Emperor Carlos V commissioned from Tiziano to bring King Felipe II's youthful and vigorous figure to the attention of Mary Tudor, in preparation for their potential marriage (fig. 6).[33] As a matter of fact, marriage was a particular occasion for which the king adapted his costuming, exploring a variety of textures, colours, and materials; a memorable occasion was the spectacular reception offered by the city of Salamanca in November 1543 to the princess Doña María de Portugal to celebrate their imminent wedding, in which King Felipe II's dress was noticed by those registering the events taking place. The chronicle of this momentous occasion illustrates the ornamental profusion in the clothes of those who, according to history, were the protagonists of these festivities, among whom the bishop and his family stood out. An entourage of squires, a trumpet, and twelve lackeys surrounded them, and the chronicler carefully annotated their livery, which made them

Figure 5 Sofonisba Anguissola, *Felipe II*, c. 1565. Oil painting, 88 cm x 72 cm (Madrid: Museo del Prado).

Figure 6 Vecelli di Gregorio Tiziano (Titian), *Felipe II*, 1550–1. Oil painting, 193 cm x 111 cm (Madrid: Museo del Prado).

look very good with their black velvet jackets and stripped perfect breeches, fur hats, cloaked in the finest black cloth with black velvet trim; after them the stable livery dressed in purple flat velvet with golden trim, yellow breeches and jackets with red cloaks and silk hats in matching colours and a thick golden trim. (*Recibimiento* fol. 13r)

The central focus of the king's own attire in the wedding ceremony was his set of white breeches and jacket, a look that nobility did not hesitate to emulate. The bride wore a 'cota de raso carmesí' (crimson satin short cape) embroidered with jewels, and rich clothes, and the ladies wore gowns made of silk and other rich clothes in a variety of colours (*Recibimiento* fols 49–52). The luminous sight of this white, red, and golden scene would be reproduced frequently, and eventually all ritual festivities of royalty and nobility follow that tradition well into the seventeenth century.

The exquisite clothing favoured by the great patron of the *Comedia*, King Felipe III, has been registered in a series of portraits that have made history, as they were designed to propagate the presence, legitimacy, and visibility of the crown's style (fig. 7).[34] This Philippine fashion, certainly a parallel universe to the fashion sported by theatrical companies, no doubt responded to the need of these subjects to impress their audiences, a trend that brought breeches centre stage in men's attire. The preference for excessive ornamentation, as was to be expected, led to a state of sumptuary degeneration in which the habit did make the monk. Juan Matos Fragoso, in a chronicle of the birth of Infanta María Teresa de Austria, recorded a symphony of clothes, colours, textures, and image whose symbolic charge surely emblematizes the evolution of breeches during the previous century and a half, and its decadent status in public spaces in the first half of the seventeenth century. The 'grosera pluma' (crude pen) of Matos Fragoso, as he self-fashions his writing, described in the year 1638 the pomp of these festivities, which included soirées, jousting tournaments, and bullfights.

The monumental *pasarelle* lasted several days of bombastic processions, among which stood out the one in which the duque de Módena appeared, as he gave his entourage the most flamboyant and handsome livery in the court: the first day twenty-four lackeys and twelve squires paraded 'dressed in green velvet, with costly ornamentation and trim made of gold, and green feathers' (*Relación de las insignes y reales fiestas* fol. A3V). On the day of the christening the duke sent a second suite wearing livery

Figure 7 Juan Pantoja de la Cruz, *König Felipe III von Spanien, bildnis in Ganzer Figur als General der Infantrerie* (King Philip III of Spain, full-figure portrait as Infantry General), 1601–2. Oil painting, 176 cm x 116 cm (Vienna: Kunsthistorisches Museum).

of flesh-coloured satin velvet, lined cloaks and bodices made of white cloth heavily embroidered, all curdled with sequins made of fine gold, a livery that rather than making the men wearing them more gallant, turned them into a sorry sight by virtue of the heavy weight they carried, and every suit cost three thousand *escudos*, white feathers, and silver chest sword sheaths, all seeded with imperial eagles with wings made of silk. (*Relación de las insignes y reales fiestas*, fol. A3V)[35]

This gallant procession, and the men whose livery should have designated them as prominent men, depicted instead a parade of figures that uncannily evoked the rows of galley slaves, because the heavy material and economic weight of their clothing 'los hazian penosos.'

Love Affair

The image of this royal baptismal festivity, produced barely a quarter of a century after the opening night of *Don Gil*, gives spectators a hint as to why the transvestite inscribed the protean sumptuary sign of power and masculinity that the breeches represented, sparing the breeched woman of the ornamental excess that spoiled the production of certain livery. The transvestite, in other words, designs her own livery; that is to say, she owns the symbolic luxury of the breeches and subverts the sumptuary laws and usage of such a garment to make her persona visible in Madrid, site of the court. This dramatic gesture does not seek to merely create another piece of clothing more in *fashionista* races (such as those led by kings, dukes, or bishops) that underscored the paternalistic values of the matrimonial and blood purity political economies.[36] Don Gil's fabrication and *industria* creates a costume that will move her dramatic figure centre stage, a scene she creates in which transvestism unleashes the subject from the crypt in which she is bound to live a life of limitation, separating the sexes and reading the contract of institutionalized matrimony as her life script. The spectacular green habit allows the comic leading lady to disarm the 'industria civil' (venal trick, cunning plot) of the false livery designed by her aborted father-in-law, Don Andrés de Guzmán (91, M 59, BM 204). Don Martín's father, blinded by his friendship with Don Pedro de Mendoza y Velástegui, Doña Inés's father, and by his desire to join in matrimony the Guzmán estate with the enormously wealthy Mendoza estate, advises his son to abandon Doña Juana. To cover the legal and moral debt which his son has incurred with the lady, the father invests him with the livery of Don Gil de Albornoz, impostor figure and Don Gil of the Green Breeches's nemesis.[37]

However, in choosing the term 'Albornoz' as the last name of the Guzmán's civil *industria* Tirso's text plays with the ambiguity of impostor signs, and forces Don Andrés's son to a crossroads virtually parallel to that of Oedipus, since the voice recalls at once the abject Muslim subject expelled from Spanish soil and the power of blood purity economics invested in Christian Spanish families (fig. 8). As it is registered in Covarrubias's *Tesoro*, 'albornoz' designates both one of the noblest families of Castille and the 'capuz cerrado de camino con su capilla, de cierta tela que escupe de sí el agua que le cae encima sin calar adentro' (closed hood worn while travelling with its short cape, made with a fabric that repels the water that falls on it without letting it permeate), a garment commonly used in North Africa (44). As Bernis documents, *albornoces* and *capellares* were pieces of clothing used by Arabic subjects, the same way that breeches were literally foreign to such attire, since Muslims covered their legs with thick, loose socks called *zaragüelles* (474–5).[38] This sumptuary difference turns the screw again on the catachrestic *albornoz* of Don Martín, moving along the (in)vested interests crafted by the green Don Gil, for as it turns out her lack of last name – which Caramanchel read as tantamount to a 'capón' (capon, immature name and manhood) (126, M 75, BM 212) and an 'hermafrodita' (hermaphroditic master) (140, M 89, BM 219) – is more valuable than the possibility of being associated with a Muslim subject. Her breeches, in other words, although as suspicious as Albornoz's uncertain lineage, generate images of consumption shown in public by the king himself, and as the lackey confesses to Don Juan, they become the most valuable possession of his master, 'en cuyas calzas funda su apellido, / que ya son casa de solar sus calzas' (Whose breeches add the title to his name, / (As they now seem to be the family seat) (261, M 203).[39]

The metamorphosis of Don Gil's green breeches – from thread to cloth to garment to home to original last name – free Doña Juana of the ancient lineages and livery systems, liberating her as well from becoming suspect of heresy.[40] True, as Covarrubias says, the Albornoz family 'en Castilla es muy ilustre' (was very illustrious in Castile) (44), but Don Martín's hood is not woven by virtue of a highly illustrious blood purity – his Gil pretension usurps the name of the Castilian Albornoces when he simulates their livery, while he dissimulates the Guzmán livery. His lack of credibility increases when Don Andrés sends him a draft for one thousand *escudos*, which he is supposed to collect from a merchant whose residence is located in the Puerta de Guadalajara in Madrid, an area of the city where vagrants gathered to *pretender* and hustle around the commercial activity of that urban zone, mostly

Figure 8 Rodrigo de Villandrado, *El príncipe Felie, future Felipe IV, y el enano Soplillo* (Prince Felipe, future Felipe IV, and Soplillo the Dwarf), c. 1620. Oil painting, 204 cm x 110 cm (Madrid: Museo del Prado).

revolving around the trade of cloth and jewels, as A. Morel Fatio's study shows (417–23). The addressed envelope, reading 'A Don Gil de Albornoz' falls through the textile cracks of Don Martín's fob and jacket, falling on the floor (194–9, M 140–4, BM 242–4). In a stroke of genius of comic chance, Caramanchel finds the letter purloined by virtue of the bad tailoring of the impostor Albornoz's suit, later delivering it to the breeched woman who, in turn, gives it to his real servant, Quintana, for collection of the small fortune it represents. With this draft the breeched woman buys Doña Inés the dresses and jewels she is meant to receive from the impostor Don Gil de Albornoz, who planned to win her hand in matrimony.

Transvestite Economics

The performative universe mobilized by the green breeches of Don Gil is of such rhetorical prowess that the pedestrian piece of cloth covering the actors' abdomens and thighs translates into a fantasy of material reproduction, staged industrially when four characters join in the simulated fun and pretend to be Don Gil: Don Martín, of whose Albornoz the breeched woman is a simulacrum, and who loses the game when he says, in the garden scene, 'calzas verdes me pongo desde mañana / si esta color apetece' (I shall don / Green breeches from tomorrow on, / If that's the colour that appeals) (161, M 107); Caramanchel, who tells his master that 'por si otra vez te me pierdes / me encajo tus calzas verdes' (In case you're lost again I'll squeeze / Inside your bright green breeches) (207, M 153); and Don Juan and Doña Clara, who join the game later in the play, him 'de noche' (as for night-time, in night attire) and her, 'de hombre' (dressed as a man) (270, 290, M 209, 223, BM 279). As if audiences were watching a persuasive commercial of Versace or Dolce and Gabbana today, the green breeches reproduce the material consumption of desire and generate with it an industrious fabrication that even today, four-hundred years after its opening night, keeps inciting people to desire and experience the breeches first-hand.[41]

The transvestite *industria* becomes even more significant if readers insist on seeing the fabrication of the breeched woman as a sumptuary banquet that pays off with great interest for many a character in the play. Early in the show Doña Juana voices her awareness of how interest is submitted to the monumental monetary value attached to Doña Inés by virtue of her sizable dowry: she describes gold, 'que es sangre vil / que califica intereses, un portillo supo abrir' (which is a baser blood / Ennobling vested interests, / Soon found the means) to tap Don Martín's vein of avarice, and hence, his having abandoned her in the first place (90, M 57). The transvestite, as Doña Elvira, does not mince words when she speaks truth to Doña Inés's face about 'el interés de tu dote' (the interest / of (in) your dowry) that explains why Don Martín abandoned her, the leading lady in drag (180).[42] Don Martín affirms, with great conviction, that the trick he has played on Doña Juana is justified because 'el interés / y beldad de doña Inés / excusan la culpa mía' (the growing interest / and loveliness of doña Inés / exonerate me from all blame) (193, M 141).[43] The byzantine tales of the transvestite, which reflect the absolute social and aesthetic value of Doña Inés as a future trophy wife culminate in a clumsy gesture on her part, when she exclaims after she and her father have agreed on her matrimonial deal, '¡Interés / dichoso!' (Dreaded / interest!) (217).[44] The transvestite's *industria* exercises a profound impact on this market of matrimonial values, distributing her (in)vested interests among many rather than concentrating wealth in one single place.

Thus, Doña Juana becomes the proud owner of the ten thousand *ducados* that constitute Don Martín's wedding gift to her, as well as the symbolic capital that comes with the intellectual, artistic, and political property of reinventing Don Juan Tenorio's tricky game. Don Juan, hardly a Tenorio, is named owner of the seventy thousand *ducados* of Doña Inés' dowry, as well as the purity of her name; she, in turn, gains a whole new perception of dress, sex, and manliness, which the breeched woman has given her as the best wedding gift.[46] Doña Clara and Don Antonio, conservative investors, profit from the knowledge they can derive from their incursion in unknown territory when she dressed as a man in her performance of the third Don Gil. Theatrical companies that have staged *Don Gil* have reaped great material profit from selling out virtually every show of this play, despite that ominous fiasco of its opening night in 1615 (see note 2); for these theatrical ensembles, the human growth that comes as collateral in the material gain is incalculable. And the many audiences who have come to see Don Gil's transvestite show, without whom there is no theatre, take the greatest treasure: a portfolio of imaginative resources with which to rethink and redraft marriage, theatre, and the law. In 'The End,' theatrical code for 'ultimately,' the transvestite accumulates and collects all those interests by virtue of the fabrication and *industria* with which she has crafted her costume. Her metonymical game of masculinity, emblematized in her green breeches, unfolds as a theatrical and performative life that lead

Doña Juana to a point in which she is able to create a character who benefits from the king's own symbolic capital. As Don Gil says very early in the play, and as this chapter opens, 'yo sólo vivo de mi hacienda,' which can be translated into a work of fabrication and *industria* that invites audiences to continue weaving, theatrically, to keep earning (in)vested interests.

Coda: The Musical Chairs of Divorce

Sustento en fin lo que escribí, y conozco
Que aunque fueran mejor de otra manera,
No tuvieran el gusto que han tenido
Porque a veces lo que es contra lo justo
Por la misma razón deleita el gusto.

(And yet, at last I must defend my plays
While knowing they are flawed in many ways
Because their vogue depended on these flaws
For sometimes something charms the taste because
It is in fact contrary to the laws.)

Félix Lope de Vega, *El arte nuevo de hacer comedias*
(The New Art of Writing Plays)

The *entremés* (hors d'oeuvre), loosely translated as 'interlude,' was the locus of bawdy dramatic representation where music, dance, foul language, desire, and sexual innuendo were unabashedly staged, in a melting pot of transgressions of the clearly defined boundaries of marital legislation.[1] This chapter analyses the interplay of characters in *El entremés del juez de los divorcios* by Miguel de Cervantes Saavedra with various linguistic and theatrical rehearsals of divorce, a farcical marriage scene that melts down into music – the only sensible curtain call for the subject stage of divorce in early modern Spain.[2] This coda imagines a staging of this short piece where the named music underscores (and is underscored by) the endless possibilities of the *fachada*, the backdrop and house of the public theatres. Following the lead casually dropped by Cervantes in the title, my short coda envisions this piece as a one-two-three game, with the *entremés*, the judge, and divorce moving around in buffoonish, clownish fashion, as in the game of tic-tac-toe. The game is also known as the game of noughts and crosses or, more aptly for 'The End' of a *comedia* – and, perhaps, for a book on marriage, theatre, and the law – hugs-and-kisses. The board is designed for two people who enter the match with the goal of placing three marks by the same player in one of the horizontal, vertical, or diagonal rows drawn usually with pencil on a napkin or some other ephemeral writing media.

The two players of the church-and-state marital game (man/husband, woman/wife and their roles of domination and submission, source and receptacle of life) unfold in the short Cervantine interlude as a myriad of possible interactive combinations that, mediated by the farcical rendition of a succession of three full courthouse hearings (and an aborted fourth one where only the husband shows up, delivering a monologue at once hilarious and fairly sad) are received by a judge and a clerk. Such are the musical chairs of divorce, for the legal frontier did not allow for the annulment of a marriage save in a few exceptional circumstances, and the theatrical frontier did not include a tradition of representing divorce.[3] Their voices, rather than staging marriage in the complex, forward action of the *comedia* (in between whose acts the *entremés* was designed to move centre stage), appear in the imaginary space of the play/courthouse combining endless duos, as in the game of tic-tac-toe: man/wife, man/judge, judge/scribe, man/member of the audience, woman/judge, scribe/man, and so forth.[4] As any player of the children's game knows, the best play is when both parties 'win' as the game ends in a draw. I invite you, idle reader, to leave behind the cerebral, academic considerations of marriage we have woven together in the previous pages and imagine Cervantes's *entremés* onstage, with each of their characters hollering along the lines of what the 'noblest' of characters, Mariana, says to mark her grand entrance onstage: 'Señor, ¡diuorcio, diuorcio, y mas diuorcio, y otras mil vezes diuorcio!' (Your Honour, divorce, divorce, and more divorce, a thousand times divorce!) (2–3).

Published in Spain during a period of consolidation of the public theatres where the *entremeses* thrived, *El juez* represents (like most of its counterparts in the genre of *teatro menor* or short plays) a bold experiment in queer audiovisual language, publicized desire, and unconcern toward reproduction – something Sherry Velasco and Peter Thompson, among others, have studied very well in their analysis of the life, work,

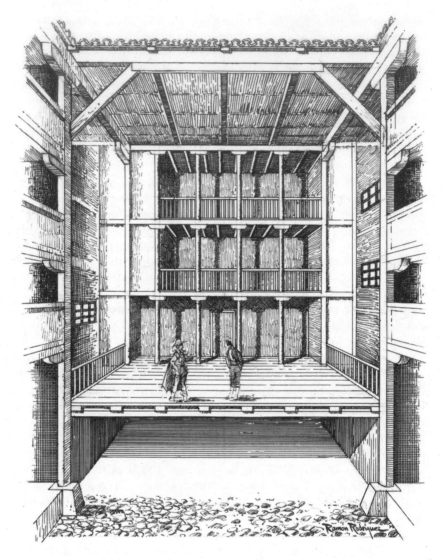

Figure 9 *Reconstrucción de un tablado de un corral de comedias con énfasis en el foso* (Reconstruction of the stage of a public theatre with emphasis on the space under the stage, known as 'the Hell' in Elizabethan theatre). Courtesy of Evangelina Rodríguez-Cuadros. 'Loci Theatrales: El edificio teatral' (Theatrical Places: The Theatre Edifice), *Ars Theatrica: Siglo de Oro*. In *Parneseo* http://parnaseo.uv.es/Ars/Imagenes/Loci/5.htm.

and performed pregnancy of Juan Rana, the gay actor of the *Comedia*, and king/queen of the *entremeses* stages.[5] With its bawdily public representation of divorce, hundreds of years before the 1978 legislative move, *El juez* mobilized subject stages other than the man-woman / wife-husband strictly bound by the prescription of reproduction spelled in the laws of the Catholic Universal Monarchy. To more fully unleash the great histrionic potential of this piece I propose to read this *entremés* as an instance of 'queering marriage' – and not to play a seemingly enlightened version of the game 'Where's Waldo' to provide us with a certain banal academic amusement, unfitting for the present occasion.

Rather than spending my time forcing homosexual subjects out of the delicious closet of the *entremés*, I insist on teasing out how *El juez* and his ensemble play a ludicrous, disparate game that in 'The End' is called *fiesta* and *música* to accompany the titanic vessel of the *matrimonio cristiano*, as the institution was beginning to sink in front of the very eyes of its artists and readers. Far from pretending that I know in advance where sexuality can be found in this *entremés*, my goal is to acknowledge a now canonized critical failure to assume anything other than a transhistorical heterosexuality in *El juez*, and to propose that readings of sexual *differánce* (in a more or less Derridean sense) in the *entremeses* can, and should, be performed.[6]

El juez unleashes a number of forbidden desires that speak of sexual recreation. Forced to sublimate such repression, its characters represent the embodiment of alternative ideas of marriage, in which biological reproduction, as the sole mandate for the union occupies, literally, no textual space; hence, the importance in this staging of using the spaces of the *fachada* as places for hide-and-seek where the irrevocability, mooring, and indissolubility of marriage would take off and mean otherwise, if only for a fleeting moment. The marriage that these characters articulate openly differs from the one explicitly desired by imperial publications such as the *cédulas* and *pragmáticas* that translated the institution of marriage to the general public in instalments such as the Decree of Tametsi. The queering of *matrimonio* staged in *El juez*, in the end, is one desired by those who, as if they were children playing tic-tac-toe or a game of musical chairs, riot against the existential mooring of a marriage dictated from the public transcript of such official stories, and instead pursue a ludicrous parody, a little farcical number along the lines of what Cynthia Herrup called 'Going to Law' in the seminar she directed at the Folger Institute in the spring of 1999. These subjects' comic class action seeks to interpellate the judge, the representative of the father and his law who in this *entremés* could be read as a Judge Judy *avant la lettre*.

To stage these games of divorce performed in the fantasyland of the pretend courthouse I follow closely an excellent analysis by Anne Cruz, who reads Cervantes's *entremeses* as artistic pieces that 'question the possibility of reproducing unmediated desire all the while deferring formal closure' (119). The conclusion proposed by Cruz – that in 'deferring the possibility of any social change' the *entremeses* lay out their own limits of subversion (125) – is critical in understanding the kind of queer marriage that *El juez* stages in print, for the professional stages of the *Comedia*. Its characters subvert the institutionalization of marriage knowing full well what its legal limits are. In that context, their adamant voicing (singing) in favour of divorce imagines a critically queer marriage that, to borrow Judith Butler's words, 'avows a set of constraints of the past and the future that mark at once the limits of agency and its most enabling conditions' (*Bodies* 228). The limits of literary and social agency in this piece have been cogently examined by Cruz, who sees the inscription of the musical theme of *la noche de San Juan* (the night of the celebration of St John's day, a night of festivals and rituals throughout the Hispanic world) and the legal occasion of the annual signing and renewal of contracts for domestic servants, as 'an economic subtext through which the (dis)order of the social body identified with the carnivalesque and expressed through women's sexual desire is subsumed under a new symbolic order that represses desire, displacing and substituting it with monetary exchange' (126).

This reading of how Cervantes contaminates legal discourse 'with the language of the marketplace' (126) leaves out an alternative kind of desire, that of the inscription of homoerotic bonds between men and women of the play. In the moment when the first husband, El Vejete, admonishes his wife, Mariana, for making such a public scene of her 'negocio' (affair), Cruz is right in reading the patriarchal authority with which the Old Man articulates his critique of her 'pendencia' (dispute) (2–3). The verb 'almodonear' (yell out) used by Mariana's decrepit husband of twenty-two years sells her out in the marketplace of the theatre, that place of danger for a woman (as chapter 4 showed earlier). This verbal trick betrays the Vejete as a complicit voice with the *moralistas*, revealing in his speech an agreement with such misogynistic articulations. At the same time, his advice that she speak otherwise, 'habla passo, por la passión que Dios passó' (speak softly, by the Passion of Christ) (2–3) betrays an enmeshment of genre, spectacle, and a sense of drag that, if detected, dissolves the very same authority with which the aging barren man speaks. As chapter 2 revealed, in Cervantes's universe of theatre, multiperspectivism and *heteroglossia*, the term 'passo' with which the husband wants his wife to speak inscribes the histrionic power of the *pasos* (short plays) from which theatre was born and from where the *entremeses* derived. Ironically, as he pushes her to look like an icon, mimicking the women gathered around Christ during the Passion and thus striking a pose of purity, the husband's sibilant command also encourages her to show her musical wares onstage, perhaps in one of the upper balconies.

The divine 'passión' that should motivate her *perfecta casada* voice could be read as El Vejete's own movie montage of Christ's Passion, a highly irreverent footnote from the part of Cervantes to the wedding of Christ with his church. As Bruce Wardropper said about *El viejo celoso* (The Jealous Old Man), 'the *entremeses* present a world of farce, in which nothing, not even marriage, is sacred' (20). 'Passó,' the verb that conveys in Spanish the agonizing process of biblical proportions through which Jesus Christ suffers before his crucifixion, disappears in the possessive 'of' in the English translation. The sibilant dragging, the contradictory subject of Mariana, and the opening scene crumble under the thunder of Mariana's voice, which competes with God himself, and his theatrical machine, the deus ex machina, for the spotlight. She, Mari-Ana, passes for God with her shrieking petition for divorce, staged in a pretend masculinist space, the courthouse in the playhouse. Undoubtedly, this is a most confusing and embarrassing event for a childless husband without sufficient leverage to control his unruly wife in public. TIC!

Mariana's response to both paternalistic figures, her own husband and the judge who holds her fate in his impotent hands, interpellates the regulatory fictions that would have her, as a wife, perfectly contained, incapable of reading matrimonial Law. With a clarity that reveals her awareness of the emerging contractual system of marital legislations and litigations, she envisions marriage as a real estate transaction that in three-year cycles 'como cosas de arrendamiento' (like a rent contract) could be dissolved to alleviate the 'perpetuo dolor de entrambas partes' (perpetual grief to both parties) (4–5). Her roaring petition for divorce is ultimately driven by the fact that El Vejete is bound to a box (a coffin, *grande morte*) because he lacks sensorial and tactile powers, while she wants to openly exercise her wifehood with her own sensorial pleasures (*petite morte*):

Encerraos vos que lo podréis lleuar y sufrir, que ni tenéis ojos con que ver, ni oydos con que oyr, ni pies con que andar, ni mano con qué tocar; que yo, que estoy sana, y con todos mis cinco sentidos cabales y viuos, quiero usar dellos a la descubierta, y no por bruxula, como quinola dudosa.

(Shut yourself up, for you can stand it; you have neither eyes to see, nor ears to hear, nor feet to walk with, nor fingers to feel with. But I'm healthy and my five senses are sound and keen, and I want to use them in open freedom, and not by guesswork, fumbling in the dark.) (6–7)

The same desire professed by Mariana to fulfil sexual, sensual, and sensorial desires within or without marriage binds all the women in the text.

As soon as the second plaintiff, by the name of Guiomar, jumps on-stage Mariana acknowledges their bond after she hears her give the soldier, her husband, the pejorative qualifier of '*deste*': '¡Bendito sea Dios, que se me ha cumplido el desseo que tenia de verme ante la presencia de vuessa merced, a quien suplico quan encarecidamente puedo sea seruido de descasarme deste' (Thank the Lord, at last my wish is granted to come before Your Honour. I beg you with all the strength of my soul please to unmarry me from this) (8–9). The Judge objects to such denigration of manhood, and asks '¿Qué cosa es *desde*? ¿No tiene otro nombre?' ('From this'? Hasn't he a name?) (8–9). Chastised by the Judge with a 'Bien fuera que dixerades siquiera deste hombre' (You could at least say 'from this man') (8–9), Guiomar responds, 'Si él fuera hombre, no procurara yo descasarme' (If he were a man, I should not try to be quit of the marriage) (8–9), adding that, in fact, he is not a man, but a 'leño' (stick of wood), for 'el no sabe qua les su mano derecha, ni busca medios ni traças para grangear vn real con que ayude a sustentar su casa y familia' (he doesn't know his right hand from his left, and he won't hustle about to earn two bits to help support his house and family) (8–9). The itinerant retort from the soldier (a rogue tale worthy of *Lazarillo*, full of dreams of chaps, unfulfilled wands of authority, saddle-bags, travelling costumes, an ass, linens, hams, and many other dreamed goodies) acknowledges that his intentions are good, but that he has 'ni oficio ni beneficio' (neither profession nor benefice) and because he is married no gentleman will employ him (8–9). His wife, in other words, speaks the truth. When she argues that she is chaste and virtuous and deserves the respect that is owed to such a woman, the soldier recants on the part of the social contract prescribed for the perfect wife analysed in chapter 1: 'Bueno es que quieran las mugeres que las respeten sus maridos, porque son castas y honestas, como si en solo esto consistiesse de todo en todo su perfeccion, y no echan de ver los desaguaderos por donde desaguan la fineza de otras mil virtudes que les faltan' (It is all very fine for women to wish their husbands to respect them because they are chaste and decent, as if their perfection of character lay in that and in nothing else; and they do not notice the leaks that siphon off the cream of a thousand other virtues that they lack) (12–13).

After alleging that Guiomar walks zombie-like around the house 'rostrituerta, enojada, zelosa, pensatiua, manirrota, dormilona, perezosa, pendenciera, gruñidoera, con otras insolencias de este jaez, que bastan a consumir las vidas de dozientos maridos' (scowling, grouchy, jealous, moody, wasteful, lie-abed, lazy, quarrelsome, grumbling, with other vices of the sort, enough to wear out the lives of two hundred husbands), the soldier performs a verbal about-face reminiscent of the operation of the *bofetones* seen in chapter 4, and says that she has never behaved like that; on the contrary, he is, after all, the lazy stick of wood, and 'doy en pleito por concluso, y holgaré de ser condenado' (I consider the case closed) (12–13). As Diana the Belflor called for a man in her house to play the role of honour-keeper, Mariana and Guiomar have searched in vain for a man in their marriage to play the two-for-two script prescribed by civil and ecclesiastical laws, to no avail. Mariana, in fact, supports the accusation that Guiomar voices against her husband: '¿Pues no quieren vuessas mercedes que llame leño a vna estatua que no tiene mas acciones que un madero?' (Do you expect me not to call him a stick? This dummy has no more action than a plank) (8–9).[7] The voices of the litigants in chapter 2, the Burgos *comediantes* in chapter 3, Mencía y Leonor in chapter 4, Diana, Teodoro, Marcela, and Tristán in chapter 5, and Doña Juana-Don Gil-Doña Elvira with Quintana in chapter 6 reverberate in the acting sound of Mariana, who in solidarity with Guiomar intervenes: 'Ésta y yo nos quejamos sin duda de un mismo agravio' (This woman and I are certainly complaining of a similar offence) (8–9). TAC!

The third wife, Minjaca, reiterates the same desire voiced by the previous two women: divorce from her husband, the Cirujano. They all want to move out, a move that in theatrical terms begins by occupying another one of the tic-tac-toe boxes. Minjaca's reasons are manifold (she counts four hundred), if they all boil down to what Mariana and Guiomar alleged before her:

La primera, porque cada vez que le veo, hago cuenta que veo al mismo
Luzifer; la segunda, porque fuy engañada quando con el me casè, porque
el dixo que era medico de pulso, y remanecio cirujano y hombre que haze
ligaduras y cura otas enfermedades, que va dezir desto a medico, la mitad
del justo precio; la tercera, porque tiene zelos del sol que me toca; la
quarta, que como no le puedo ver, querría estar apartada dél dos millones
de leguas…

(First, because every time I look at him I think he is Lucifer himself; second,
because I was deceived when I married him, for he said he was a bona fide
doctor, and he turned out to be only a barber-surgeon, a man who sets
bones and treats slight illnesses, which means that he is nothing like a
regular doctor; third, because he is jealous of the sun's rays when they
touch me; fourth, I can't endure the sight of him, and I want to get two
million leagues away from him …) (14–15)

In this third legal farcical game, with allegations that bring us back to
the senseless merry-go-round of bureaucracy seen in chapter 1, and the
suspicions of adultery that ended badly in chapter 3, the representatives of the legal system intervene in what seems to be a structural melt-
down; first, the Procurador (prosecuting attorney) cheers the husband's
nonsense with '¡Bastantissimamente ha prouado su intencion!' (He has
proved his cause to the utmost sufficiency!), and second, the Escribano
(clerk) derails the wife's farcical deposition by screaming '¿Quién diab-
los acertara a concertar estos reloxes, estando las ruedas tan desconcer-
tadas?' (Who can ever make these two clocks keep time together, when
their wheels are so out of gear?) (14–15).

England and the Reformation were on their 'road to divorce,' but
Spain was to wait until the latter twentieth century, and so the Judge,
with no time left for a series of decisions for which the only solution is to
adjudicate the case with the legal phrase 'no ha lugar' (there is no case
here) gives his farcical class-action, ludicrous verdict: 'Señora, señora, si
pensays dezir aqui todas las quatrozientas causas, yo no estoy para.es-
cucharlas, ni ay lugar para ello. Vuestro negocio se recibe a prueua, y
andad con Dios, que ay otros negocios que despachar' (Hold on, woman,
if you are going to enumerate all four hundred causes, I am in no mood
to listen to them, nor is there time to do so. Your case will be taken under
advisement, so farewell. There is other business to attend to) (14–15).
The Cirujano speaks for all of them, including the silenced four hundred

reasons of his own wife, as well as all other subject stages staging 'other business to attend to': '¿Que mas prueuas, sino que yo no quiero morir con ella, ni ella gusta de viuir conmigo?' (What more testimony do you want, besides the fact that I do not wish to die with her, and she does not wish to live with me?) (14–15). It may be four couples, four hundred reasons, four thousand clerks and attorneys, and four million judges; in the end, 'Si esso bastasse para descasarse los casados, infinitissimos sacudirian de sus ombros el yugo del matrimonio' (If that sufficed to part married couples, an infinite number would shake from their shoulders the yoke of matrimony) (14–15). TOE!

To the tic-tac-toe Cervantes adds one last intervention, an addendum that throws off the rhythmic beauty of the children's game. In a ghostly imprint of what a desire for divorce would feel like, the wife's voice altogether disappears in the fourth pretend lawsuit. In theatrical terms, this lack of presence of the wife onstage eerily reminds audiences of the void left by Mencía in the scene of uxoricide. As a fourth woman in a series of defeats when facing a masculinist scheme, this fourth 'case' presented to the judge in the divorce court is intensely and contradictorily reminiscent of the future character composed by Tirso de Molina, Doña Ana de Ulloa, the wife-to-be of Don Juan Tenorio, whose only appearance onstage is as the object of a proposed marital negotiation between the king of Spain, and Don Gonzalo de Ulloa, Doña Ana's father. As will happen in *El burlador*, the homoerotic circulation of power, energy, and desire between men is released immediately as the fourth husband, the lone ranger Ganapán, elicits a pronouncement of solidarity with the Cirujano: 'Ya conozco yo a la mujer deste buen hombre, y es tan mala como mi Aldonza; que no lo puedo más encarecer' (I am acquainted with this good man's wife, and she is as mean as my Aldonza; I can't make it any stronger) (16–17). Aldonza Lorenzo, the debased real woman who constitutes the undesirable raw material for Don Quijote's fantasy of Dulcinea, remains as the final emblem of all women in *El juez*. The hatred for each other in this farce about the labours of love lost between men and women could constitute in any reasonable scheme grounds for reconsideration if not of the bond in itself, at least of the terms in which it is prescribed and institutionalized. Be that as it may, the farcical representative of the state, taking his best notes from the stultifying forms and formats for history afforded to him by the *capitulaciones* and the *facultades de mayorazgo*, concludes that never-ending bureaucracy is the only solution for his court. Kafka would be proud:

Mirad, señores: aunque algunos de los que aqui estays aueis dado algunas
causas que traen aparejada sentencia de diuorcio, con todo esso, es menester que conste por escrito y que lo digan testigos, y assi, a todos os recibo
a prueua ...

(Look, my good people; although some of you who are here have ad-
duced reasons sufficient for divorce, none the less it must all be set down
in writing and witnesses must testify; so I will take all your cases under
advisement.) (16–17)

As Cruz has noted, there are tangible differences between the networks of men and women in the text. The most notorious of them is
without a doubt the fact that the male officers of the law perform their
duties in frank solidarity with the husbands, while the three wives
present in the courthouse are forced to endure scolding, corrections to
their speech, or orders to be silent – perhaps the reasons why the fourth
one does not even bother to show up in court. If readers pay close attention to the rhythm of the *entremés*, honouring the author's call in his
Adjunta al Parnaso that he wanted to deliver these pieces 'a la estampa
para que se vea de espacio lo que pasa apriesa' (to the press so that
what happens in a rush is seen in slow motion) (116), the interruption
of the demanding, vocal wives by the men onstage constitutes the single constant beat of the piece. As Mary Gaylord argues, this is emblematic of the genre since the social order represented in the *entremeses* was
literally designed to interrupt the dramatic convention of the multiple
wedding scenes with which many *comedias* called the curtain.

In closing, I would like to drive this point even further, noting that
the litigation and oral pleasure *interrupti* with which these women are
represented does not actually stop their interventions. What brings
them to a halt is the eruption of yet another case of marital litigation to
be heard, a relentless artistic interruption of what Hilaire Kallendorf
has cogently analysed as a key dynamic of the Spanish *Comedia*: casuistry, or case morality, by virtue of which subjects were able to pose, as
they played, fundamental questions about life, love, and other matters.
But even with those interruptions in the forum (funny thing must have
happened to them on their way there), these women find ways to connect with each other. The *fachada*, that space that allows them at once to
connect and separate, is the place where nine discrete blocks allow four
men and three women, as well as the title character of the judge and his
legal entourage, to play games, at a fundamental level like those played

by the characters, actors, and readers we have seen in the previous chapters of this book. Cervantes plays with the web of drama and theatre, linking his cast of characters to the worlds of print and stage, divorcing the bodies and souls of readers and players (pun intended) from the marital ideologies studied in the previous chapters. In the tectonic-plate move to make contractual *nouveau marriages* more visible, parodied in the three-step tragicomic dance of marriage inhabiting the space/time world of the *comedias*, the failed interruptions in *El juez* stand as a self-referential gesture to further turn the screw of interpretation on marriage.

This delicious *guarnición* (side dish), in particular, defers the charac-·ters' desires as an alternative economic exchange of marriage emerges in that grandest (and most regulated) public marketplace of the body: the theatre. Perhaps with the Alcaldes engaged in satisfying their own bodily needs or desires in-between acts, *El juez* speaks directly to the occupants of the *patio* or the *cazuela*, much along the lines of the members of the *I salonisti* band playing to the occupants of the Titanic, which in *El juez* presents audiences with a burlesque tune. With this I do not intend to argue in favour of reading Cervantes as advocating divorce, or to argue that queer subjects were considered card-carrying members of the Counter-Reformation club. History has it that the band did play on, for in 1615, the year of publication of these *entremeses*, Milton had not even started with *The Doctrine and Discipline of Divorce*. As Lawrence Stone has amply documented, in England the 'road to divorce' was long and tortuous, despite the manic force with which Henry VIII advocated, with words and actions, for such social change. In Spain, the eight wanting characters of *El juez* would have to wait until 1978 to have their desired sentences of divorce granted, and at the time I first wrote these lines (April of 2004) for a talk at the Cervantes symposium at the Newberry Library organized by Sherry Velasco, Judge Zapatero insisted on burning the midnight oil to carve the way to the altar of the *Cortes* to achieve the next step in this legal frontier: granting legal status to same-sex marriages.

There is no doubt that in *El juez* Cervantes puts together a hell of a band to play tic-tac-toe and musical chairs, incorporating in the space of the farce those who knew that, in their lifetime, such subversion would be legally limited. Parodying the dictatorial frame of Counter-Reformation marital ideologies, the cast of *El juez* imagines a world of fantasy that flies in the face of authoritarian laws, daring to sing their own queer desires in public. It is now up to Hispanists to listen to such tunes and see the poetry of citation that the liturgy of marriage truly is capable of achieving for all subjects; alternatively, they may choose to ignore it and focus on trying to rescue the inevitably sinking mammoth ship of the *matrimonio cristiano*, amply loaded with taxing antics such as the romanticized reading of a languishing patriarchy performed, in their moment, by scholars such as Marcel Bataillon.[8] I, for one, intend to join the party of the *apaciguados* (chilling dudes) and those playing *conciertos* whose rhyming of *justo* and *gusto* (laws and flaws), as Lope said in the epigraph, played a fair game. In a queer version of marriage Cervantes's tic-tac-toe represents, like many other voices heard in this book, subjects refusing to return to their households according to the binary logic of the Catholic Universal Monarchy Laws, choosing instead to build a place where honour is revived with 'el gusto, que estaba muerto' (love, once dead) and 'Amor es el sabio más experto' (Cupid, the most expert of judges) (18–19). Let the games begin.

Conclusion

My first research trip for this book took me to the Archivo General de Simancas, a small town near the city of Valladolid, in the fall of 1993. The Archive is housed in the Castle of Simancas, where it has been located since 1545 when King Felipe II established it as the depository of documents pertaining to all the institutions and representatives of the crown – the first Royal Archive of the Crown. The castle, originally commissioned in the fifteenth century by Don Fadrique Enríquez, admiral of Castile, was built among the ruins of an old fortress occupied alternatively by Arabs and Christians above the Pisuerga River. From New York city, where I lived and taught at the time, I travelled to the AGS in search of unedited documents that would help me prove what I thought was a sensible working hypothesis for the study of early modern Spanish cultural and literary history: that the unruly event of theatre stood in frank opposition to the 1564 Spanish legislation that, in making the words from the Council of Trent the law of the Spanish land, had defined marriage forever.

At the time, the larger goal of my study was to disprove that seventeenth-century Spanish theatre was designed as propaganda for the absolutist Habsburg monarchy, a widely held premise in the scholarly study of the *cultura del barroco* canonized about forty years before in the scholarly work of José Antonio Maravall. Having gone through a meagre four years of my own marital journey and three as a tenure-track assistant professor, I was committed rather vehemently to proving that the classical theatre of Spain – which since my childhood and youth in Spain I had considered a living part of a cultural past, and not the pawn of academic and canon wars that it has come to be – was not a mere prop for marital dominant ideologies. Literature had given me ample evidence to refute Maravall's story, but I wanted to investigate further the legislative documents that I had found scattered throughout a pretty dysfunctional bibliography. In Simancas and in the archives that I visited thereafter I found a much richer, more complex panorama of marriage; this has driven my critical inquiry for the past decade and a half; a series of research questions has unfolded as the debates about marriage have propagated, and continue to rage, on both sides of the Atlantic.

As always happens with archival journeys, that first trip to Simancas was initially a fracas and it raised more questions than the answers it was supposed to provide for my research. As soon as I set foot in the castle-archive and told the *archivero* that I was looking for documents pertaining to the legislation and administration of marriage, he drew a blank and virtually invited me to leave. I had decided to travel to Simancas because since its establishment as Royal Archive in 1545 and through 1844 (when the crown opened the Archivo Nacional de Alcalá de Henares and closed Simancas to the public), the castle was the deposit for all official documents produced by the crown's representatives and institutions, among them the Valladolid and Granada *Chancillerías*, the *corregidores del reino*, the *Consejo de Castilla*, the *Alcaldes mayores*, and various ambassadors. I thought that I would find for sure a treasure trove of materials on marriage generated by judges such as the *Alcaldes mayores* or those in the *Chancillerías*. The first thing I stumbled upon was the realization that marriage – as opposed to war, navigation, justice, economics, and other affairs more traditionally characteristic of, and visible in, the official, public spaces of the *Monarquía* – is not a question or topic that people came to Simancas to research. Those topics, and not marriage, were the ones that drove researchers to endure the difficulties of conducting research in such a remote place. I refused to believe that this massive, comprehensive archive of monarchic administration (the collection on the *Consejo de Castilla* alone has over 3,000 *legajos*) would not have materials significant for a research project on marriage in early modern Spain. Honouring stubbornness as a trait of good archival research, two *archiveros* to whom I am forever in debt – Javier Álvarez Pinedo and Inmaculada Delgado – suggested that I not waste my time looking for legislative documents, most of which have already been published in modern editions, but that I look at *facultades de mayorazgo*, the legal documents that noble families petitioned for in order to found estates for future marital negotiations.

This opened the door to what sixteen years later has become the present book: a study of correspondences between marriage, theatre, and the law in early modern Spain that engages – as precisely as possible in one book – the enormous referential wealth of this cultural event. The nearly 200 documents I harvested in Simancas only touched the tip of an iceberg that has enveloped my intellectual and professional life for over a decade, and that I can only present here in very partial terms. *Subject Stages* does not seek to be a definitive history of this institution in early modern Spain, parallel to the lifetime work that Lawrence Stone published in his two volumes, *The Family, Sex and Marriage in England, 1500–1800* (1977) and *The Road to Divorce* (1990); although Stone's larger conclusions about marriage, sex, and the family in early modern England have been largely debunked, his two studies nonetheless remain critical sources of reference for this subject matter in ways that have not yet been articulated for marriage in early modern Spain. *Subject Stages* neither defends nor condemns this institution, and neither is it interested in proving that the discourses and practices of law or theatre were (or are) institutionally or personally better or worse than the other in representing marriage; rather, it seeks to analyse the variety of ways in which tensions in theatrical, legal, and political arenas informed each other in the process of production and reproduction of marriage in these three arenas of literature and society that still find resonance in the current debates and legal reform of this institution.

The *Comedia's* reiterated inscription of marriage in a variety of political and aesthetic venues mobilized a citational obsession with primal scenes of relations between the sexes and, according to many laws, despite them a virtually compulsive theatrical gesture with which the phenomenon of theatre built a variety of alternative legal imaginaries that revolved around the birth and development of this institution. It was an artistic and economic gesture that would find profound reverberations in future times. In another time and place, far removed from what Margaret Greer has cogently analysed as 'the place of theatre' in Madrid, television in the United States has revisited the *Comedia's* recreation of law and theatre in the late twentieth-century with productions such as *LA Law*, *Allie MacBeal*, and *Boston Legal*, as well as the splintered drama running continuously since 1990, *Law & Order*, and its two spinoffs, *Criminal Intent* and *Special Victims Unit*. The film industry has also experimented with the content and the form of the legal drama, but neither TV nor the movies has engaged the representation of marriage with the systematic, centre stage intensity that the Spanish *Comedia* once did.

The scenes of marriage produced by subjects in the stages of theatre in early modern Spain reproduced, as we have seen, the marital ideologies of the absolutist Catholic Universal Monarchy. They did so to keep their shows going while they at the same time portrayed current scenes of the law, as audiences of *Law & Order* and the other TV legal dramas see on a daily basis. In a much more controlled artistic and social environment than today in the United Sates and other parts of the world, though, the *Comedia* also showed the clear and present danger of resistance to marital ideologies, producing in 'The End,' scenes of marriage for future generations of viewers, readers, and citizens to see, read, consider, and remember. In this sense, this theatre foretold another legal drama, the one Shoshana Felman has termed the 'juridical unconscious' of the twentieth century – a 'hidden link between trials and trauma ... more visible and more dramatically apparent' to signal 'civilization's most appropriate and most essential, most ultimately meaningful response to the violence that wounds it' (*The Juridical* 1–3). By this I do not mean to conclude that what Felman cogently spells for twentieth-century U.S. and world culture is literally to be read in sixteenth- and seventeenth-century Spanish theatre or the law. Felman's findings about the juridical unconscious, as she reads them in the 1961 Eichman trial in Jerusalem and the 1995 O.J. Simpson trial in Los Angeles, as well as by the story of Walter Benjamin's suicide in September 1940, with resonances in writings by Tolstoy, Freud, Benjamin, and Arendt, are stages of evolution (psychological, social, cultural, and political) inherent to twentieth-century world history.

However, understanding the premises that bear upon and are part of the emergence of the juridical unconscious (civilization dealing with violence and inequality, subjects dealing with private/public matters when confronted with conflict determined by race and sexuality, legal meaning interrupting consciousness, among others) is a process that may help untangle some of the assumed premises of the study of Spain's Golden Age. As Felman says, 'The complexity of culture, I submit, often lies in the discrepancy between what culture can articulate as legal justice and what it articulates as literary justice. What, indeed, is literary justice, as opposed to legal justice? How does literature do justice to the trauma in a way the law does not, or cannot?' (*The Juridical* 8). By exposing the hidden link between the trials, tribulations, and traumas of marriage in early modern Spain, theatre and the law offered spectators of all times a potentially legal way out of marital violence, patrilineal distribution of power, and a sense of closure that differed from an irrevocable contract between a man and a woman for strict purposes of procreation, the formula stipulated as the only legal basis for marriage in Catholic Spain since 1564.

The group of *comediantes* who entertained Anna de Austria and her subjects in Burgos made a monumental scene with a *mujer esquiva* at the centre of the comedic stage. This scene of marriage was, as seen earlier, a gesture charged with great political and artistic meaning that had the potential to help marital law become, as mentioned earlier, a catalyst for more generalized reforms. In theatrical terms the *comediantes'* art of resistance was, to be sure, such a catalyst, as it gave symbolic birth to a torrent of new artistic strategies that eventually came to be canonized as the Spanish *Comedia*, while at the same time it presented theatregoers with scenes of marriage radically different from the static dual role of dominant husband and submissive wife that the Catholic Universal Monarchy sought to implement during the sixteenth century. The question is, how much of the new understanding and alternative ways of representation of marriage staged in this show contributed to what kind of 'progress'? Oriana's playing of a *mujer esquiva* (woman eluding marriage) in 1570 Burgos was a splendid feat of theatrical experimentation that surely inspired a variety of cathartic moments pertaining to the representation of marriage; at the same time, her mothering act was a sixteenth-century tragedy of the kind that Fineman spells for family law in twentieth-century America.

Progress in the legal reform of marriage in Spain became barely visible in 1978, when divorce was recognized as a legal option, and more recently and unexpectedly in 2005, when marriage among members of the same sex was legalized. During the sixteenth and seventeenth centuries church and state continued to be the strangest matrimonial bedfellows, a process best emblematized centuries later after the legal reforms of 1978 and 2005, in the decisions and inaction of rogue judges intent on sabotaging the legality of same-sex marriage, who claim that such perversion of the marital contract and ceremony goes against their moral standards because it represents perdition. These decisions, a parallel (if not similar at all) universe to those made by the *comediantes* when showing marriage plays, reveal an intimate correspondence of law and theatre in the matrimonial arena. Legislation usually seeks to control subjects with words of finality, binding, and irrevocability, while litigation, arguments, acts of protest, and theatre open up new questions about such processes. The chapters of this book have explored how the negotiation and staging of marriage took place in the spaces of the theatre and the law, in order to show how these areas of cultural production became interrelated in representing marriage in the early modern period in ways critically relevant for the unfolding of history in contemporary Spain.

In aesthetic terms, Oriana's act in Burgos set an important precedent for a host of ingenious characters in the theatrical workshop of the *Comedia*, a Spanish hall of fame populated with *graciosos*, *galanes*, and *damas* that for virtually a century trotted from town to town in Spain and the Americas and established the foundation for an artistic arena that even today continues to move massive audiences. A high point during this founding stage took place in 1659 with a feast of the senses and political acumen as monumental, if not more, than the Burgos *ceremonial* of 1570: the celebration of the marriage between Louis XIV and the infanta, María Teresa, a ceremony peppered with the poignant drama of adultery composed by Pedro Calderón de la Barca in his *La púrpura de la rosa* (The Blood of the Rose). This mythological tale of triangulation, fidelity, and vengeance with early operatic music by Juan Hidalgo was first staged to celebrate the nuptials of the French king with the Spanish infanta, a union that emblematized the Peace of the Pyrenees. In 1680 *La púrpura* was staged again in the context of another Franco-Hispanic wedding, this time Carlos II and Marie Louise D'Orleans. In a deliciously ironic twist of this affair of marriage, theatre, and imperial politics, Don Melchor Portocarrero Laso de la Vega, viceroy of Perú, commissioned Lima's *maestro de capilla*, Tomás Torrejón y Velasco, to stage *La púrpura* in 1701 on the occasion of the eighteenth birthday of the recently crowned King Felipe V.

José Antonio Maravall, one of the most insightful and influential Spanish social historians of the twentieth century, argued that, to define himself as original and modern, the baroque man pretended to reject rules, but that 'por debajo de su apariencia libre y sin normas, se halla sujeto a un fuerte principio de unidad y subordinación' (under his unbound and unrestricted appearance, he is subject to a strong principle of unity and subordination) (*La cultura* 295). The only logical conclusion to this reasoning was that the engine behind the Iberian stages of the sixteenth and seventeenth centuries was one hegemonic, orthodox angle of the marital union, a conclusion rendered unsustainable both by the dramatic texts and their contexts. The bizarre marital plots, unlikely couplings, and twisted matrimonial scenes rendered visible on the stages of the *comediantes* showed their audiences a variety of matrimonial images considered illicit by the Catholic Universal Monarchy and its most vocal group of representatives, the *moralistas*, thus restoring social order at 'The End' only in appearance, as seen here.

This book has shown how dramatic fabrications of the adultery of marriage (within and without the boundaries of actual adultery) represented a component of what Wlad Gozich and Nicolas Spaddacini have termed 'literature among discourses': the mobilization of subjects visible in the early stage of the ceremonial entry of Anna de Austria, and thereafter in numerous other *comedia* texts such as *La púrpura*. These scenes of marriage were composed with artistic units that questioned the monologic prescription legislated by the Catholic Universal Monarchy. In the space of theatre, marriage was staged as well in numerous instances of litigation, and although those were not sufficient to further legal marital reform and achieve visible progress, they certainly constitute a body of evidence that students of marriage, theatre, and the law must take into account.

For over four hundred years of cultural solitude before that momentous 'pretend' occasion of adulteration of marriage, actors impersonating a variety of characters on- and offstage played with ideologies of marriage designed to reproduce and sustain the imperial agendas of the monarchy. These scenes of marriage, theatre, and the law written, published, and performed in Spain and its American colonies differed radically from those produced in other European countries during that period. In England, for instance, women would not join the *tablados* legally until the middle of the seventeenth century, when Milton would be carving the 'road to divorce' with his *Doctrine and Discipline*. This scenario no doubt informed the development of the transvestite drama that Sidney Donnell has generously analysed, which in turn is tangible in the tic-tac-toe games of Cervantes's imagination and his readers, as it has been in audiences thereafter. Despite the opposition of *moralistas*, women went from the restrained spaces of the emerging domestic urban homes, where the Catholic Universal Monarchy and its advocates relentlessly sought to keep them, to the public and court theatres, to act and pretend – married, to be sure – and to watch, and to be watched, from the latter part of the sixteenth century; so did men, and all other subjects desperately seeking a stage.

That the public women's figures were constantly assailed by different strands of *moralismo*, *arbitrismo*, and other regulatory fictions is a testament to the resilience and power of the dominant ideologies of 'manual control,' as Navarro called them. The catalyst for the Schism was a difference of opinion between the British king and the Vatican over terms of indissolubility of his royal marriage, and the *Monarquía Católica* was forged in overt and deep commitment to the Roman side of this great divide. This commitment, founded upon a solid rhetorical base, gridlocked the study of early modern Spanish literature and culture in a revolving door of subalterity to Catholic nobiliary dogmas. Be that as it may, as the previous chapters demonstrate, marriage and the law still found their way to the theatrical forum, and many a funny thing ensued from that voyage. *Entre burlas y veras*, between the tricks of the imagination and the truth of the senses, the Spanish *Comedia* forged subject stages which allow us to think again about marriage and the law.

Acknowledgments

It has taken three *lustra* and residence in three *tierras* – Madrid, New York, Atlanta. Whenever these axes intersected an ensemble gathered, marriages of sorts.

First, a cast of characters to whom I owe everything I know about the Spanish *Comedia*: Denise DiPuccio (*magistra inter pares*), Harry Vélez-Quiñones, Laura Bass, Elizabeth Wright, Sherry Velasco, Sidney Donnell, John Beusterien, Rogelio Miñana, José Cartagena-Calderón, and Julio González-Ruiz, fellow actors in the global *Comedia* travelling theatre. Their questions, Harry's candy, theme songs, jokes, critiques, acts of recognition and intervention, and sheer solidarity have nurtured my body and soul.

A second stage, at the Shakespeare Library. With travel grants from the Folger Institute I was able to engage scenarios with colleagues in a variety of other disciplines. I benefited greatly from these discussions wisely lead by David S. Kastan.

Staff members at the AGS, the AHN, the Biblioteca Marqués de Valdecillo, and the BNE patiently guided my numerous tours into archival labyrinths. Whenever I played dead dog they taught me to be patient with the *legajos* so I could properly locate materials in the Spanish *Red de Archivos* – that exciting and bizarre mix of Derridean fantasies, Cartesian nightmares, and Borgesian tales. I am especially indebted to Inmaculada Delgado, Javier Álvarez Pinedo, and Isabel Aguirre at the AHN. María del Carmen Ortega, my fabulous Middle School philosophy teacher in Madrid, came back into my life in the Interlibrary Loan Office at the Biblioteca Nacional. Luis Corteguera guided me through some of the twists and turns of the historical riddles.

Laura Bass and Sidney Donnell gave me indispensable advice about where to start with the requests and permissions for the Illustrations; José María Ruano de la Haza at the University of Ottawa in Canada, Concha Ocampos Fuentes at the Museo del Prado in Madrid, Florian Kugler at the Kunsthistorische Museum in Vienna, Rachel Foss at the British Library in London, Evangelina Rodríguez Cuadros at Parnaseo. com kindly confirmed the location of such illustrations, and without any further ado granted the permissions to reprint the images here. Sections of chapter 3, 'The Birth of the *Comedia* and the Bride Onstage,' chapter 4, 'Foundational Violence and the Drama of Honour,' and chapter 6, 'Woman in Breeches,' have been previously published in journals or edited collections in Spain, Canada, and the United States: 'Here Comes the Real Bride: Anna de Austria and the Birth of the *Comedia*' (*Revista de Estudios Hispánicos* 40 [2006]: 113–44); 'The Burden of Evidence: Performances of Violence, Marriage, and the Law in Calderón de la Barca's *El médico de su honra*' (*Revista Canadiense de Estudios Hispánicos* 26.3 [2003]: 447–68); 'Mencía (in)visible. Tragedia y violencia doméstica en *El médico de su honra*' (*Hacia la tragedia áurea. Lecturas para un nuevo milenio*. Eds. Frederick de Armas, Luciano García Lorenzo y Enrique García-Santo Tomás. Madrid: Universidad de Navarra y Editorial Iberoamericana-Vervuert, 2008, 429–48); and 'Intereses (in)vestidos. Fábrica, industria y vestuario en *Don Gil de las calzas verdes*.' *Materia crítica: formas de ocio y de consumo en la cultura áurea*. Ed. Enrique García-Santo Tomás. Madrid: Iberoamericana-Vervuert, 2009, 385–405). I thank editors Akiko Tsuchiya, Jesús Pérez-Magallón, Enrique García-Santo Tomás, Luciano García Lorenzo, and Frederick de Armas for granting the permissions to reprint these materials.

Luciano García Lorenzo, Enrique García Santo-Tomás, Adrienne Martin, Fred de Armas, María José del Río Barredo, James Amelag, Evangelina Rodríguez Cuadros, Margaret Greer, Ignacio Navarrete, Jorge Mariscal, Luis Avilés, Jacques Lezra, Anne Cruz, Emilie Bergmann, Mary Gossy, William Clamurro, Gigi Dopico, Yolanda Martínez San Miguel, and Edward Friedman are models of scholarly rigour and humanity.

Colleagues at Columbia and Emory fostered institutional environments where this book made sense. I am especially indebted to Ruth Hill, Gus Puleo, Diane Marting, Tina Brownley, Carole Hahn, Martha Fineman, Rosemarie Garland-Thompson, Nick Fabian, Jonathan Goldberg, Michael Moon, Frances Foster, Lynn Huffer, and Cris Levenduski. Martha Grace Duncan was both Virgil and Beatrice; thanks for the invitations, the music, the challenges, and the love.

Students at Columbia and Emory asked really good questions and laughed really hard with these scenes. José A. Rico-Ferrer, Rocío Rodríguez, Ryan Prendergast, Amy Austin, Anjela Cannarelli-Peck, María del Mar Rosa-Rodríguez, Gloria Hernández, Margaret Boyle, and Manuela Ceballos have left indelible marks. Dara, Patrick, Gabriel, Arnaldo, Ma-Márgara, Camila, Ana, and Omar: *monstruos de una especie y otra*. At UPR, Gretchen Torres-Cintrón, the best.

Sandra Still, Sarah Shortt, and Anne Bunger told me I could write a book, laugh, and live. To Berky Abreu and Zinnia Johnston, thanks for always being your beautiful selves and knowing what to do with the university's backstage maze.

At Emory, the University Research Committee, the Faculty Development Office, and the Institute for Comparative and International Studies supported travel and research. The College of Arts and Sciences granted me an Associate Professor Completion Leave during which I was able to ready the manuscript for publication; the Emory College and the Graduate School of Arts and Sciences gave generous funding to subsidize it.

Eight editors received proposals to publish this book. Some said yes, but Richard Ratzlaff at the University of Toronto Press was best among equals; so were the anonymous readers and members of the copy editing and design crews at UTP (especially Miriam Skey, Barbara Porter, and Patricia Camoes), best prompters for this stage. The errors, naturally, are all mine.

José Quiroga played infallibly best colleague, mentor, and editor. None of that kept him from being a dear friend. I may have brought you to Cuba, but you bring me back. Friends and colleagues played stories, music, and games: Tess O'Dwyer, Emily Honig, Lourdes Alvarez, María Rosa Menocal, Mayra Maldonado, Eyda Merediz, Leyla Rouhi, Sandra Vicenty, Fernando Calderón, Aurora Lauzardo, Dámaris Otero, Lala Mendoza, Daniel Torres, Beatrice Pelloni, Licia Fiol-Matta, Merce Rivas, and Izaskun Álvarez-Cuartero.

Emilia Navarro banned me from ever thinking about forgetting the centrality of pleasure in life, especially when dealing with warrior princesses and uppity women. In sickness and in health, it has been thanks to Emilia and our dear friends Ralph Vicero, Bernard Hunt, Les and Deedee Real, and Larry Saunders that the academic sidewalks at Emory and living in Atlanta – both of which could have been otherwise dreadful events – seemed ever so gleeful, a discovery, a step forward in making a home away from a long lost homeland. Bernard, Emilia, Larry *in memoriam*, I know you would have laughed.

María M. Baralt, my mother, retired from an inane clerical job she held to support her kids, deserves special recognition for listening with infinite patience to my ramblings; they must have sounded like such small potatoes next to her wisdom and love. To the Rheingans and Carrión families, really, without you there would be none of this.

To the *voluptates* and joy of our lives, Roman and Camilo, thanks for your patience; here's your pretend sibling, alas, at last.

It's going to be twenty years since Rick and I went to the chapel and got married – motorcycle diary, Dwight Chapel, Madonna, Old Campus, Pink Floyd, Us and Them. Rick, you know the best and the worst, the sickness and the health; here's looking at you, kid.

Notes

Introduction

1 As it is tradition among theatre professionals in Spain, the term *cómico* (comic) refers here to the theatrical enterprise as a whole, and not strictly to a local genre in dramatic literature. The terms 'theatre,' 'comedy,' and *'Comedia'* will appear indiscriminately, alas, not to suggest a lack of boundaries, but to insist on histrionics as a key sign in these texts. Malcolm Heath traces the Aristotelian origin of the definition of 'comedy' as 'an imitation of inferior people' (1). Richard Janko, on the other hand, finds traces of the lost second book of the *Poetics* in a later treatise, the *Tractatus Coislinianus*. Janko reconstructs Aristotle's views on comedy from the *Tractatus* – a thesis vehemently discredited by Heath and others. Michael S. Silk summarizes the conclusion of this debate quite sensibly, arguing that 'there is precious little sign of an intelligent interest in comedy in *Poetics* as we have it' (44). His book turns to Aristophanes to search for clues about the theoretical possibilities and internal mechanics of comedy. Silk's chapter 'Comedy and Tragedy' offers clear and insightful comparisons of these two forms.

2 José María Izquierdo Martínez charts a collection he titled 'Field notes for a juridical anthology of the *comedias*.' Bermejo Cabrero compares, as his title suggests, 'penal justice and Baroque theatre' as well as the 'duels and challenges in Law and Literature' (91–126) González Echevarría, Dopico Black (*Perfect Wives*), Kartchner, and Armon analyse what they see as the presence and function of the Law in literature, inquisitorial hermeneutics, deceptive idealism, and courtship in the representation of marriage in narrative, metafiction, conduct handbooks, drama, poetry, and short novels. Susan Byrne examines the function of the Law as legal commentary in *Don Quijote*.

3 Margaret Greer has effectively deconstructed this theory: 'While this is an understandable perspective given Maravall's historical situation under the Franco regime, it is based on a peculiar assortment of texts and an insensitivity to the plurality of potential interpretations available in most powerful dramatic texts. Effective drama depends upon the presence of a convincingly forceful opponent, whose vigour and magnetism may not be contained by the reimposition of order and a didactic concluding pronouncement' ('A Tale' 407–8).

4 Dennis Kezar economically summarizes the predicament of my intentions and methods: 'The "law and literature movement" describes a space in which institutional momentum and interdisciplinary inquiry meet with often intriguing but frequently short-lived and theoretically inarticulate results. Few can define this "field" compellingly or lastingly enough to describe what would amount to an orthodoxy, let alone an intervention' (2). As I examined the premises that would have supported a book about the representation of marriage in theatre and how law informed such dramatic production, I grew more and more disenchanted with the prospect of publishing merely 'intriguing' results. The possibility of achieving a more theoretically and historically articulate result, then, became my guiding light.

5 The *Código Civil de España*, or first Civil Code of Spain was initiated in the 1811 Cortes, and it was not promulgated as Law until 1889.

6 I use the term 'reproduction' to convey three distinct and interrelated meanings that converge in the production of marriage: first, to refer to the dissemination of these two roles through the publication of Trent documents, royal decrees, *pregones* (cries), priests, and others invested in such publication; second, to denote how the Law deployed biological, 'natural,' and futurist reproduction to characterize the subjects of husband and wife; and third, to expose how husband and wife were reproduced along the lines of what Walter Benjamin once called the 'aura,' that component of artistic production before 'the Age of Mechanical Reproduction' that led the work of art to a 'parasitic dependence on ritual' because lineage, ownership, or cultural value – and not the work of art itself – defined its inherent capacity to communicate (217–30). With a little help from my mechanical reproducing friends, my take on 'reproduction' in this book seeks to redefine the aura of the two marital subjects, to expose meaning for them as works of art once dependent on ritual.

7 In its search for 'the science of the just and the unjust' Justinian's *Institutes* separates natural from civil law, as stipulated above. Marriage falls under the former, sealing the fate of this institution as something dependent on

observations of, at best, natural philosophy, but more often than not on unexamined premises. These traditions from time immemorial locked sex and gender in what Judith Butler termed 'the crypt,' a corporeal space derived from a refusal of any sex or gender outside the heterosexual matrix; the refusal, says Butler, is 'compelled by social taboo and appropriated through developmental stages' and enclosed, as a result of a melancholic structure, in the 'crypt established through an abiding denial' (*Gender Trouble* 88). In the founding legal text, nature 'teaches to all animals' what law is, and as such, natural law belongs to all creatures; from it, not from civil or common law (the two areas of law regarding men and nations) 'comes the union of the male and female, which we term matrimony; hence the procreation and bringing up of children' (*Institutes* 13). Be that as it may, this merely 'natural' legal premise will be deployed as a critical component of nation-building, one of the many notes taken from the *Corpus* to establish the Law in early modern Spain, with which theatre and the law will play.

8 Marriage was represented in Greek New Comedy as an affair in theory designed for life in which no event or domestic usage caused 'a husband to pass out of the affections of his wife or to cause separation' (Lee 30). Mutual devotion between spouses characterizes the marriage stage in the New Comedy, as Menander's *Epitrepontes* illustrates.

9 Hokenson's thorough study examines 'the arc from ethical to social conceptions,' which he traces from 'the classical' to 'the Renaissance' attitudes through to 'early modernist theory'; in all of them, says Hokenson, there is a great deal of resistance to understand comedy as its own idea (23–63). The dismissal of comedy as theory and critique has transcended well into contemporary aesthetic and critical arguments, from Schiller to Northrop Frye and beyond (64–108), which has yielded numerous unexamined premises in the reading of comic theatre such as the *Comedia*.

10 For a number of good reasons Mariscal dismisses the importance of theatre in the study of subjectivity in early modern Spain: 'I posit the subject as a content-free form that is "filled in" differently according to specific social and historical conditions. My argument, therefore, dissolves the notion of a unified individual, even a role-playing individual, just as it erases the absolute *cogito* of Cartesian thought as well as ideas about "pure consciousness" or the desiring ego, the products of phenomenology and psychology respectively, which, in their more generalized form as "self," continue to exert tremendous influence over a traditional literary scholarship' (5). Although in agreement with most of these premises,

I differ from Mariscal's dissolution of the role-playing individual, a key unit of my own argument.

11 Cascardi clearly articulates the complex web of referents that for centuries have favoured hegemony and have made it virtually impossible to read Mariscal's 'contradictory subjects': 'It is more or less well known that the formation of a Spanish "national identity" was staked on the political suppression of the differences among the various cultures, languages, races, religions, and histories that came together on the Iberian peninsula. The elevation of the interests that centered in Castile and in Christianity into a national ideology was a crucial part of this process' ('Beyond' 139). Alberto Moreiras edited a collection of essays in which various scholars explored the world of what he saw as Spain's 'nation formation' period: 'Moriscos, *indianos*, military queers, gypsies and fake Spaniards, body parts, whores, saints, and actresses, female eunuchs, and endangered bums; as Steven Hutchinson would say, like most authorities on those subjects, we know almost nothing about them. This monstrous collection, which opens onto non-knowledge, organizes the present special issue on Spanish nation formation' (5). See also Cascardi ('On the Subject') and Lezra. Continuing these scholarly lines of thought, *Subject Stages* seeks to further elucidate how marriage, theatre, and the law played a key role in the formation of Spain as a nation.

12 Cascardi proposes the analysis of 'the ways in which institutions, discourses, and practices enable concrete subjects to exist' as a critical strategy to understand this question of hegemony that has marked the study of early modern Spain for so long ('Beyond' 143–4). The following pages seek to contribute to such an analysis, by engaging the questions Cascardi raises for those seeking to reach a better understanding of early modern Spain: 'What enables religious institutions, the family, literature and the arts, and the political system (all of which Althusser calls "Ideological State Apparatuses") to function in a unified fashion? And how do these in turn enable the formation of concrete subjects?' ('Beyond' 144).

1 Marital Law and Order in Early Modern Spain

1 Justinian's 'Of Paternal Power' (translated elsewhere as 'The Power of Parents') stipulates that children are the property of the parents, a tale of national definition spoken between men and inherited by the men in the family – despite the fact that women are implicitly involved in the title, as the alternative translation may suggest, and in the production of children: '*Our* children whom *we* have begotten in lawful wedlock are in *our* power ...

The power which *we* have over *our* children is peculiar to Roman citizens, and is found in no other nation. The offspring then of *you and your wife* is in *your* power, and so too is that of *your* son and *his* wife, that is to say, *your* grandson and granddaugher, and so on. But the offspring of *your* daughter is not in *your* power, but in that of *its* own father' (*Institutes* 12; emphasis mine: I have emphasized the pronouns that mark the shift from an implied sexual couple, an 'us' involved in the production of children, to a 'you' or male addressee of the law that reifies the female descendant).

2 Susan Treggiari cites from a version of the *Institutes* different from both the Latin used by Covarrubias and Moyle's translation: 'Nuptiae … sive matrimunium est viri et mulieris coniunctio individuam vitae consue-tudinem continens' (Marriage or matrimony is the union of a man and a woman, implying the undivided conduct of life) (10n).

3 The word *coniugatio* chosen by Covarrubias engages a wide spectrum of terms mobilized by theologians, lawmakers, and philosophers attempting to define marriage. Although her review does not mention *coniugatio*, Treggiari considers a few of them: *consortium, communicatio, coniunctio,* concubinage, and cohabitation, among others (8–11).

4 This *translatio* of *marem et mulierem* (male and woman) is, in turn, the legacy of Augustine of Hippo, from *De virginitate beatae Virginis*: 'Matrimo-nium est legitima societas inter virum et feminam, in qua ex pari consen-sus semetipsum alter alteri debet.' The *Magister Sententiarum* (Lib 3 Distinct 27) reads: 'Matrimonium est viri mulierisque coniuntio maritatis inter legitimas personas, individuam vitae consuetudinem retinens.'

5 On Roman law and marriage, see Bierkan et al., and Evans Grubbs. For an introduction to Canon Law and marriage, see McAreavey. Reynolds and Witte have edited an invaluable collection of essays on the documentation of marriage in Western Christendom, with studies on consent, celebration, and property; the latter Roman Law period; the *Tabulae Nuptiales* in Roman North Africa; dotal charters and dower charters; and marital contracts and agreements in medieval France and England, Renaissance Florence, and Reformation Geneva.

6 Covarrubias draws the quote from Palude's *In quartum* (Lib 4 Distinct 26 Quaes. 1). Henricus of Segusio, also known as Cardinal Hostiensis, prefigured Palude's premise in *De matrimonium*, the segment he wrote about marriage in his *Summa super titulis decretalium* (also known as the *Summa Hostiensis* and *Summa aurea*), composed between 1250 and 1271 while he was archbishop of Embrun: 'Unde dicatur? A *matre et munium*, id est officium; dicitur enim matrimonium quasi matris officium, quia dat mulieribus esse matres. Et ideo licet pater generationis sit auctor et pene

uxoris dominus, tamem matrimonium plus ascribitur matri quam patri, quoniam ejus officium plus apparet in matrimonio quam officium viri' (Where was it said? From mother (*matre*) and duty (*munium*), because such is the moral obligation; it is called indeed matrimony as it is the duty of the mother, for it allows women to be mothers. And for that purpose it is allowed that the father of the offspring be author and almost the lord of the woman, but marriage refers more to the mother than to the father, whereas her duty is more apparent in matrimony than the duty of man) (344; my translation).

7 Treggiari aptly summarizes this tradition: '*Matrimonium* is an institution involving a mother, *mater*. The idea implicit in the word is that a man takes a woman in marriage, *in matrimonium ducere*, so that he may have children by her. He joins her to him by marriage, or by "his" marriage, or by marriage with himself. He keeps her in marriage, *in matrimonio habere*. Her family may give her into marriage, *in matrimonium dare* or *collocare*. The husband receives her, *accipere*. The word *matrimonia* may also be used almost as the equivalent of "married women." There is a tendency, then, to stress the woman's position in relation to marriage, not the man's. Only a woman can enter into *matrimonium* or a *matrimonium*, a relationship which makes her a wife and mother. A man cannot' (5).

8 Emperor Justinian's *Corpus Iuris Civilis*, a cornerstone of Western legal culture, of which the *Institutes* is one part, divided public from private law, and the latter into natural, civil, and common law, which pertained respectively to nature (animals), communities, and the nations (3–4). The *Corpus* also separated written from non-written laws; those written could be *leges* (proposed by a senatorial magistrate, passed by the Roman people); *plebiscita* (proposed by a plebeian magistrate, passed by the plebs); *senatusconsulta* (orders of the senate); *constitutiones* ('what the Emperor determines has the force of a statute'); *edicta* (edicts of the praetors); or *responsa* ('the opinions and views of persons authorized to determine and expound the law') (4–5). Finally, the *Corpus* defined unwritten laws as those 'which usage has approved: for ancient customs, when approved by consent of those who follow them, are like statute' (5–6).

9 As Kagan says about the study of law in early modern Spain (particularly in Castile, as the place of centralization of regional and ancient legal systems during the sixteenth century), 'Castilian law of the early modern period is best approached through the study of Castilian law in the Middle Ages' (258). The *Fuero Juzgo*, the *Fuero Real*, the *Siete Partidas*, the *Fuero Viejo*, the *Ordenamiento de Alcalá*, the *Leyes*, the *Estilo*, and the *Ordenanzas Reales de Castilla* must be collated, as Kagan rightly argues, with the

'*cédulas, edictos, pragmáticas,* and other laws issued by the crown' that do not figure, for instance, in the 1569 *Recopilación* nor in the various *Cuadernos de leyes añadidas* issued between 1581 and 1620' (258). Natividad Moreno y Garbayo published in 1977 a valuable *Colección de Reales Cédulas* found in the AHN, dated between 1366 and 1801. The *Noticia bibliográfica de textos y disposiciones legales de los reinos de Castilla impresos en los siglos XVI y XVII* published in Madrid in 1935 began to address this problem, but as Kagan concludes on this matter, 'an authoritative edition of the royal *cédulas* and *pragmáticas* issued by the Habsburgs is still lacking,' and there is no parallel source for the study of civil law, or for family law (259–60). The study of municipal laws faces similar obstacles, although Tomás y Valiente (*El Derecho penal*) and Clavero (*Mayorazgo, propiedad feudal*) have conducted excellent studies on penal law and on the laws of primogeniture so necessary to understand marital law.

10 All quotes from the *Nueva Recopilación* come from the Lex Nova facsimile edition of the 1640 reprint of these Laws by King Felipe IV, grandson of King Felipe II; the Laws in the 1640 edition are the same as those drafted in the mid-sixteenth century, but to them the editors added a few edicts, orders, and other legal decisions made in the century that separates the two printings. Pedro López de Alcocer, Pedro López de Arrieta, Bartolomé de Atienza, and other jurists and attorneys put together the original compilation between 1537 and 1567; the 1640 printing names Joseph Gonçalez and Fernando Piçarro as responsible for putting together the addenda. The source of the laws cited here will be indicated in parenthesis as *Nueva Recopilación* with the book, title, and folio number in which they can be found in this edition. For a clear explanation of this process of compilation, printing, and reprinting, see Tomás y Valiente, 'El movimiento recopilador en los siglos XVI y XVII' (The Compiling Movement in the Sixteenth and Seventeenth Centuries) (*Manual de Historia* 263–81) and Kagan, 'In the Cretan Labyrinth' (*Lawsuits and Litigants* 21–32).

11 On a study about the relationship between legitimacy of the Law and compliant behaviour, Tom Tyler argues that figures of authority in social groups know that 'their effectiveness depends on their ability to influence the behavior of the group's members' (161). When King Felipe II speaks of the authority of the Laws in the *Nueva Recopilación* authorized by him, the lengthy explanation of chaos and disarray in which he saw the Law, and the much shorter but highly persuasive command for a clear legal document that will separate good from evil and those who are to practise the former and refrain from the latter shows the king's attempt to influence the behaviour of his group's members, as Tyler says. Legitimacy, as Tyler also

acknowledges, is 'the normative factor of greatest concern to authorities,' which, in the case of legal authorities, is determined by an expectation that people will obey the Law (161). Whether or not the subjects of the crown believed in the whole legal spectrum that defined marriage, the king's desire to establish marital law and order – a matrimonial deus ex machina – met with significant histrionic elements in courthouses and playhouses that played with these notions of legitimacy and compliance.

12 Margaret Ferguson, A.R. Buck, and Nancy E. Wright published an important collection of essays entitled *Women, Property, and the Letters of the Law in Early Modern England* that consider gestation, legal contracts, female litigants, property and popular cultures, prostitution, primogeniture, patrilineage, poverty, marriage and identity, estates, epistolary practices, women's wills, nunneries, female surnames, and aristocracy, among other issues.

13 The Spanish original by Castillo de Bobadilla reads 'Finalmente, para qué hemos menester ejemplos extraños para sublimar el sacro Tesoro de las letras y la importancia de la ciencia legal para los gobiernos políticos, pues como dijo con razón el obispo Simancas, nunca España tuvo paz ni a las leyes y gobernadores fue tan obediente … como después que ha sido gobernada por consejos y hombres de letras' (quoted in Bennassar 42). Roger Merriman summarizes the overwhelming power of the *Corregidor*, who 'represents the persona of the king, and may sit in judgment and mete out punishment for any sort of crime … and condemn the guilty party to confiscation, or death, or the galleys, or a fine to be paid to the Cámara del Rey, and in all such cases the Corregidor has a free hand, even though the accused be a titled lord or a noble of the realm' (quoted in Chamberlain 224n).

14 Darci Strother analyses the representation onstage of 'family matters,' which she defines as 'the formation of a family unit through marriage, the alternatives available to those who could not or did not wish to marry, and the relationships between parents and children' (13).

15 Inmaculada Vivas Tesón cogently argues that in the drafting of the modern Civil Code in 1889 women still remained relegated to a second plane with respect to men, a frame of inequality that translates into disparities for men and women as legal subjects. The historical span of this inter-sex difference is quite vast. Heath Dillard has analysed 'brides, weddings, and the bonds of matrimony,' 'wives, husbands, and the conjugal household,'and finally, the 'numerous class' of the widows of the Reconquest in medieval Castile (36–126). Marilyn Stone, on the other hand, focuses on the nexus marriage-friendship as stipulated in the *Siete Partidas*. Isabel Testón Núñez has

studied the nexus of 'amor, sexo y matrimonio' in the midlands of the west of Spain, Extremadura. Perry (*Gender and Disorder* 53–74) and Dopico Black (*Perfect Wives* 48–108) have examined the historical implications of the powerful concept of the *perfecta casada* during this period; Thomas O'Connor has analysed the correspondence of conjugal spirituality and the antitheatrical polemic, and Henry Sullivan has explored the intersection between matrimonial regulations, love, and desire in *El burlador de Sevilla* ('Love'). Lawrence Stone has thoroughly documented the history of sex, marriage, and family in England, as well as this country's 'road to divorce' between 1500 and 1800 (*Family* and *Road*).

16 There is a dire need for a systematic analysis of how playwrights, actors, *autores*, and other members of theatrical companies 'expected that laws and judicial tribunals should deliver justice in a fair and timely fashion, that justice should emanate from the monarch down through the system of justice, and that judges should conform with their offices' dignity,' as Luis R. Corteguera has noted about Barcelona master artisans and their familiarity with the law (1023). The present study argues that such expectation is evident in the marriage scenes composed by litigators and those representing marriage scenes onstage.

17 A collection of essays edited by Asunción Lavrín studies 'the scenario, the actors, and the issues' of sexuality and marriage in colonial Latin America (1–47), considering honour, illegitimacy, church hierarchy, witchcraft, colonialism, the Inquisition, partnerships, politics of marriage, 'la mala vida' (prostitution), family, and divorce, among others.

18 For marriage in Canon Law, see *Manual de Derecho Matrimonial Canónico*, edited by Álvarez Cortina et al., with chapters on marriage and Law; canonic jurisdiction over marriage; natural law and marriage and the freedom to exercise it; goals and essential properties of marriage; formalities before and after marriage; matrimonial impediments; impediments due to crime and consanguinity; matrimonial consent; consensual incapacity; simulation in the consent; error and ignorance; violence and fear; conditioned consent; matrimonial form; marriage annulment and its corroboration; marriage dissolution in canonic order; canonic regulation of matrimonial separation; and procedures for marriage annulment.

19 The cornerstone of the *Nueva Recopilación*, rhetorically positioned as the very first Law, 'De la Santa Fè Catolica' (Of the Holy Catholic Faith) said: 'The holy Mother Church teaches, and preaches, that every faithful Christian reformed by the holy Sacrament of Baptism firmly believes and simply confesses that there is one only and true God, eternal, immense, unchanging, omnipotent, ineffable, Father, Son, and holy Spirit three

Persons and one essence, substance, or nature: the Father unattainable, the Son engendered by the Father alone and the holy Spirit breathed from high simplicity, proceeding likewise from the Father, and the son in essence, equal in omnipotence: and one beginning principle of all visible and invisible things' (*Nueva Recopilación* Lib 1 Tit 1 Ley 1).

20 David Caudill argues that language is a decisive factor for 'the subject of law' (42–65). In the field in which Caudill works, contemporary contract theory, the issue of gaps and filling them is a textual problem 'on two obvious levels: first, a written contract inevitably betrays missing provisions (e. g., addressing possible contingencies) that the parties to a contract intentionally or accidentally ignored; second, a court hearing a contract dispute is often called upon (when an unaddressed contingency arises) to apply a generalized "default" (i.e., absent an instruction) rule to a specific contract. A gap in the contract (and sometimes in contract doctrine) is thus filed in by each judicial construction of a contract' (43). A number of historical specificities separate Caudill's subject of legal interest and mine, but his consideration of language, missing provisions, contingencies, and judicial constructions in contract design resonate with the present reading of the way subjects of law in early modern Spain wrote and read marriage Law. The fact that Spain's early modern 'subject of the law' contracted with 'the Holy Catholic Faith' at its foundation established a peculiar set of gaps with which litigation and theatre could play substantially. In theory, this subject was bound to believe all the Articles of Faith, 'que todo fiel Christiano deue saber: los Clerigos explicitamente, y por extenso; los lego implicita, y simplemente, teniendo lo que tiene y enseña, y predica la santa Madre Iglesia' (which all Christian must know: the clerics, explicitly and extensively; laymen, implicitly and simply, having what the holy Mother Church has, teaches, and preaches) (*Nueva Recopilación* Lib 1 Tit 1 Ley 1).

21 'De la santa Fè Catolica' clearly stipulates this point: 'And if any Christian with pertinatious and obstinate will were to err, and insisted in not having, and believing what the holy Mother Church has, and teaches; we order that he is subject to the punishment stipulated in our laws of the *siete Partidas*, as well as those contained in this book in the title about heretics' *Nueva Recopilación* Lib 1 Tit 1 Ley 1).

22 Dopico Black (*Perfect Wives*) considers wide-ranging strategies of reading present in de León's text, given his own confrontations with the Inquisition. At once, the fact that this is a conduct handbook paves the way for the ideological containment of women as future wives.

23 Aurora Morcillo Gómez, speaking of the presence of the *Institutio* in the educational reform of Francoist Spain, says: 'The new education system

aspired to forge true Catholic womanhood by appealing to Spanish historical tradition. First, the regime sought to revive sixteenth-century devotions to saintly female figures – such as Santa Teresa de Jesús or the Virgen del Pilar – and hoped to repopularize Renaissance treatises on the character and proper education of women by Fray Luis de León and Juan Luis Vives' (55). Asunción Lavrín notes the parallel impact and transcendence of the *Institutio* in the development of highly conservative perspectives on sexuality and marriage in colonial Latin America: 'While no civil or ecclesiastical legislation endorsed forced marriages, the preservation of social status and the general social order through marriage between equals was preached through the literature of advice and education' (17). Sakari Sariola also analyses the impact of Vives's humanism in colonial Latin America (264–5).

24 Although critics have identified the wifely stage of Rosaura in Caro's play as an image of the Catholic Queen Isabel de Castilla, I have elsewhere argued that the text stages the deferral of marriage as a feminist rhetorical strategy reminiscent of Elizabeth I of England, and that the Virgin Queen's political theatrics of matrimony significantly inform *El Conde Partinuplés* – in ways considered heretic by the crown ('Portrait of a Lady,' 241–2).

25 Helen Rawlings examines the strange marriage of *arbitristas* and the church, an alliance that lead to the development of theoretical and practical instances of anticlericalist philosophy.

26 For other aspects of this legal network, see Alcalá, Avilés, and Tomás y Valiente (*La tortura en España*) on the Inquisition; Tomás y Valiente (*El Derecho Penal*, 'Delincuentes y pecadores,' and *Manual de Historia*), DuBoys, and Bartolomé Clavero on the penal system; and Villalba Pérez on the administration of justice in the court in Madrid, especially the *Sala de Alcaldes*.

27 The *Curia* (originally published in Lima, Perú, in 1602) was the most widely used handbook of legal practice. Other important manuals included the *Práctica criminal y civil* by Gabriel de Monterroso y Alvarado (published in Valladolid in 1566), the *Libro de la práctica judiciaria del reyno de Aragón* by Pedro Molinos (published in Zaragoza in 1575), the *Práctica para procuradores para seguir pleitos civiles e criminales* by Juan Muñoz (published in Madrid in 1618), and the *Práctica y formulario de la real chancellería de Valladolid* by Manuel Fernández de Ayala (published in Valladolid in 1667).

28 Quevedo engaged an intense and literarily brilliant staging of matrimony in his burlesque and satirical poetry. As Ignacio Arellano has noted, such a vision of marriage 'is integrated in the larger frame of misogynistic *burla*

(invective), but it has its own demarcations and definitions,' such as its debt to Latin satirical writing by Juvenal and Martial and the satire against the corruption of good manners common in Quevedo's time ('El matrimonio' 12). Arellano's remark, 'marriage is tiresome because of its monotony, so it ages and bores those who engage it, and it pushes the married one to miss the care-free diversity' insightfully reveals the bases for Quevedos's satirical and burlesque poetic work on marriage, which was also the stage on which many other subjects created their own scenes of marriage ('El matrimonio' 13).

2 Marriage Scenes in the Archives

1 I cite litigation materials by the first words of the title of the case (as listed in Works Cited), followed by the name of the collection from the Spanish archive where I located the case, the bundle number ('Leg.'), and the page number (fol.'). The present quote is drawn from the case entitled *Sobre el violento casamiento tratado [de] efectuar de Doña Elvira Enriquez, Vda de Dn. Alvaro de Borja Marques de Alcañices, con don Enrique Enrriquez. 1588–1589*, located in the collection 'Cámara de Castilla. Procesos y Expedientes Criminales' of the Archivo General de Simancas, bundle 1604, case 1, page 1 (*Sobre el violento casamiento* CCPEC, Leg. 1604, fol.1). Some *expedientes* (case files) have no case number, or no pagination, in which case the reference will not include either the 'Fol.' or 'fol.' notation. To avoid repeating the lengthy names of archival collections, I cite with the corresponding abbreviations as stipulated in the List of Abbreviations.

2 When language and discourse cannot represent certain subjects, as frequently happens with peasants, witches, or mad persons, the understanding of the past runs into an unsurpassable obstacle. When a case is legal and psychiatric, for instance, not even a public confession from a murderer is legible: 'The possibility of interpreting this text is specifically ruled out,' says Ginzburg, 'because it is held to be impossible to do so without distortion or without subjecting it to an extraneous system of reasoning. The only legitimate reactions that remain are "astonishment" and "silence"' (xviii).

3 Luis de León, author of *La perfecta casada*, wrote 'En el nacimiento de doña Tomasina' (On the Birth of Doña Tomasina), a poem in honour of the fourth child of Doña Elvira and Don Álvaro, who would marry Don Juan de Vega y Toledo, first count of Grajal (117–19). Doña Elvira and her second husband, Don Juan de Tovar Enriquez de Castilla had one more child, María-Jacinta de Tovar Enriquez de Almansa, half-sister of Tomasina.

4 Bertrande de Rols, the wife of Martin Guerre accused of complicity in the plot to create an imposter husband during the absence of her true husband, lived in a parallel universe to that of Doña Elvira. Although in vastly differing socio-economic and cultural contexts, both women knew the benefits of marriage and family only to see them vanish. In such absence (permanent for Doña Elvira due to Don Álvaro's death, and seemingly permanent in the cases of Bertrande de Rols and Penelope due to the disappearance of their husbands), they all became intimately acquainted with the pressures of managing a house/family by themselves, and with the rituals of unwanted courtship. In Bertrande's case Roman Catholic Canon Law stipulated that she could not remarry after abandonment, which one could argue was a protective shield of sorts for her; however, such a shield may have played a role in her acceptance of the imposter husband by her side. For further details on these issues see Davis (*The Return of Martin Guerre* and 'On the Lame') and Finlay ('The Refashioning').

5 The rhetorical and formal structure of bureaucratic documentation limits both the writing of marriage scenes as well as their reading. As Alexandra Parma Cook says, notarial information has tremendous pitfalls for researchers that only educated guesses and sheer luck can help overcome: 'The scribal script [*letra procesal*] is often the most difficult of all for even the most adept palaeographer. Thousand of pages of transactions, contracts, or wills, for example, might be included in a notarial bundle for a single year, especially in a major city, and there are usually no indexes. Notarial research is monotonous; a clue may be followed by hundreds of pages of irrelevant entries' (xiii).

6 In cases of litigation over a *mayorazgo*, the language of origins and foundations surfaces to control the possible histrionics of succession. See, for instance, the 1489 provision granted by Catholic Queen Isabel so that the duke of Nájera, Don Pedro Manrique, did not alienate the assets of his estate (*Provisión* CCD, Leg. 39, Fol. 47). If a *mayorazgo* was not inherited by anyone in a family, a lawsuit would ensue, as shown in the document 'Execution of the lawsuit between D. Antonio Miguel de Montenegro, resident of Tuy, and the Marquis of Castelar over the possession of the estate founded by Tristan de Montenegro, 1541,' left vacant due to the death of the Count de Maceda) (*Ejecutoria del pleito* D Gral Leg. 241).

7 Other *mayorazgo* documents in the AHN reiterate incessantly the priority of male over female subjects. See, for instance, the cases of D. Antonio Pazos Montenegro (*Ejecutoria del pleito* D Gral Leg. 241), Don Sarmiento de Valladares (*Ejecutoria ganada* D Gral Leg. 243), and Doña María Manuela de Puga y Gago (*Memorial ajustado* D Gral Leg. 248). The *tenutas, títulos,*

and other documents speak of transcendence through time, since the possession was designed to last through many generations to come. The disputes could last quite some time, in some cases even centuries; thus, for instance, the case of Don Antonio Miguel de Montenegro, a lawsuit pertaining to a *mayorazgo* founded in 1541, executed and sealed on 27 May 1788 (*Ejecutoria del pleito* D Gral Leg. 241).

8 For Carol Gilligan, men and women do not allow women to voice their experiences, building relationships based on silences, men's 'disconnection from women and women's not knowing their dissociation from themselves' (xx). In early modern Spain, the Law stated time and again its disconnection from women. Litigation, theatre, and even bureaucracy opened up spaces where marriage could be heard in different voices.

9 I mean the word 'voice' in the theoretical dimension suggested by Gilligan: there is a voice when the subject who speaks is clear, apparent, and perceptible, for 'those who are being spoken about have no voice' (xix). In the theatre, voice is 'the means by which you communicate your inner self' by virtue of a number of physical and psychological factors that, as Cicely Berry argues, contribute to its making (12). For Kristin Linklater the first law of theatre is that 'the voice is inherently an erotic organ' (*Vox Eroticus* n. p.). Remembered oral/aural traditions keep the voice alive in the body, because as Linklater says, 'the voice *mechanism* is in the body ... [it] depends on breath passing through the vocal folds in the throat to create the vibrations which are ultimately recognized as an individual voice ... It is not metaphorical to say "the body breathes"' (4).

10 Gilligan's title, *In a Different Voice: Psychological Theory and Women's Development*, refers to a relational voice that must be exercised 'so that psychological separations which have long been justified in the name of autonomy, selfhood, and freedom no longer appear as the *sine qua non* of human development but as a human problem' (xiii).

11 The connection with other subjects, and with herself/himself is theorized in the letter and spirit of both civil and ecclesiastical Laws: marriage is a mysterious union of man and woman by means of which they become one juridical, spiritual, and material entity. However, the design of the roles of husband and wife in the Law did not respect the integrity of this connection, favouring the role of the husband as the referential centre of the institution.

12 The development of a voice is best understood as a process that evolves in stages, Berry says, of which the first gives the subject proof of the potential sound s/he has and the second requires that the actor discard what is comfortable and find the energy and how to use it (12–13). Finding a voice, Berry notes, is a matter of finding a balance, which does not mean one

single point (12). Subjects in marital litigation and theatrical scenes of marriage engaged these and other points of tension in the search for voice effectiveness, sensuality, freedom, energy, truth, and predictability as part of their performances of man, fool, transvestite, lady, husband, or whatever role the script they had at hand required.

13 Traditionally meaning 'understanding,' *entender* has come to be an encoded term of communication between and about queer subjects. Bergmann and Smith explain this range of meaning. Translation, as they argue, plays a critical role in elucidating what they call the 'questions of homosexuality – questions of Hispanism.' After all, 'homosexual' and 'gay' are words 'alien and irrelevant to Spanish-speaking cultures,' a context in which *entender*, 'a slang term also used beyond Spain in some parts of Spanish America,' contributes to a better epistemological approach to this matter, for it 'is clearly a cultural, not a natural category' (11–12).

14 Barahona's analysis is indispensable reading for anyone seeking to understand the complex correspondences of what he summarizes as 'courtship patterns, sexual practices and attitudes, and violence and aggression against women' (xix) in early modern Spain. Taylor focuses on a more direct liaison between the literature of the *comedia*, law, and honour, considering the latter not a code but a 'rhetoric employed to convey information about the way [early modern Castilians] viewed themselves, their place in the community, and their judgments on proper and incorrect conduct in social relations among their neighbors' (21). Since Taylor relates this rhetoric to the homoerotic ritual of the duel, his study does not focus on sexual crimes, but rather on how men and women separately related to honour.

15 'Fribolas' qualifies the excuses given by Mr Mateo, which according to the definition given by Covarrubias in the *Tesoro*, meant they had neither 'calor ni sustancia como razón frívola, que no concluye' (warmth nor substance, like frivolous reason, which is inconclusive) (561).

16 Barahona acknowledges that *amancebamiento* (cohabitation) was the only sex crime that offended a number of parties: 'God, royal justice, the community, and morals' (96). Neglect, abandonment or mistreatment of wives, says Barahona, was also a key concern: for the authorities in Vizcaya, 'the connections between cohabitation and domestic discord and abuse were indisputable' (101).

3 The Birth of the *Comedia* and the Bride Onstage

1 There are numerous accounts of these kinds of festivities that illustrate the emerging correspondence between marriage and theatre. N.D. Shergold

(*A History of the Spanish Stage*) quotes the 1599 *Fiestas nupciales* by
G. Aguilar about King Felipe III's marriage festivities, among others.

2 Anna de Austria is the name chosen by the queen and favoured by
historians both in Spanish and English. As Kamen notes, 'This is the
correct form of her name, and she always signed this way. As far as I know,
she never used the Spanish form "Ana." See her letters in *HHSA. Spanien,
Hoftkorrespondenz*, karton 2, mappe 12, f. 15' (*Gran Duque* 317n).

3 Teresa Ferrer Vals notes how this text is termed a *comedia* by one of the
chroniclers, a sign that this was a 'courtly conception of spectacle, in which
the staging is tied to a concrete circumstance and the pomp that from it are
derived' (195n). Action, says Ferrer Vals, must not have been too elaborate,
because the interesting elements of this piece must have resided 'in the
visual aspect and in a sophisticated poetic word' emplotted in a dramatic
structure of 'an open end' (195n).

4 The craft of the *comediantes* shows a tangible concern with what Richard
Schechner calls 'the efficacy, entertainment braid' (120–4), an aspect of
theatrical texts that demands public negotiations of movement, subjects,
opinions, economics, fun, and other units of a *polis* in some sort of recognizable, habitual designations of time/space.

5 The expression 'oppositional reception' comes from Stuart Hall's theories
of encoding and decoding cultural, media, and linguistic events (128–38).

6 The original passage in Latin reads: 'Sic rite Psyche conuenit in manum
Cupidinis et nascitur illis maturo partu filia, qua*m* Voluptatem nomina-
mus' (*Les Métamorphoses* 93). 'And thus Psyche was married to Cupid, and
after in due time she was delivered of a child, whom we call Pleasure'
(*The Golden Ass* 285). Paul Vallette and W. Adlington, the translators of
Apuleius's tale into French (*Les Métamorphoses*) and English (*The Golden
Ass*) rendered in those two languages the wedding scene in which Psyche
marries Cupid. Lisardo Rubio translated 'conuenit in manum Cupidinis'
(*Les Métamorphoses* 93) into Spanish with the following passage: 'Así,
regularizada ya su situación, quedó Psique en poder de Cupido' (*El asno de
oro* 187) (Hence, once her situation was regularized, Psyche remained
under the power of Cupid. *The Golden Ass* 285). All translations agree in
the meaning of 'maturo partu' as a birth 'in due time.' The daughter,
named 'Voluptuosidad' in Spanish and 'Voluptuosité' in French, is
'Pleasure' in English.

7 The definition of the *vulgo* (public, audience) in the *Comedia* begins with
the tensions inherent in putting a show together: who speaks? for whom?
to whom? when? how? For Lope de Vega, the production and reception of
theatre had to be performed in sync, an event that could only be done with

people. These people were different from the mad characters of the Greek tragedies and the Latin comedies, and this difference was precisely what motivated his writing: 'Los que el vulgar aplauso pretendieron / Porque como las paga el vulgo, es justo / Hablarle en necio para darle gusto' (Those who sought the vulgar applause / Because since the vulgo pays, it is only fair / That we speak stupid to please them) (*Arte Nuevo* 285).

8 In 1853 Juan Tejada published the first bilingual edition (Latin-Spanish) of these documents with the intention of supporting the *Clero*'s 'first and most essential duties' in serving the Spanish crown (5).

9 As Jean-Pierre Amalric argues in the prologue to this study, the king's move reflects 'the active function that the monarch relentlessly assumed in the redefinition of the Catholic Church facing the Protestant Reform' (15).

10 For futher details on how this loss of privacy translated into a point of liability for women in seventeenth-century Madrid, see Pilar Tenorio Gómez (43–77).

11 Parker and Sedgwick misquote this passage as a direct citation from a previous study by Sedgwick; however, this particular segment does not appear in a previous study. See 'Introduction: Performance and Performativity' (10) and 'Queer Performativity' by Sedgwick (3–4).

12 James Scott calls this fantasy the 'public transcript,' a text where the self-indulgent impression of control of dominant groups over subalterns is entertained (45–6).

13 Citing the critical contributions of Sherry Velasco, Matthew Stroud, Harry Vélez-Quiñones, and Julio González Ruiz, among others, José Cartagena Calderón economically reviews the crisis of masculinity and the surveillance of gender as the building blocks of what he terms 'the drama of masculinity in imperial Spain' (9–53). The 'masculinities under construction/masculinities in plays' that Cartagena cogently analyses (which, in turn, are based on a number of scholarly works he cites in his study) offer a solid scholarly foundation for the present queer reading of the roles of husband and wife.

14 In Stroud's apt words, expressions of alternate sexualities were most tangible in acts of gender undecidability, of which there is considerable evidence (*Plot Twists* 20).

15 José Ruano de la Haza and John J. Allen charted the history of the commercial theatres with the development of the *Comedia*, offering readers a useful handbook for the study of the artistic, cultural, and economic landscape of this theatre (*Los teatros comerciales*).

16 Rennert traces the complex road to the *tablas* that actors and actress had to travel during the latter sixteenth century and the first half of the seventeenth.

The *moralistas* condemned the troupes' licentiousness and *desenboltura*, especially those of the actresses, and recommended that the king, officers, and administrators of the *corrales* close them, or at least regulate them heavily. See Rennert's comprehensive analysis of 'women on the stage' in France, England, Italy, and Spain (137–58), as well as his 'characters of the actors and actresses' to get a glimpse of the various stages of the controversy about theatres, the decrees to regulate them, and the companies that ensued as a result (206–28). Margaret Wilson has compiled an excellent synthesis of 'the controversy' (*Spanish Drama* 24–37), and Dopico Black has explored the interconnected symbolic projections of 'the body of the Golden Age actress, the body of Mary Magdalen, and finally the body politic' ('Public Bodies' 82).

17 Greer performs a comparative reading of theatre and politics in Calderón's *La piedra, el rayo y la fiera* and Don Juan José's role in the drama of palatial control and rulership (*The Play*). In 1677 Don Juan José displaced queen regent Mariana de Austria and her *valido* Fernando de Valenzuela from their posts in court and appointed himself prime minister.

18 In addition to the study by Shergold mentioned above, see McKendrick (*Theatre*) and Ferrer Vals.

19 For Kamen this triple alliance was a step trying to avert a 'total war' (*Philip* 125).

20 Kamen draws the term *menuda* from Gachard's study, *Carlos V*: 'her face is small and she is not very tall' (137n). All other terms seem to be Kamen's own.

21 The term 'queer' is used here to understand how these actors exposed the relative power of the binary marital system, by engaging a premise that for Stroud lies at the heart of *Comedia* productions: it 'may include heterosexual or nonsexual activities as well but may nonetheless present certain challenges to the reigning orthodoxy of seventeenth-century Spain' (*Plot Twists* 22). The queer subjects that this book takes into account are a sample of what the correspondence of marriage, theatre, and the law yielded: a *mujer esquiva*, an absent king, a vocal wife, an obsessive-compulsive husband, a masochist and sadist noblewoman and her secretary, a *mujer varonil*, and a bunch of hilarious, quixotic subjects screaming for divorce.

4 Foundational Violence and the Drama of Honour

1 Pedro Calderón de la Barca, *El médico de su honra*, ed. Don W. Cruickshank. For the translations I cite the English version of *The Surgeon of His Honour* by Roy Campbell. Cruickshank's edition follows the text printed by María de Quiñones for Pedro Coello; this printing, known as QC, is the authentic

edition of the 1637 *Segunda parte*, the second collection of printed dramas authorized by Calderón (*El médico* 11). Cruickshank mentions two performances of plays with this title staged in the Salón de Palacio in 1629 and 1635, the first one possibly by Lope. According to J.E. Varey and N.D. Shergold, Agustín Manuel and his company also brought a play with the same title before 1688 to the Cuarto de la Reina (*Comedias* 159). I have found no evidence to date of a performance of this dramatic text in a *corral*. For an overview of Calderón plays staged during the twentieth century, see Luciano García Lorenzo.

2 As Robert Johnston argues, the central motive (and motif) of this play is the 'narcissistic, illusionary, and self-destructive idea' that control of women equals control of the self (44).

3 This administration of justice, different from the spectacular turn of judicial events in 'peasant honour plays,' such as Lope de Vega's *Fuente Ovejuna* or Calderón's *El alcalde de Zalamea*, portrays a kingly figure with undesirable traits; in *El médico*, as Jodi Campbell argues, 'although the king leads the plot to its conclusion to the satisfaction of all the (surviving) characters, the outcome is a grim warning of the consequences of having justice depend on a king who is willing to twist it for the sake of appearances' (112). This instance of a 'theater of negotiation,' as Campbell's study is titled, was produced in a time when questions about the legitimacy of monarchy were being posed, and art, like the political treatises of those seeking reform, or *arbitristas*, sought to advocate good kinship and to 'evince a clear concern for the primacy of law over the arbitrary whims of a ruler' (12). To formulate this premise, Campbell cites the two best studies on kingship and Calderón's theatre to date: those by McKendrick (*Playing the King*), Rupp, and Fox, who see the ludic dimension of these royal figures as signs representing limits of conformity, detect traces of anti-Machiavellian traditions, and examine characterization and political theory in his plays. The thorough analysis of kingship under the rulership of Philip III (1598–1621) by Antonio Feros (*Kingship*) is an invaluable source on this matter.

4 For Cruickshank, the staging of Pedro I in this play as Justiciero, ultimately authorizing and condoning Gutierre's performance of violence, poses some of the finest instances of irony in the text ('Calderón's King Pedro' 113). The historical moment remembered by Gutierre's order of execution is King Pedro's order for his wife, doña Blanca, to be put to death after being falsely accused of adultery with Prince Enrique. The irony is completed by the play's implied reference to the historical event of the king's death in Montiel shortly after his visit to Seville. His half-brother,

the bastard Count Enrique of Trastámara, murdered him to win the crown of the kingdom of Castile. Lloyd King and Carol Kirby Bingham review these and other historical dimensions of this character.

5 Steven Wagschall persuasively argues that honour and jealousy are intrinsically related in the *casos de la honra* represented in honour dramas (23).

6 Vision, optics, politics, and science collaborated in early modern Spain in ways that are not self-evident for contemporary readers. For an insightful study on this subject matter, see García-Santo Tomás.

7 The terms of domination and the arts of resistance as political performances are key in understanding my reading of the various ways in which subjects in this text and context not only produce but also, most importantly, resist, this violence. I am not interested in exploring violence as a self-portrait of absolutist Habsburgs or their dominant elites; rather, my goal is to point out what James Scott calls 'a politics of disguise and anonymity that takes place in public view but is designed to have a double meaning or to shield the identity of the actors' (19), in an attempt to tease out the political and aesthetic resistance of these characters to various performances of marriage, violence, and the Law.

8 For a thorough overview of the evolution of this debate, from Roman Law until the Constitution of 1978, see Álvarez Cortina (*Violencia*).

9 Renato Barahona and Scott Taylor have contributed significantly, if differently, to this question. Taylor, guided by a matrix of dueling, considers violence as one more tool 'to be picked up and used at the discretion of the user – insults, gestures, symbols such as hats and mustaches, and violence were all a part of a loose but well-understood repertoire of moves and emblems that allowed early modern Castilians to pursue disputes over truth and reputation' (227). Honour, the rhetoric, helped 'managing relationships when problems occurred,' says Taylor (227). According to him, this management of relationships has been ill understood due to an over-reliance on gender, which 'important as it was' is not a good tool for predicting behaviour (228). No doubt women 'protected their families, and they also maintained credit and debt relationships,' but their actions certainly should not be used to erase the fact that on- and offstage violence against women, as Barahona well documents, was a social issue – not by means of the frequency of the assaults, but by the mere fact that they could actually happen in the name of the Law. Although coercion, physical force, and violence 'hardly surfaced in most of the lawsuits' he examines, Barahona says the 'numerous *estupro* (ravishment, defloration, rape) lawsuits contain unmistakable elements of threats, intimidation, insults, and verbal harassment, while others involve explicit instances of physical

violence and aggression both before and during the commission of sex acts,' as well as abduction and transfer of the victim to have sexual relations with her (59). Family and friends, socio-economic pressures, and the condition and status of the victims became coercive elements against women, who, despite their resistance and conflict of will, more frequently than not lost the battle in a field where, as Barahona concludes, the male was 'invariably presented as the more aggressive and dominant of the two' and seductions were pursued by them with 'highly ambiguous and contradictory components of courtship, promise of marriage, consent, coercion, and violence' (59–60).

10 Rather than suggesting any direct influence of this case over the process of composition of *El médico* by Calderón, my intention in bringing it forth is to illustrate the kind of violent language and discourse employed in a secular tribunal to debate a key issue in marriage during this period: that of the woman's consent to matrimony. Hence, my interest at this time is not to look at the plot of this case, but rather to focus on the linguistic and discursive tools employed by both parties. I thank David Armitage for pointing out the methodological problem of suggesting a direct influence of a 1588 court case on a dramatic text of the 1630s. The case is in the Archivo General de Simancas, in the section of Cámara de Castilla, Procesos y Expedientes Criminales (CCPEC).

11 Barahona's description of his journey to this data resonates with my access to this case: on the one hand, 'I was especially taken by the documents' vivid details and by the protagonists' dilemmas, travails, and punishments' that 'seemed to trump the pens of even the mightiest novelists and playwrights of the Golden Age,' while at the same time, the absence of comprehensive, reliable catalogues, gaping holes and lack of uniformity makes was utterly disheartening. This case, although fairly well preserved, is a fair example of what Barahona called 'documentary jigsaw puzzles' that characterize this kind of historical legal research.

12 See the studies by Barahona and Taylor cited in chapter 2.

13 Matthew Stroud concurs with Lope in seeing these *casos de la honra* as blockbusters (*Fatal Union* 13). The question of their interpretation, Stroud argues, is complex. Unitary meaning in these texts must be undermined, says Stroud, and a single moral stand must be avoided in order to avoid the traps of the fatal union (20–3).

14 I have argued the correspondence of honour and tragedy in 'Mencía (in) visible.' On Calderonian tragedy, see Hermenegildo, Fischer, Hernández-Araico, Ter Horst, MacCurdy, Parker, Ruano de la Haza ('Más sobre la tragedia' and 'Hacia una nueva definición'), Saffar, and Wardropper.

15 Hilaire Kallendorf articulates insightful readings into the rise of casuistry in Spain, Jesuit school drama, and the education of Spanish playwrights. This interpretive toolbox would be an invaluable source for rereading honour and violence in the wife-killing plays.

16 Cascardi links social rigidity and immobility in early modern Hispanic culture to the fact that Muslims, Jews, and Christians interacted according to their caste and racial identification, not class differences, which made legitimate social mobility virtually impossible ('The Subject' 140). These differences were not physically visible, but determined by faith and performative gestures such as clothing, food habits, or the way in which men and women arranged their hair. Hence, says Cascardi, 'as it is manifestly evident both in the workings of the Spanish Inquisition and in the "honor plays" of the Golden Age, the impossible pursuit of unattainable certainties generated a collective psychology of suspicion and fear that the analysis of caste in purely structural terms could not fully explain' ('The Subject' 140).

17 Milton clearly saw that considering sexual and economic control, as well as procreation, and not love, the primary ends of the marital institution could only lead to its deterioration. However, as Stone has rightfully noted, Milton's argument that the union of a man and a woman had to be driven by 'the apt and cheerful conversation of man with woman, *to comfort and refresh him* against the solitary life' clearly denotes his assumption of the subordinate function of married women (*Family* 138; my emphasis).

18 The codification of honour as a central referent for this and other texts produced in seventeenth-century Spain has been so pervasive that it could be argued that it has become a foundational fiction for the discipline of Spanish 'Golden Age' Studies. In 1959, Gustavo Correa's piece on the '*doble aspecto de la honra*' brought honour to a virtually fossilized status. Cyril Jones and McKendrick effectively disarticulate this reading, the former arguing that honour was 'a historical phenomenon, convention, and artistic motive,' the latter underscoring its literariness and establishing a correspondence between the fictional tragic events of sexuality in the *dramas de honor* and the equally tragic scrutiny of race and ethnicity in the ideological programs of *limpieza de sangre* ('Honour / Vengeance' 312).

19 René Girard's theorizing of violence and the sacred speaks of the need to secure the unanimous approval of society – at least, nominally – for a violent event to qualify as sacred.

20 Cruickshank ('Pongo mi mano en sangre bañada'), Parker, Sullivan, Dunn, Oostendorp, Neuschäfer, Hesse, Casa, Ter Horst, Soufas, Johnston, Smith,

Benabu, and Lauer have analysed various aspects of this text, such as honour, poetry, and psychoanalysis.

21 Their common source is Agustín de Amezúa, who argued that the source for the play was an incident recorded in the *Casos notables de la ciudad de Córdoba* (398–403).

22 Curiously, in his translation of *El médico* Campbell added the words '(*Room in the Alcazar or Royal Palace of Seville*)' (Calderón, *The Surgeon* 17) before the stage quotation, signalling a space like the ones envisaged by Greer (*The Play of Power*) and Kagan.

5 Punishing Illicit Desire

1 This chapter explores the intersection of race, empire, corporality, and the visual arts that, as Peter Erickson and Clark Hulse argue, are key points in the study of the cultural production of Europe, Africa, and the Americas in the sixteenth and seventeenth centuries.

2 Being officially recognized as a subject of pure blood was a requirement *sine qua non* to function socially in sixteenth- and seventeenth-century Spain, as Albert Sicroff rightfully concluded (173). This racist system added two new layers to the causes for discrimination in the new imperial territories of South America: indigenous and African blood, both more visibly impure than the often-times masked impurity of Muslim and Jewish subjects.

3 These scenes emblematize a resistance to such segregation rhetoric and constitutional discourses that was tangible, for instance, in what Trevor Dadson sees as 'official rhetoric versus local realities' in the 1609–13 expulsion of the *moriscos*. Alexander Samson has also analysed the existence of bridges of tolerance, interfaith sexuality, and *converso* culture present in the case of the affair between Hurtado de Mendoza and the *judía de Venecia* (62).

4 Frida Weber de Kurlat established this categorization of the play in 1975. Cañadas disagrees with this encasing of the play, which misses its radical interpellation of the *Estatutos*. The discernment of blood traits in early modern Spain was very different from modern genetics, where the examination of blood yields data about genotype or inheritable, internally coded information. George Mariscal has logically argued for the need to connect these dots and see the importance of early modern Spanish racist ideologies in the formation of modern race theories. Baltasar Fra Molinero sees black subjects in early modern Spain, both on- and offstage. And John Beusterien examines the complex games of visibility-invisibility

deployed by both officers of the crown and artists to represent race in the Spanish *comedia*.

5 Iván Cañadas has argued that the *comedia palatina* mobilizes critical correspondences between playwrights, ambiguity, marginality, theatre, and drama, constituting 'a carnivalesque interrogation of rank and gender' in which the subject lacking in *limpieza de sangre* becomes a critical agent of the (in theory) impossible process of social mobility (32). Cañadas adds that irony and humour lead to ambiguity and ambivalence, 'allowing radical or potentially dangerous or offensive positions to be expressed with some license' (33). Some of these potentially dangerous or offensive positions without a doubt include the queer patronage established between Lope and the duke of Sessa, because as Cañadas also acknowledges, 'from his ambiguous social position as a professional writer and the client-servant of a duke, Lope explored issues involving hierarchy, social mobility and honor' (32). A review of Lope's artistic life – which Elizabeth Wright has read as a journey through 'pilgrimage to patronage' – proves that, although his authorial figure and artistic production never fully engaged the higher spheres of court space, he also 'exploited the playwright's power to stage ambition; in so doing, he publicized his desire for the position of royal chronicler, a sinecure that he envisioned as a suitable reward for his exceptional talents' (111).

6 Félix Lope de Vega y Carpio, *El perro del hortelano*, ed. A. David Kossoff. For the translations I have consulted two English versions of *The Dog in the Manger*: those by Victor Dixon and Jill Booty. Dixon's translation, although not rendered strictly in the same poetic forms as the Spanish original, reflects the poetic quality of the language used by Lope and is more appropriate for my citations; passages from Dixon's translation will appear marked with 'D.' There are a few passages in which Booty's translation contributes worthy meaning to the play in the English language, and I will mark the corresponding quotes with 'B.' In a few instances I will offer a translation of my own in order to underscore the presence of my critical terms in Lope's text; in those cases, readers will know it is my translation because the citation will only indicate page numbers in the Spanish original.

7 For Ruano, the *comedia* was not merely an auditive theatre but rather a highly sophisticated and thickly layered feast of multiple senses ('Hacia una metodología' 82). Other special effects, such as character props, stage props, different *atrezzo* and costume schools, *bofetones, escotillones, palenques*, sound effects, animals, birds, at times even insects, and music granted enormous referential audiovisual wealth to the *comedia* as text

onstage, and the interactive correspondence of these theatrical signs
constitute the surface over which the message was composed by the
collaborative of playwrights, directors, actors, technicians, and audiences
that is the theatre. For further information about this theory, see his
valuable handbook, *Los teatros comerciales de Madrid*, with John Jay Allen.

8 That Teodoro is a secretary and not a butler, as in the drama about the
duchess of Amalfi with her *mayordomo* (butler) also by Lope, is rather
telling on a number of levels. The most important one, as Elena del Río
Parra and Mercedes Maroto Camino have argued, is the fact that as
prescribed by a number of secretarial handbooks of the time, the figure of
the *secretario* was tantamount to that of the keeper of secrets in a household, which as these two studies show, increased exponentially the
possibilities of this *comedia* to represent sex and gender.

9 *La dama boba* has received a great deal of critical attention. *El perro*, on the
other hand, has elicited studies about its deployment of satire (Wilson,
'Lope'); comedy as genre (Sage, Wardropper, 'Comic Illusion'); love,
honour, and *burla* (Rosetti); and silence and rhetoric (Carreño).

10 There is an interactive structure of conversion, clientage, and the performance of masculinity that also finds a literary medium in *El perro*. As
Alison Weber says about the *Rimas*, the ideal secretary assumed a level
of self-abnegation that she identifies as a performance of masculinity
common at the time. The relationship between Diana and Teodoro cannot
be taken as a literal or autobiographical inscription of Lope and Sessa;
be that as it may, as Camino's article demonstrates, the feminization of
Teodoro as the 'keeper of secrets' of the House of Belflor is without a
doubt a great icon for the crisis of masculinity that Weber rightly says that
Lope was experiencing at the time, and that took him to proactively
engage in multiple gender performances – 'as a biological woman ... the
puto of the Gongorine satire, and the ephebe-lover of the second bucolic'
all signs that 'by 1614, clientage had become a kind of thralldom for the
duke's secretary' (410).

11 For an introductory overview of masochism and its relations to fantasy,
instinct, power, character, excitement, art, narcissism, compulsion, masculinities, and anxiety, see Glick and Meyers, *Masochism: Current Psychoanalytic Perspectives*, as well as Mansfield, *Masochism: The Art of Power*.

12 Michael Sells has translated *The Interpreter* as well as other poems by Ibn
'Arabi (*Stations of Desire*). Sells is also the author of an extensive analysis
on the relation of poetry with love in courtly, popular, and Bacchic
scenarios (which produced numerous hauntingly lyrical images of exile,
longing, camps in the desert, ruins, and intense desire for the lost love)

particularly in the Arabic tradition of the *qasidas*; he has resumed this sprawling cultural and literary history in an economic essay aptly entitled 'Love.'

13 Julio González Ruiz analyses the various stages in which Lope de Vega used the audiovisual language of theatre to represent homoerotic desire, another forbidden type of human relation. The free theatre that González Ruiz reads in other plays by Lope is parallel to Diana's *monstruo ambiguo*, who illicitly desires to mix blood from different social strata.

14 Luis González-Cruz has analysed this series of sonnets in the text of *El perro*, and deemed them signs that convey the thematic essence of this dramatic piece.

15 Michael Spiller documents the development of the sonnet as a form, which combines Ovid's *Metamorphoses* with Virgil's *Aeneid*, Sicilian courtly poetry such as that of Giacomo da Lentino, and Provençal *canso* poems, in which the female figure had already been positioned as an elevated figure to be adored (14–15).

16 Social rank plays an important role in the unfolding of courtly love, which Capellanus divides by gender and social class (33–150).

17 For a reading of misogyny as a therapeutic strategy for the sickly courtly lover in medieval Iberia, see Solomon.

18 Jean Howard reviews the economics of theatregoing, spectacle, and what that meant and represented for women. Jane Albrecht studies the composition and significance of audiences in the *Comedia*.

19 Natalie Zemon Davis used this expression to refer to the cultural traditions that draw on images of disorderly and unruly women as signs of resistance to unjust rules ('Woman on Top').

20 Diana, in a sense, could be enacting – another turn of the screw – a scene of punishment of the effeminization of the Spanish male, which Donnell, Stroud (*Plot Twists*), Vélez-Quiñones, Cartagena-Calderón, and myself ('Men With Style') have seen as a crisis of masculinity emblematized in the theatre.

21 See Ruano de la Haza, *Los teatros comerciales* (with John Jay Allen), *El corral del Príncipe (1583–1744)*, and *La puesta en escena de los teatros comerciales del Siglo de Oro* for a comprehensive overview of the critical role played by architecture in the theatres.

22 Stroud (*The Play*) explores the symbol of the mirror as a motif that yields rich psychoanalytic data about the Spanish baroque theatre. McKendrick, on the other hand, considers portraits, glass, and mirrors as images of honour, desire and captivity for women in the *Comedia* ('Retratos' in *Identities* 151–70).

23 The reference of the *lienzo* as a handkerchief, favoured by both translators, no doubt evokes Othello's gift to Desdemona. This adds another turn to the *limpieza de sangre* screw, tying the illicit desires harboured by Diana and Teodoro to issues of race, honour, and uxoricide. The *lienzo*-as-canvas mobilizes one of the richest sources of material for the *comedia*, ekphrasis, which Frederick de Armas has studied so generously and extensively (*Quixotic Frescoes*, 'Painting with Blood,' and *Cervantes, Raphael, and the Classics*).

24 Two studies by John Beusterien clarify this visual. In 'Jewish Male Menstruation,' Beusterien shows that 'in seventeenth-century Spain … the Jewish body supposedly leaked impure blood' (447). And in 'Blood Displays' he traces the contradictory subject of blood, race, and menstruation, which for the church 'was a sign of sickness' (*An Eye on Race* 66–7).

25 Devin Stewart offers an economic view of this and other points in the poetry of Ibn Zaydûn.

26 As Fuchs rightly argues ('Virtual Spaniards'), the daunting challenges of inscribing themselves in history faced by *moriscos* more often than not yielded a Spanish identity more virtual than real – a point no doubt at the core of identity politics in *El perro* and the games its people play.

6 Woman in Breeches

1 Tirso de Molina, *Don Gil de las calzas verdes*, ed. Vicente. For the translations I have consulted Minter's bilingual version entitled *Don Gil of the Green Breeches*, and Browning and Minelli's *Don Gil of the Breeches Green*. In different passages each translation contributes worthy meaning to the play in the English language; hence, I will refer to one or the other with the letters 'M' (Minter) and 'BM' (Browning and Minelli) followed by the page number from the respective translation. In a few instances, as in this paragraph, I will offer a translation of my own in order to underscore the presence of my critical terms in Tirso's text; in those cases, readers will know it is my translation as the parenthesis will only indicate page number from the Spanish original. The words 'hacienda' and 'pretender' are key to the unfolding of the play; the former refers to both material property and the process of self-making (or, to borrow Stephen Greenblat's apt term for this occasion, 'self-fashioning'), and hence I have translated it as 'my own resources,' while the latter can signify both 'to seek' and 'to assume another identity,' two meanings with which I will play critically in this chapter. 'Hacienda' is correctly translated by both M as 'lands and rent' (73) and BM as 'estate' (211); however, neither one utters the lady's

agency and resourcefulness in making the room of her own. 'Pretender,' on the other hand, is translated as 'to seek' by both translators, although M adds an extra verse to indicate that Don Gil wants 'to claim a coat of arms.' The fact that such coat does not belong to her implicitly ties in the impostor (pretend subject) with her claims and aspirations (pretence), thus hinting at the dual nature of the word in the play.

2 Francisco de San Román cites the contracts signed to stage this play in the Mesón de la Fruta (Fruit's Inn) of Toledo in the year 1615, by Pedro de Valdés's company. Valdés was married to the famed actress Jerónima de Burgos, on whose age and large frame the fiasco of opening night was blamed (210).

3 The translations for the terms 'pelón' and 'moscatel' follow the meanings listed by María Inés Chamorro in her *Tesoro de Villanos: Diccionario de Germanía* (595, 643). It is interesting that 'pelona,' which would be the grammatically correct signifier for doña Juana's anatomy, referred to a woman with syphilis in *germanías* or street slang in early modern Spain.

4 According to Covarrubias a 'librea' (livery) was a kind of clothing once reserved only for the king's servants, and by the seventeenth century the custom was evolved 'para ser distinguidos y diferenciados de todos los demás; y porque éstos tienen muchos privilegios y libertades' (to be distinguished and differentiated from all other folks; and because those with livery have many privileges and freedoms) (714). By the beginning of the eighteenth century the *Diccionario de Autoridades* furthers that definition, defining livery as the 'uniform clothing that Kings, those belonging to Great Families, Nobles, and Gentlemen gave respectively to their Guards, Pages, and those downstairs servants, with the colors of the arms and shield of the one who granted it. It used to be embroidered, or adorned with stripes of different ornaments ... By extension livery is the name give to uniform clothes that Gentlemanly formations wear public festivities, such as *Cañas*, masks, etc. Livery uniforms were made of velvet of various colors, and many of them were embroidered; I remember my father and his companions wearing livery made of black velvet' (399).

5 For Covarrubias, a 'paje' was a 'muchacho que sirve algún señor' (young lad who serves a master) (795), while the 'lacayo' (lackey) was a 'mozo de espuelas que va delante del señor cuando va a caballo' (spurred young man placed in front of the master when he rides his horse) (696).

6 Carmanchel characterizes Don Gil with terms doubting his manliness: 'capón' (castrated man, lacking a last name or a beard) (126); 'hermafrodita' (an adolescent who, according to myth, because of his wandering and curiosity was transformed into man and woman at once) (140); 'prima y

bordón' (strings of a vihuela or guitar, or on the one hand, a well-endowed female acrobat bird that surpasses hunters, and on the other, the staff or cane of the pilgrim's bundle (140); 'toronjil y perejil' (celery and parsley) (140); and 'tiple' (third voice) (128). Caramanchel also uses costuming terms to question Don Gil's masculinity: among others, 'cenojil' (thread with which the half-breeches were tied under the knee) (140) and 'cambray' (a cloth even thinner than the finest *holanda*). The definitions are from the *Tesoro*.

7 The translators choose longer and wordier renditions of the quick, witty expression 'de damisela en varón' uttered by Quintana, perhaps seeking to cope with the complex web of layers of signification posed by the original: 'female form in manly dress' (M 51) and 'woman's form / ... appearance of a man' (BM 201). The verb 'disfraza' is beautifully translated as both 'disguise' (M 51) and 'cloak' (BM 201).

8 The 'hábito de encomienda' sought by Doña Juana–Don Gil, as it will shortly become apparent, corresponds with its most visible, legal, and domesticated meaning of 'livery,' that is to say, clothing that would identify a subject as the member of a publicly recognized institution. For Covarrubias 'encomienda' means 'entrusting something to another,' which reflects Doña Juana's entrusting her life and honour to the Don Gil she plays, who interacts with Don Martín's version of Don Gil (469). The one who received the livery of the *encomienda* was called a *comendador*, 'because the rents obtained are given to him as a trust, and not in titles as clerics, gentlemen and commoners, who were incapable of having pure ecclesiastical titles' (337).

9 As Stroud points out, the point of cross-dressing in the *Comedia* was to unleash by means of humour the questioning of the rigid gender categories prescribed in orthodox Counter-Reformation Spain, a complex affair; on the contrary, he says, comic turns 'exemplify Butler's notions that heterosexuality produces a great deal of drag for its own consumption, figures to laugh at but not to take seriously as a threat to social customs and norms' (*Plot Twists* 31).

10 For an overview of the politics of rage in cross-dressing, the body of the warrior, magic and theatre, and the adulteration of male gender, see Levine.

11 González Ruiz has cogently argued how Lope de Vega inscribes the woman in male disguise as a sensational theatrical device with which he 'attacks the dominant patriarcal system, subverting not only certain well defined patterns of social acting and imaging, but also the discourses that conceptualized and defined sexual normativity imposed by such system' (47).

12 McKendrick (*Identities* and *Woman*) and Bravo-Villasante analyse what in their important, pioneer studies they called, respectively, the 'mujer varonil' (manly or masculine woman) and the 'mujer vestida de hombre' (woman dressed as a man), noting how these types of women imitated man as defined in the binary and polarized ideological construct of sexuality and gender of that context.

13 This 'way of growing by means of conflict and schism' is, according to Schechner, 'a major agency of human cultural growth' (167).

14 'Fábrica' and 'industria' are here materials for the couture of an image that will be virtually reproduced with such success that it will actually surpass the wildest fantasies of the figure who in principle creates it – as happens, for instance, to Mickey Mouse in the film *Fantasia*. For Covarrubias, 'fábrica' is a sumptuous building that with time requires repairs, but that in its original design was 'well traced, measured, planned, with great distribution, joyful, well-proportioned, solid, well-finished and attended ... with great lights' (531); on the other hand, 'industria' is 'skill, diligence, and pride with which one does anything more effortlessly than others,' for he knows how to produce it 'promptly and largely' (666).

15 Covarrubias associates 'pretender' with pretension and the Italian *pretensa*, related to the scribe or church doctor who once upon a time had the authority to interpret sacred scriptures, or theologians in Tirso's time (495).

16 BM translates 'industria' in this passage as 'diligence' (263), which rightly verbalizes the lady's agency in devising the multiple 'ardides' (lies, tangled web) that constitute the 'shrewd plan' that M cites (187).

17 For Ruano, clothing onstage was 'artificial, conceived not so much to reproduce realistically the dress of a peasant or an emperor, but to communicate clearly and succinctly to the audiences, as if they were tags, the social condition of the character' (*Los teatros comerciales* 295).

18 Bernardo García García argues that the evidence of design, confection, traffic, and consumption of theatrical costuming harbours 'great possibilities of archaeological recovery of the appearance, textures, and coloring' of Spanish baroque theatre (189). This, adds García García, would in turn further the study of documentary sources, which could be used 'in the analysis of character typology and the symbolism of the accessories, comparing them with artistic and emblematic iconography' (190). Such readings, like the present one, about the green breeches, could, ultimately, fill the archival gap that the lack of images from the *Comedia* represent for the study of this theatre and its socio-political, economic, and cultural context.

19 Lope advises in his dramatic manifesto titled *Arte nuevo de hacer comedias* that 'las damas no desdigan de su nombre; / y si mudaren trage, sea de

modo / que puedan personarse, porque suele / el disfraz varonil agradar mucho' (The ladies naturally we would expect / To be in character. If they change their dress, / Let it be seemly done, for I confess, / The crowd is always pleased by male disguise) (288, 142). In 1608 the *Reglamentos de teatro* (Theatre's Regulations) included an order stipulating that 'no woman shall go onstage to dance, nor to perform in man's clothing' or she will risk a fine of 20 ducats; this order was revised in 1615 and again in 1641, when the *Regulations* dictated that 'women shall perform in decent women's clothing, and they should not go onstage to act in their underskirt only; instead over that they should wear other clothes, like a long coat or overskirt, loose or attached to the skirt, and they shall neither perform in men's clothing, nor act their part, neither should men, even the young ones, act the parts of women' (quoted in Varey, 48, 56, and 92).

20 Without confusing the generic boundaries of the *comedia* and the *entremés* (see chapter 5), readers and spectators of *Don Gil* can see how this text participates in the deconstructing process of theatrical costume typical of the short plays – known as *teatro breve* or brief theatre – which, according to Evangelina Rodríguez Cuadros, used to mark 'stable social behaviors at once always turned toward the kind of sarcasm typical of the satirical literature of the period, which played with the baring of appearances and value hierarchies in the Baroque' ('El hato' 115).

21 Regueiro (32–8) and Donnell (33), among others, have demonstrated the need to read these final scenes otherwise, not merely as scenes of a literal, wholesome restoration of a social order imposed by the Catholic Universal Monarchy.

22 By insisting on the term 'fábrica' I am not encasing *Don Gil* in the taxonomical frame defined by Bances y Candamo in 1690: *comedias de Fábrica* 'are those that somehow intend to prove something with the event staged, and their characters are Kings, Princes, Generals, Dukes, etc., and prominent persons who remained nameless or had no fixed name in the histories, and their artifice rests on various turns of Fortune, long pilgrimages, duels of great Fama, great conquests, elevated Loves and, finally, strange and higher and wondrous happenings than those that take place in the scenes that, not long ago, I called domestic' (33). Although there are contact zones between *Don Gil* and the *comedias de Fábrica*, my reading aims beyond the boundaries of generic taxonomies.

23 Garber (1–17), Juárez Almendros (19–40) and Sifuentes-Jáuregui (1–14) elaborate this key theoretical concept in the development of the transvestite in several different geopolitical and historical contexts.

24 Velasco cogently examines Erauso's 'hybrid spectacle,' in which les-
bian desire, monstrosity, passing, and crossing of sexual desire, as well
as the manly woman play key roles (*Lieutenant* 13–86). That spectacle,
and not merely 'being' a man is what informs the likewise spectacular
transvestite figure of don Gil in Tirso's play. See also Juárez Almendros
(128–43).

25 The original document cited by Postigo, located in the collection 'Grace
and Justice' of the AGS (Leg 890), reads: 'Batállase en este Consejo sobre el
honor, prenda la más estimada de la vida, batállase sobre la vida misma,
que no la hay sin el honor, y entre el honor y la vida se batalla sobre la
hacienda que no se desprecia poca en semejantes pretensiones' (13).

26 Pérez Castañeda y Couto de León define this process, according to which
those seeking to join the religious order had to 'prove that their ancestors
had not been, or been related to, Muslims or Jews, or been condemned by
the Inquisition, nor had belonged to any "bad sects"' (3).

27 Among the women who had been ordained 'in old times' Da. Ana de
Guzmán, born in Toledo (1524), Da. Inés de Barrientos, from Valladolid
(1525), Da. Juana Panda de la Carta, from Valencia (n. d.), María de Isla,
from Becerril (1528), Da. Catalina de Peonosa (n. p. n. d.), Da. María de
Luna, from Calabazas (1533), Da. Catalina de Rivera, from Seville (n. d.),
Da. María de Castañeda, from Valtierra (1535), Da. Leonor de Quiñones,
from Madrid (1538), Da. Mayor Bibero, born in Toledo (1539), and Da.
Isabel Mexia, from Casa Rubios, among many others. The 'Index' of livery
granted to women between 1524 and 1698 – which includes also those
obtained by means of marriage – registers ninety-eight requests, almost all
of them granted.

28 Sumptuary laws, according to Hunt 'connect "backwards" with the
medieval world by contributing a critique of the luxury and a generalized
moralization of social relations represented in and by religious discourses,
but it also points "forward" to a change in the concern with "economics"
and in that, with the role of the State, which involves a radically different
way of thinking and understanding in which social relations are built and
reinforced by multiple governing projects' (10).

29 The variety of different breeches of that time produced a lexical treasure
compiled in part by Bernis: 'velvet with *fajas*, 1589; black velvet with
stockings, 1595 and 1609; with wider or narrower *fajas*, 1598; black velvet
'lined with satin,' or 'with its satins,' 1604, etc.' (152–3).

30 Arellano qualifies Don Gil's economics of costume management: 'It is
notable that many characters penned by Tirso de Molina display a notable
desire to play dramatically, and a well-tested histrionic skill; is Doña

Juana/Don Gil but the author of a recital of theatrical performances, a gamut of roles and characters that she herself invents and lays out?' ('Las máscaras' 11).

31 Bernis analyses how black breeches were the thing to wear in sixteenth-century Spain, as illustrated in the repressed colour palette in portraits such as Sofonisba Anguissola's *Felipe II* and Juan Pantoja de la Cruz's *El archiduque Alberto* (141) and effigies such as those of the brothers Francisco and Luis de Ortega y Vallejo, from Valdepeñas, Francisco de Hermosa, from San Lorenzo de la Parrilla, the father and sons in Mayor Pedro Monresin de Alhange's family, in Granada, and the family of Don Alonso Gonçalez, from Madrid and el Cardoso, all of which appear in the cover of their letters of *hidalguía*t (153 and 155). These uniform, homogeneous breeches showing little ornamentation stand in ample contrast to the gay spirit of the breeches that were in fashion in King Felipe III's court, worthy heirs of the French court fashions.

32 Bernis quotes Vargas Machuca, who in his 1619 *Teoría y ejercicios de la jineta* (Theory and Practice of the Nasri Sword) lamented that with the tight and tied-up breeches 'men were so stiff and constrained that they were incapable of bending their body or using their extremities) (203).

33 As Laura Bass shows in her insightful study about theatre and visual culture in early modern Spain, 'in very real ways portraits produced and reproduced the monarchy,' for not only did they stage genealogies visual and otherwise, but they also were used as tools to forge monarchic alliances, and in the absence of the king they inscribed a virtual presence of the crown and helped prop the subjects' loyalties (*The Drama* 79).

34 There is copious evidence of this style. See the beautifully striped and adorned breeches of the *Archiduque Leopoldo de Austria* and the *Retrato de Felipe III*, both by Bartolomé González; the ones with the straight bottom border in the *Retrato de Felipe III* by Juan Pantoja de la Cruz; the long breeches of the *Retrato ecuestre del Duque de Lerma* by Pedro Pablo Rubens; and the voluminous, elaborate, golden ones of the portrait of *Felipe IV y el enano soplillo* by Rodrigo de Villandrando; all these portraits are in the Prado Museum in Madrid. The invaluable volume by Bernis shows reproductions of all these images (140, 139, 149, 145, 143, and 157 respectively).

35 Bernis points out that, although the *valones* (three-quarter length pants) were more commonly used among squires and lackeys, these servants also used breeches; the painting *La Dieta de Augsburgo* by Juan de la Corte, in the Museo Municipal de Madrid illustrates this comparison (shown in Bernis, 167).

36 Stallybrass bases his reading of clothing and theatre on the premise of livery, which he considers 'the industrial basis of production of cloth and circulation of clothing' in England, where clothes and fabrics also became currency that inscribed messages of power and memory in subjects' bodies (289). For Stallybrass, 'if the livery system was an attempt to inscribe memory in the body, theatre dis-placed immediately such memory' (305). Hence, my translating Doña Juana/Don Gil's reason to travel to Madrid, 'un hábito de encomienda,' as 'livery' and not as 'a title of nobility' (BM 211) or 'a coat of arms … a grant of letters patent' (M 73).

37 In his Spanish edition of the play Vicente notes the context of marriage between members of powerful families, a binding of estates that became a characteristic institution of Spanish society that 'made the first born son the heir of the father's wealth, to the detriment of the remaining children of the family,' which also, by virtue of the strategic negotiation of some marriages, 'gradually moved the wealth of the country into a few hands and lead to important changes in the social body' (129).

38 For two insightful readings on the ambiguity of certain sartorial signs such as *aljubas* (long shirts), *mantillas* (veils), *zaragüelles* (baggy trousers), *camisas* (chemises), *tocas* (headdresses), *almalafas* and *marlotas* (two types of cloaks) and how these and other garments related to self-fashioning, ornamentation, dating, and provenance of textiles and clothing, see Fuchs (*Exotic*), Bass and Wonder, and Feliciano.

39 Browning and Minelli focus their translation in the real estate aspect of 'solar de sus calzas:' 'his breeches are the basis of his name / (you see, his breeches are his house and lands)' (270).

40 In 1641 Granada, a city ordinance banned Muslims from working as sock makers. Bernis, who quotes the law, illustrates the differences between Muslims and Christian subjects with images from Juan de Acelga's *Libro de Geometría, práctica y traça, el qual trata de lo tocante al oficio de sastre* (Book of Geometry, Its Practice and Traces, Regarding the Occupation of Tailor) dated 1580, and the detail of one of the royal characters who wears a handsome *albornoz* richly ornamented in *La adoración de los Reyes* (*The Adoration of the Three Kings*), a sixteenth-century altarpiece in the parochial church of Orobia (474–8).

41 In the twentieth and twenty-first centuries *Don Gil* has been staged in the Hubert de Blanc Theatre of La Habana, by the company Teatro Corsario and on other stages in various locales and by the student troupe of Brigham Young University in Utah. The Compañía Nacional de Teatro Clásico (CNTC) staged José Caballero Bonald's adapted version in 1994, and again in 2006, when Eduardo Vasco directed it. In the annual rite of the

Festival de Teatro Clásico in Almagro, Corsario, the CNTC, and other companies have also represented *Don Gil*. Notoriously, the play does not appear registered in the catalogue of plays staged in the border Festival de Teatro del Siglo de Oro celebrated annually in Chamizal Park, near El Paso, Texas.

42 The two translations do not underscore the intersection of monetary interest and spectacular interest (curiosity, desire) of which the Spanish line 'interés / de tu dote' speaks in reference to Inés's dowry: 'fine dowry' (M 127) and 'the dowry that entailed' (BM 235)

43 In the Browning and Fiorigio translation Don Martín merges with Doña Inés in sexier market terms: 'If I'm at fault in this, / Inés's worth and beauty are to blame' (BM 241).

44 BM translate freely these terms of engagement of the material and spectacular, turning 'interés / dichoso' into 'O happy union!' (252), while M stays closer to the original: 'And I'm repaid / With interest' (161).

45 According to Covarrubias, Inés is 'nombre de mujer, del nombre latino AGNES, vale tanto como pura, casta y santa, del verbo αγγεύω' (a female name, from the Latin Agnes, which is equivalent to pure, chaste, and saintly, from the verb 'angeo') (666).

Coda: The Musical Chairs of Divorce

1 In the early stages of development, the word for this dramatic and theatrical form referred to mime routines performed, like little dishes, between the main courses of a banquet in medieval times. This inter-course soul food became a highly protean subject stage, composed of characters of dubious positions in society standing next to proper ladies and court representatives, whose predicaments were supported by disparate mixes of poetic, cultivated forms with the language of *germanías*. The tradition began with a strong gestational period in which authors of other short dramatic forms (such as the *auto* and the *paso*) contributed to develop the *entremés* as an integral part of the emerging theatrical world of sixteenth-century Spain. During the consolidation period of the *Comedia* the *entremés* moved centre stage, in a manner of speaking: the cost of having one in a *Comedia* was dear, but *autores de comedias* would pay handsomely for them, since they knew that a good *entremés* could sell the lousiest of *comedias*. Such a theatrical platform became the site of production of highly desirable actors, among whom Cosme Pérez, also known as 'Juan Rana' (John the Frog) stands out. As a written form, the *entremés* was cultivated by all kinds of different *poetas* (poets and playwrights): Castillo Solórzano, Salas

Barbadillo (also authors of picaresque novels), Antonio Hurtado de
Mendoza and Francisco de Quevedo (authors of poetry as well), and Luis
Vélez de Guevara (a key player in the writing of *comedias*). In the second
half of the seventeenth century, Jerónimo de Cáncer and Agustín Moreto
wrote numerous *entremeses*, and contributed to the phase in which its form
evolved to be known as the *comedia burlesca*, characterized by high self-
parody and monumental set design, due in great part to the demand for
these events in court. For a long period of time, as happened with the
evolution of Old into New Comedy, the *entremés* virtually disappeared
from the stages until it finally was replaced by a modern form: the *sainete*.
At the end of the nineteenth and during the early twentieth century the
entremés went through a period of resurgence in Spain, where it reappeared
in the writing of Ramón María del Valle Inclán, the Álvarez Quintero
brothers (Serafín and Joaquín), Carlos Arniches, and, after the end of the
war, Max Aub and Lauro Olmo, among others. Cotarelo y Mori, Shergold
(*A History of the Spanish Stage*), Asensio Asensio, and Buendía offer a rich
critical overview of this evolution.

2 Miguel de Cervantes y Saavedra, *Entremés del juez de los divorcios*, ed.
Sevilla Arroyo. *The Judge of the Divorce Court* appears in Spanish and
English in the collection *The Interludes of Cervantes* compiled and translated
by Morley. Although two other translations have appeared before this (*The
Judge of the Divorce Court* by Edith Fahnestock and Florence Donnell White,
The Colonnade 13.5 (1919), and Willis Knapp Jones in *Poet Lore* 45.2 (1939), I
cite Morley's translation because both his Spanish and English versions are
impeccably executed, and rendered in one economic bilingual edition.

3 In his brief chapter '"Divorce" and Greek New Comedy,' Lee reviews the
scant theatrical evidence we have on this subject. Although the staging of
separation and divorce was minimal and may seem insignificant when
compared to the tenor of mutual love and theatrical conventions of closure
that this comedy may suggest, divorce was present, and not insignificant,
in these comic texts. For instance, if the son-in-law's conduct was improper
or wrong, says Lee, the father was within his right 'to withdraw his
daughter from her husband's control and bring her to his own home,' even
against her will, 'but it is represented that it was done only after attempts
at reconciliation had failed' (30). If the wife left the husband, that action
was 'represented as regrettable and as done only as a last resort' (30). The
exception was represented when she left him for 'infidelity or ill usage,' in
which case her conduct would be proper, and her property could go with
her (31). If, on the other hand, the plot revealed that the wife had not been
chaste before entering the marriage covenant, or if the husband found her

guilty of infidelity, he had the power to divorce her and was 'compelled to dismiss her' (30). Lee notes that in those cases 'no legal process, beyond the summoning of witnesses, was necessary' (31). The great elliptical strategy of theatre, composed as a delay in the scene, more often than not served the deferring purpose of producing miraculous new data that would help the husband reconsider, so he, his wife, and everyone could live happily ever after (30).

4 As Patricia Kenworthy has noted, the *entremeses* of Cervantes are substantially invested in representing the illusory world that the dramatic/theatrical medium can communicate by extending 'the limits of subject matter available for dramatic treatment' ('The *Entremeses*' 12). This, as Cory Reed has argued, translated into a poor reception of his dramatic work, which is imitative neither of classical forms of theatre nor of Lope de Vega's parameters of the *comedia nueva*, but an innovative form that 'brings many of the thematic and structural characteristics of prose narrative to the composition of his 'novelized' drama' (69). By combining the threads of composition of marriage with those of the composition of theatre, Cervantes is inscribing performative aspects also present, as scholars have noted elsewhere, in the literary surface of the novel. For this last point, see Carrión, 'El amor en tiempos de cólera' and 'Don Quijote's *ingenio.*'

5 Cosme Pérez, great actor that he was, realized the potential for play that the presence of the body had onstage at a time when gender and sexuality were heavily controlled by various state apparatuses. The *Entremés del juez de los divorcios* parades a variety of body parts that, by showing up onstage and being uttered in more or less explicit fashion, articulate a critique to such control of gender and sexuality: face, anatomy (body), back, cheeks, chest, mouth, foul breath, teeth, stomach, eyes, ears, feet, hands, the five senses, and phallus (named as 'a stick of wood'), among others.

6 My reading, although focusing on gender and sexuality in relation to marriage, also refers to the artistic component of its dramatic texture. I continue along the lines of inquiry proposed by Mary Gaylord Randel and Silvia Rossi de Castillo, who have noted the presence of poetry and poets in these *entremeses* in corresponding fashion to the ways in which Reed and Francisco J. Martín have pointed out the correspondences with the discourses, structures, and textual strategies of the novel in these short theatrical pieces. In a parallel literary analysis, Stanislav Zimic related the *entremeses* to the narrative form of the *exempla*; however, his argument runs contrary to what Gaylord, Reed, and others see in the intertextual relationship between Cervantes's *entremeses* and the novel. For Zimic, all of Cervantes's texts should be analysed according to their intention to

ejemplarizar (set an example), 'understanding that *ejemplaridad* (exemplarity) means implicit or explicit exaltation of reason, common sense, virtue, and morality' ('La ejemplaridad' 444). The dramatic conflict between these meanings of *ejemplaridad* could not be more poignant than in the staging of divorce in an *entremés*.

7 The dynamics of this collaboration of women, grandly theatric and in line with what Edith Villarino and Elsa Fiadino have seen as bridges between verbal and non-verbal lines in the *entremseses*, is yet another sign of the 'libertad femenina' (feminine freedom) noted by Chul Park in his reading of this *entremés* and *El viejo celoso* (The Jealous Old Man) – another interlude in which Cervantes also explores gender relations dynamics. On how these negotiations of verbal and non-verbal referential networks foretell Brecht's theatrical theories and practices in the *entremeses*, see Jean Canavaggio.

8 Marcel Bataillon, trying to recover a 'historical comprehension' of Cervantes, deems him neither a revolutionary nor a 'reaccionario' (his quotation marks), but grants the 'matrimonio cristiano,' religious mystery and sign, the status of central, determining referent for all the texts of this author: '¿Hay muchos momentos en los que Cervantes sea más plenamente él mismo que en estos desenlaces tan elaborados y en sus epílogos? Son como la firma del novelista. Pero la concepción del matrimonio cristiano se halla incorporada a ellos como ciertos rasgueos de pluma que son rasgos de época y confieren a una rúbrica su estilo' (Are there many other moments when Cervantes is more plentifully himself than in these elaborate endings and epilogues? They are like the novelist's signature. But the conception of Christian marriage is incorporated in them like certain pen strokes that are signs of a certain time and confer such rubric its own style) ('Cervantes' 255). Theresa Ann Sears has deconstructed this monolithic view of Cervantes's writing and recovers the 'told story' of his *Novelas ejemplares* on a 'literal level': 'it is an uncomfortable one, involving forms of coercion from imprisonment to kidnap to rape, as well as narrative sleight-of-hand designed to obscure the nature and purpose of that coercion' (8).

Glossary

Alcaldes de Casa y Corte Judges *togados* who as a judicial body constituted the fifth Courthouse of the *Consejo de Castilla*.

Alcaldes mayores Assistant judges, usually advisors to the *corregidores*.

alcázares Royal palaces. Type of space where court plays were staged.

alguaciles Policemen in charge of public order in theatres, among other public places.

autores Owners / producers / directors of theatrical companies or *Cofradías*.

autos Primitive theatrical pieces usually based on liturgical texts.

autos de fé Public shows of trial and punishment of heretics by the Inquisition.

Buffone Buffoon in the *commedia dell'arte* troupes. Joker, fool, *gracioso*.

capitulaciones matrimoniales Prenuptial agreement, contractual terms of possession and distribution of assets and liabilities to enter the marital contract and state.

Catecismo Romano Official Catholic handbook for prelates to administer the sacraments.

cazuela Stewpot. Restricted area in the public theatres for common women.

Chancillería Chancellery or higher court in the Spanish legal system. The two most important were located in Valladolid, once the capital of Spain, and Granada.

ceremoniales Public shows of royal or noble power with complex ceremony protocols.

coliseos Early modern theatres that were neither public (*corrales*) nor courtly, where many developments of set design and building took place.

Comedia First professional theatre written and produced in early modern Spain.

comedia One specific text belonging to the *Comedia*.

comediantes Members of the *Comedia* – actors, playwrights, directors, *autores*, and technicians. Today, *comediantes* is also used to refer to *Comedia* scholars.

cómicos Actors and members of a professional theatre group.

cómites Galley ministers in charge of the orders and punishment of the slaves.

commedia dell'Arte Italian early modern theatre organized around the power of expression of gesture, costume, colouring, and symbolism.

compañías de teatro Theatre companies, also known as *cofradías*.

Consejo de Castilla Superior body of government that assisted the king in concrete terms on the administration of justice, but also in more general matters of administration in his kingdom. The *consejos* were named according to the territory or subject matter of their judicial and administrative competence: for matters pertaining to the peninsula, the *Consejo de Castilla* and *Aragón*; for the Flemish territories, the *Consejo de Flandes*; for the colonial territories, the *Consejo de Indias*; and for the Treasury, the *Consejo de Hacienda*.

Consejo de Estado The highest consultative body of government pertaining to political and administrative matters in Spain and its former colonies.

corrales Early modern Spanish public theatres.

Corregimientos del Reino Royally appointed judges.

cofradías Incorporated theatrical companies in early modern Spain.

cristiano viejo Old Christian, that is to say, one of pure old Christian blood, as opposed to a *converso* (convert from Judaism), *morisco* (convert from Islam), or Protestant.

desenboltura (modern spelling *desenvoltura*) Forwardness, confidence in body movement frequently invoked by the *moralistas* as the root of theatre's evil.

dottore Neighbour and rival to Pantalone in the *commedia dell'arte*. Dottore e Pantalone routines usually represent self-serving and hypocritical wisdom.

Etiqueta Borgoñona Court etiquette highly representative of the Habsburg imperial court of the last Sacred Roman Emperor, Maximilian. His son, Charles I of Spain and V of Germany, first incorporated *borgoñón* rituals into the Spanish court.

facultad de mayorazgo Royal licence approving the foundation of an estate.

festaiuoli Italian directors of festivals, worthy of greatest respect in these gatherings.

galán Male lead actor or character. *segundo galán* Male secondary actor or character.

gracioso Stock character in the Spanish *comedia*. Alter ego to the first *galán*, always his servant, much along the lines of the *Zanni* and the *Buffone*. From his dispossessed place as servant and physically a lesser subject than his master, the *gracioso* grants the *comedia* in which he appears all the irony it needs. As a result, his performance is rather empowered and carries the potential of being likewise empowering.

gran teatro del mundo The great theatre of the world. Phrase equivalent to the Elizabethan theatre's 'All the world's a stage.'

impostoría Passing, dragging, or other kinds of performance of an impostor identity.

licenciado Someone licensed, like an attorney or a college graduate.

mayorazgo Estate, comprising titles, land, and any other material or immaterial assets that constitute the legal wealth owned by a family.

misterio An inexplicable scene or event in the liturgy or other cycle of prayer. A primitive theatrical piece based on these particular texts, also known as *consuetas* or *representaciones*. The mystery of marriage, and the mystery of theatre.

momeries Short plays derived from *momos* or ideas; primitive theatrical pieces.

Monarquía Católica Universal Universal Catholic Monarchy, Spain's imperial state.

moralistas Politicos, priests, and writers who published relentless attacks against the theatre and other public engagements.

mujer esquiva A woman, a woman who eludes, shuns, or eschews marriage, as in a swerving, symbolical motion.

Pantalone The employer in the *commedia dell'arte*, inseparable from the *Dottore*, his neighbour and rival. Although he gives the orders, he does not move the action.

pasos Primitive theatrical piece, a secular one-act play. A specific scene in a *consueta*.

Patronato A board, council, or sponsorship founded by a royal or noble subject.

prelopistas Playwrights preceding Félix Lope de Vega in chronological order.

primera dama Female lead actor/character; *segunda dama* Female secondary actor/character

Real Cédula Royal edict.

Sala de Alcaldes de Casa y Corte The policing and judiciary arm of the *corrales*.

señorío Seigniory, estate, authority, and power of a *señor* (seigneur, Lord).

Siglo de Oro The Spanish Golden Age, 1515–1680

tablas Wooden planks. Term used in Spanish to refer metonymically to the theatre.

teatro breve One-act plays.

tenuta y posesión Title and possession, usually of a *mayorazgo* and its assets.

tertulias and *desvanes* Two levels of seats at the public theatres that in the modern, bourgeois theatres evolved into boxes and balconies.

valido A post loosely equivalent to the modern prime minister, who runs government in representation of (and oftentimes at odds with) the king.

vestuario Dressing room.

Zanni Servant male character in the *commedia dell'arte*

Works Cited

Manuscripts and Facsimiles

Alegaciones de la causa entre Beatriz de la Palma, de una parte, y de la otra Gaspar Suárez, sobre matrimonio. Sixteenth century. AHN, Inq., Libro 1225, fols 179–92.

Capitulos para el matrimonio de D. Francisco de los Cobos con Da. Ana Feliz de Guzmán. Sixteenth century. AGS, CCD, Leg. 39, Fol. 15.

Carta del Cardenal Manrique arzobispo de Sevilla. Sixteenth century. AGS, CCD, Leg. 39, Fol. 39.

Castillo de Bobadilla, Jerónimo. *Política para Corregidores.* Medina del Campo: Por Christoual Lasso y Francisco Garcia, 1608.

Ejecutoria del pleito entre D. Antonio Miguel de Montenegro, vecino de Tuy y el Marqués de Castelar. AHN, D Gral, Leg. 241.

Ejecutoria ganada por … Sarmiento de Valladares en el pleito seguido con la Marquesa de Astorga sobre tenuta y posesión de los mayorazgos pertenecientes a la casa y estado y marquesado de Valladares y sus señoríos. 1754. D Gral Leg. 243.

Erasmus, Desiderius. *Encomium matrimonii. Opera Omnia (Commendations of Matrimony. Complete Works).* Amsterdam: North Holland Publishing, 1975.

Escritura de concierto otorgada entre D. Diego Enriquez de Guzmán … D. Enrique de Guzmán … y d. Diego Enriquez de Guzmán … con D. Pedro Fernández Manrique. 1552. AGS, CCD, Leg. 39, Fol. 46.

Escrituras de censo, 1415–1696. AHN, D Rueda, Notarial, Leg. 114, Fol. 4.

Gómez, Antonio. *Compendio de los Comentarios extendidos a las ochenta y tres leyes de Toro.* Ed. Pedro Nolasco de Llano. Madrid: Imprenta de Don Manuel Martín, 1777.

Gómez Cornejo, Diego. *Opus praeclarumet utilissimum super legibus Tauri* (*Excellent and Useful Work about the Laws of Toro*). Salamanca: Hermanos Juan y Andrea Renaut, 1598.

Hurtado de Mendoza, Diego. *Guerra de Granada: Hecha por el Rey de España don Felipe II contra los moriscos de aquel reino, sus rebeldes… publicada por Luis Tribaldos de Toledo*. Lisbon: Giraldo de la Viña, 1627.

López, Gregorio. *Las siete Partidas del Sabio Rey Don Alonso el Nono*. 4 vols. Salamanca: Domingo de Portonaris, 1576.

Mayorazgos de Mariño y Pazos. 1783. AHN, D Gral, Leg. 260.

Memorial ajustado… entre Da. Maria Manuela de Puga y Gago… y Da. María Ignacia Gago. AHN, D Gral, Leg. 248.

Molina, Juan de. *Sermón breve en loor del matrimonio*. Trans. of Juan Gersón, *De doctrina christiana*. N.p.: Jorge Costilla, 1528.

Nueva Recopilación de las Leyes destos Reynos hecha por mandado de la Magestad Catolica del Rey don Felipe Segundo nuestro señor, que se ha mandado imprimir, con las leyes que después de la vltima impression se han publicado, por la Magestad Catolica del Rey don Felipe Quarto el Grande nuestro señor. Madrid: Por Catalina de Barrio y Angulo y Diego Diaz de la Carrera, 1640. Facsimile: Valladolid: Editorial Lex Nova, 1982.

Ortiz de Zúñiga, Don Diego. *Annales eclesiásticos, y secvlares, de la muy noble y muy leal ciudad de Sevilla, metropolis de la Andalucía* … Madrid: Imprenta Real, 1796.

Palude, Petrus de. *In quartum sententiarum*. Venice: Bonetus Locatellus, 1493.

Pleito de Iñigo López de Anaya con Aldonza de Guevara. 1504. AGS, CR, Leg. 26, Fol. 13.

Pleito de Juan Pérez de Marquina, en apelación de una sentencia dada contra él por el licenciado Martín de la Villa, alcalde de Casa y Corte y juez pesquisidor, en el proceso que se le siguió a petición de la priora y monjas del monasterio de la Encarnación, extramuros de Bilbao, por haber sacado de él violentamente a Catalina Marquina, su hija, y casándola con Martín de Leguizamo. 1522. AGS, CR, Leg. 128, Fol. 6.

Pleito de la Infanta doña Mencía de la Vega con el infante don Fernando de Granada. 1511–1512. AGS, CR, Leg. 41, Fol. 15.

Pleito de María de la Cruz, hija de León Picardo, pintor, con Machín de Placencia. 1532. AGS, CR, Leg. 47, Fol. 8.

Pleito de Pedro de Bilbao, 1494. AGS, CR, Leg. 93, Fol. 1.

Pleito de Rodrigo Pacheco, señor de Minaya, con Alonso Pacheco, su hermano, Pedro Ruiz de Alarcón y Alonso Montoya, vecinos de La Parrilla, sobre haber sacado a su hijo mayor, Juan Pacheco, engañosamente de su casa y llevándole por fuerza a La Parrilla donde trataban de casarle contra su voluntad. 1516. AGS, CR, Leg. 83, Fol. 1.

Premática y nueva orden: De los vestidos y trajes, así de hombres como de mujeres. Madrid: en casa de Pedro Madrigal, 1600. Repr. *Semanario Pintoresco* 19 (1854): 242.

Procesos: heridas, daños materiales (tierras y animales), desacato a la autoridad, injurias, usurpación de oficios, fugas de prisión, agresiones, violación y abusos deshonestos, robo, etc. AHN, D Rueda, Penal, Leg. 100, Fol. 35.

Procesos: injurias e insultos, daños materiales (tierras y animales), amancebamiento, heridas, hurto, resistencia a la autoridad, agresiones, adulteraciones en el abasto, fuga de prisión, etc. 1637–1657. AHN, Div Rueda, Penal, Leg. 98, Fol. 25.

Provisión de la Reina Católica para que D. Pedro Manrique, Duque de Nájera, no enajenase los bienes de su mayorazgo. 1489. AGS, CCD, Leg. 39, Fol. 47.

Querella de Juan de Amores. 1568. AGS, CR, Leg. 136, Fol. 25.

Real Cédula de confirmación de mayorazgo de D. Francisco Hernández de Córdoba y Benavides. 1567. AHN, D Gral, Leg. 229, caja 26, no. 19.

Recibimiento que se hizo en Salamanca a la princesa doña María de Portugal viniendo a casarse con el Príncipe don Felipe II. 1543. BNE, ms 4013, fols 13–59.

Relación de las insignes y reales fiestas que se celebraron en esta Corte desde el 21 de octubre hasta 25 deste año de 1638 por el nacimiento de la Serenísima Infanta Da. Ma. Teresa de Austria… Impreso 1638. AHN D Gral, Leg. 343.

Relación verdadera de las más notables cosas que se hizieron en la ciudad de Burgos, en el recibimiento de la real Magestad de la muy católica reina nuestra señora, en veinte y cuatro días del mes de octubre, de mil y quinientos y setenta años. Impreso en Sevilla: en casa de Alonso Escribano, s. a. BNE, ms R 34.182/16, n. p.

Relación verdadera del recebimiento que la muy noble y muy más leal ciudad de Burgos, cabeça de Castilla, y cámara de su Magestad hizo a la Magestad real de la reina nuestra señora doña Ana de Austria, primera de este nombre … Impresso en Burgos: en casa de Philipp de Iunta, 1571. BNE, sig. R 4969, fols 33–52.

Segusio, Henricus de (Cardinalis Hostiensis). *Summa Hostiensis super titulis decretalium; cum summariis et adnotationibus N. Superantii.* Lyons: Jacques Herion, 1537.

Sentencia en el pleito que litigaron Arias Gonzalo de Avila, Juan Arias de Avila, su hijo, D. Pedro Arias de Avila, D. Antonio Arias de la Cerda y D. Juan Arias de Puertocarrero, Conde de Puñonrostro, 1580. AGS, CCD, Leg. 39, Fol. 48.

Sentencia en el pleito seguido entre Da. Beatriz de Figueroa … 1544. AGS, CCD, Leg. 39, Fol. 45.

Sobre el violento casamiento tratado [de] efectuar de Doña Elvira Enriquez, Vda. de dn. Alvaro de Borja Marques de Alcañices, con don Enrique Enrriquez. 1588–9. AGS, CCPEC, Leg. 1604, Fol. 1.

Título de mayorazgo que … fundaron D. Francisco Vela de los Cobos y Da. Catalina Mexia su mujer … en favor de Sr. D. diego Vela de los Cobos su hijo y sus sucesores. 1585. AHN, D Gral 1, Leg. 157, No. 1.

Transacción … . AHN, D Gral 1, Leg. 241.

Transacción … . AHN, D Gral 1, Leg. 248.

Drama Texts

Calderón de la Barca, Pedro. *El médico de su honra. Segunda parte de Comedias de don Pedro Calderón de la Barca.* Madrid: Por María de Quiñónez, 1637. BNE, Sig. TI/156, fols 94v–116v.

– *El médico de su honra.* Ed. D.W. Cruickshank. Madrid: Clásicos Castalia, 1989.

Caro Mallén de Soto, Ana. *El Conde Partinuplés.* Kassel, Germany: Edition Reichenberger, 1993.

Cervantes Saavedra, Miguel de. *Entremés del juez de los divorcios. Ocho comedias, y ocho entremeses nueuos, nunca representados.* Madrid: Viuda de Alonso Martín, a costa de Iuan de Villaroel, 1615. BNE, Sig. CER/SEDO/8698, fols 220v–24r.

– *Entremeses.* Ed. Nicholas Spadaccini. Madrid: Cátedra, 1982.

– *The Interludes of Cervantes.* Trans. S. Griswold Morley. New Jersey: Princeton UP, 1948.

Lope de Vega Carpio, Félix. *Arte nuevo de hacer comedias en este tiempo.* Ed. Enrique García-Santo Tomás. Madrid: Cátedra, 2006.

– *The New Art of Writing Plays.* Trans. Marvin Carlson. *Theatre, Theory, Theatre: The Major Critical Texts from Aristotle to Zemi and Soyinka and Havel.* Ed. Daniel C. Gerould. Milwakee: Hal Leonard, 2003. 135–45.

– *El perro del hortelano. Onzena parte de las Comedias de Lope de Vega Carpio.* Madrid: Viuda de Alonso Martín de Balboa, a costa de Alonso Pérez, 1618. BNE, Sig. R-14104, fols. 1r–27v.

– *El perro del hortelano. El castigo sin venganza.* Ed. David Kossoff. Madrid: Clásicos Castalia, 1995.

– *El perro del hortelano: A Critical Edition.* Ed. Victor Dixon. London: Tamesis, 1981.

– *El perro del hortelano.* Ed. Vern Williamsen. Comedia Homepage. http://www.comedias.org/textlist.html#Lope

– *The Dog in the Manger.* Trans. Victor Dixon. Ottawa: Dovehouse, 1990.

– *Five Plays (Peribáñez, Fuenteovejuna, The Dog in the Manger, The Knight of Olmedo, Justice Without Revenge).* Trans. Jill Booty. Ed. R.D.F. Pring-Mill. New York: Hill and Wang, 1961.

Menander. *Aspis, Georgos, Dis Exapaton, Dyskolos, Encheiridion, & Epitrepontes* (The Shield, George the Farmer, Twice a Swindler, The Peevish Fellow, The Dagger, and Men at Arbitration). Ed. And trans. W. Geoffrey Arnott. Cambridge, MA: Harvard UP, Loeb Classical Library, 1979.

Tirso de Molina (Téllez, Gabriel). *Don Gil de las calzas verdes. Quarta parte de las comedias del maestro Tirso de Molina recogidas por don Lucas de Avila, sobrino del autor.* Madrid: María de Quiñonez, a costa de P. Coello y M. López, Mercaderes de libros, 1635.

– *Don Gil de las calzas verdes.* Ed. Enrique García-Santo Tomás. Madrid: Cátedra, 2009.

– *Don Gil de las calzas verdes.* Ed. A. Zamora Vicente. Madrid, Castalia, 1990.

– *The Bashful Man at Court. Don Gil of the Breeches Green. The Doubter Damned.* Trans. John Browning and Fiorigio Minelli. Ottawa: Dovehouse, 1991.

– *Don Gil of the Green Breeches (Don Gil de las calzas verdes 1615).* Trans. Gordon Minter. London: Arix & Phillips, 1991.

Secondary Sources

Albrecht, Jane. *The Playgoing Public of Madrid in the Time of Tirso de Molina.* New Orleans: UP of the South, 2001.

Alcalá, Angel. 'Inquisitorial Control of Humanists and Writers.' *The Spanish Inquisition and the Inquisitorial Mind.* Ed. Angel Alcalá. Boulder: Social Science Monographs, 1987. 321–59.

Alonso Romero, María Paz. *El proceso penal en Castilla. Siglos XIII–XVIII.* Salamanca: Diputación-Universidad, 1982.

Alvarez Cortina, Andrés-Corsino, et al. *Manual de derecho matrimonial canonico.* Madrid: Editorial CoLex, 2002.

– *Violencia y miedo en el Código Civil español: Su aplicación al matrimonio.* Oviedo: Publicaciones Universidad de Oviedo, 1982.

Amezúa, Agustín de. 'Un dato para las fuentes de *El médico de su honra.*' *RevHisp* 21 (1909): 395–411.

Apuleius, Lucius. *El asno de oro.* Trans. Lisardo Rubio Fernández. Madrid: Gredos, 1983.

— *The Golden Ass: Being the Metamorphoses of Lucius Apuleius.* Trans. W. Addlington. Loeb Collection. Cambridge, MA: Harvard UP, 1971.

— *Les Métamorphoses. Livres IV–VI.* Vol. 2. Trans. Paul Vallette. Paris: Société D'Édition Les Belles Lettres, 1940.

Arellano, Ignacio. 'Las máscaras de Don Gil.' *Don Gil de las calzas verdes de Tirso de Molina. Versión y dirección Eduardo Vasco.* Textos de teatro clásico de la CNTC No. 44. Madrid: CNTC, 2006. 11–13.

– 'El matrimonio en la poesía satírica y burlesca de Quevedo.' *El matrimonio en Europa y el mundo hispánico. Siglos XVI y XVII.* Ed. Ignacio Arellano y Jesús María Usunáriz. Madrid: Visor Libros, 2005. 11–26.

Armon, Shifra. *Picking Wedlock: Women and the Courtship Novel in Spain.* Lanham, MD: Rowman & Littlefield, 2001.

Asensio Asensio, Eugenio. *Itinerario del entremés desde Lope de Rueda a Quiñones de Benavente. Con cinco entremeses inéditos de D. Francisco de Quevedo.* Madrid: Gredos, 1965.

Ashcom, B.B. 'Concerning "La Mujer en hábito de hombre" in the *Comedia.*' *HR* 28 (1960): 45–62.

Aubrun, C.V. 'Sur les débuts du théâtre en Espagne.' *Hommage à Ernst Martinenche.* Paris: n. p., 1939. 293–314.

Avilés, Miguel. 'The *Auto de Fe* and the Social Model of Counter-Reformation Spain.' *The Spanish Inquisition and the Inquisitorial Mind.* Ed. Angel Alcalá. Boulder, CO: Social Science Monographs, 1987. 249–64.

Azanza López, José Javier. 'Símbolos y alegorías matrimoniales en el retrato renacentista y barroco.' *El matrimonio en Europa y el mundo hispánico. Siglos XVI y XVII.* Ed. Ignacio Arellano y Jesús María Usunáriz. Madrid: Visor Libros, 2005. 211–95.

Bances Candamo, Francisco. *Theatro de los theatros de los passados y presentes siglos.* Ed. Duncan Moir. London: Tamesis, 1970.

Barahona, Renato. *Sex Crimes, Honour, and the Law in Early Modern Spain: Vizcaya, 1528–1735.* Toronto: U of Toronto P, 2003.

Bass, Laura. *The Drama of the Portrait. Theater and Visual Culture in Early Modern Spain.* University Park: Penn State UP, 2008.

Bass, Laura, and Amanda Wunder. 'The Veiled Ladies of the Early Modern Spanish World: Seduction and Scandal in Seville, Madrid, and Lima.' *HR* 77.1 (2009): 97–144.

Bataillon, Marcel. 'Cervantes y el "matrimonio cristiano."' *Varia lección de clásicos españoles.* Madrid: Gredos, 1964. 238–55.

– *Erasmo y España.* México: Fondo de Cultura Económica, 1960.

Benabu, Isaac. 'Who is the Protagonist? Gutierre on the Stand.' *IJHL* 2.2 (1994): 13–25.

Benjamin, Walter. 'The Work of Art in the Age of Mechanical Reproduction.' *Illuminations.* Trans. Harry Zohn. New York: Schocken Books, 1986. 217–53.

Bennassar, Bartolomé. *La España del Siglo de Oro.* Barcelona: Editorial Crítica, 1983.

Benvenuto, Sergio. 'Freud and Masochism.' *JEP* 16 (2003): 113–23.

Bergmann, Emilie, and Paul Julian Smith. *¿Entiendes? Queer Readings, Hispanic Writings.* Durham: Duke UP, 1995.

Bermejo Cabrero, José Luis. '"Justicia penal y teatro barroco" and "Duelos y desafíos en el Derecho y la Literatura."' *Sexo barroco y otras transgresiones premodernas*. Madrid: Alianza Editorial, 1990. 91–126.

Bernis, Carmen. *El traje y los tipos sociales en el* Quijote. Madrid: El Viso, 2001.

Berry, Cicely. *Voice and the Actor*. New York: Wiley, 1973.

Beusterien, John. *An Eye on Race: Perspective from Theater in Imperial Spain*. Lewisburg, PA: Bucknell UP, 2006.

– 'Jewish Male Menstruation in Seventeenth-Century Spain.' *BHM* 73.3 (1999): 447–56.

Bierkan, Andrew T., Charles P. Sherman, and Emile Stocquart. 'Marriage in Roman Law.' *TYLJ* 16.5 (1907): 303–27.

Bouza, Fernando. *Imagen y propaganda: Capítulos de historia cultural del reinado de Felipe II*. Madrid: Ediciones AKAL, 1998.

Bradbury, Gail. 'Irregular Sexuality in the Spanish *Comedia*.' *MLR* 76 (1981): 566–80.

Bravo-Villasante, Carmen. *La mujer vestida de hombre en el teatro español: siglos XVI–XVII*. Madrid: Sociedad General Española de Librería, 1976.

Brownlee, Marina S. 'Introduction: Cultural Authority in Golden Age Spain.' *Cultural Authority in Golden Age Spain*. Ed. Marina Brownlee and Hans Gumbrecht. Baltimore: Johns Hopkins UP, 1995. ix–xii.

Buendía, Felicidad. *Antología del entremés (desde Lope de Rueda hasta Antonio de Zamora). Siglos XVI y XVII*. Madrid: Aguilar, 1965.

Butler, Judith. *Bodies That Matter: On the Discursive Limits of Sex*. New York: Routledge, 1993.

– *Gender Trouble: Feminism and the Subversion of Identity*. New York: Routledge, 1999.

Byrne, Susan. 'Cervantes' *Don Quijote* as Legal Commentary.' *Cerv* 27.2 (2008): 81–104.

Calvete de Estrella, J. Cristóbal. *El felicísimo viaje del muy alto y muy poderoso Príncipe Don Felipe*. Ed. M. Artigas. Madrid: Sociedad de Bibliófilos Españoles, 1930.

Campbell, Jodi. *Monarchy, Political Culture, and Drama in Seventeenth-Century Madrid: Theater of Negotiation*. Aldershot: Ashgate, 2006.

Cañadas, Iván. *Public Theatre in Golden Age Madrid and Tudor-Stuart London: Class, Gender, and Festive Community*. Aldershot: Ashgate, 2005.

Canavaggio, Jean. 'Brecht, lector de los entremeses cervantinos: La huella de Cervantes en los *Einakter*.' *Cervantes: Su obra y su mundo: Actas del 1 Congreso internacional sobre Cervantes*. Ed. Manuel Criado de Val. Madrid: EDI-6 1981. 1023–30.

Canons and Decrees of the Sacred and Ecumenical Council of Trent. Trans. Theodore Alois Buckley. London: George Routledge and Co., 1851.

Capellanus, Andreas. *The Art of Courtly Love*. Trans. John Jay Parry. New York: Columbia UP, 1990.

Carreño, Antonio. 'Lo que se calla Diana: *El perro del hortelano* de Lope de Vega.' *El escritor y la escena*. Ed. Ysla Campbell. Juárez: Universidad Autónoma de Ciudad Juárez, 1992. 115–28.

Carrión, María M. 'El amor en tiempos de cólera, o el arte de esperar en *Don Quijote*.' *USA Cervantes. 39 cervantistas en Estados Unidos*. Eds. Georgina Dopico Black and Francisco Layna Ranz. Madrid: Editorial Polifemo, 2008. 305-332

– 'The Burden of Evidence: Performances of Violence, Marriage, and the Law in Calderón de la Barca's *El médico de su honra*.' *RCEH* 26.3 (2003): 447–68.

– 'Don Quijote's *ingenio*: Marriage, Errantry, and Queerness in Early Modern Spain.' *1605–2005: Don Quixote across the Centuries*. Ed. John Gabriele. Madrid: Iberoamericana-Vervuert, 2005. 93–103.

– 'Here Comes the Real Bride: Anna de Austria and the Birth of Theatre in Early Modern Spain.' *REH* 40 (2006): 113–44.

– 'Intereses (in)vestidos. Fábrica, industria y vestuario en *Don Gil de las calzas verdes*.' *Materia crítica: formas de ocio y de consumo en la cultura áurea*. Ed. Enrique García Santo-Tomás. Madrid: Iberoamericana-Vervuert, 2009. 385–405.

– 'Men With Style. *Sprezzatura*, Costume, and Movement for Men in the Spanish *Comedia*.' *Early Modern Masculinity in Italy and Spain*. Ed. Gerry Milligan and Jane Tylus. Toronto: Centre for Reformation and Renaissance Studies, forthcoming. 353–81.

– 'Mencía (in)visible. Tragedia y violencia doméstica en *El médico de su honra*.' *Hacia la tragedia áurea. Lecturas para un nuevo milenio*. Ed. Frederick de Armas, Luciano García Lorenzo, and Enrique García Santo-Tomás. (del y) Madrid: Universidad de Navarra y Editorial Iberoamericana-Vervuert, 2008. 429–48

– 'Portrait of a Lady: Marriage, Postponement, and Representation in Ana Caro's *El Conde Partinuplés*.' *MLN* 114.2 (1999): 241–68.

Cartagena-Calderón, José. *Masculinidades en obras: el drama de la hombría en la España imperial*. Newark, NJ: Juan de la Cuesta, 2008.

Casa, Frank. 'Honour and the Wife-Killers of Calderón.' *BCom* 29 (1977): 6–24.

Cascardi, Anthony. 'Beyond Castro and Maravall: Interpellation, Mimesis, and the Hegemony of Spanish Culture.' *Ideologies of Hispanism*. Ed. Mabel Moraña. Nashville, TN: Vanderbilt UP, 2005. 138–59.

– 'The Subject of Control.' *Culture and Control in Counter-Reformation Spain*. Ed. Anne J. Cruz and Mary Elizabeth Perry. Minneapolis: U of Minnesota P, 1991.

Castro, Américo, and Hugo Rennert. *Vida de Lope de Vega (1562–1635)*. Salamanca: Editorial Anaya, 1969.

Caudill, David S. *Lacan and the Subject of Law: Toward a Psychoanalytic Critical Legal Theory*. Atlantis Highlands, NJ: Humanities Press, 1997.

Chamberlain, Robert S. 'The *Corregidor* in Castile in the Sixteenth Century and the *Residencia* as Applied to the *Corregidor*.' *The Hispanic American Historical Review* 23.2 (1943): 222–57.

Chamorro, María Inés. *Tesoro de Villanos. Diccionario de Germanías*. Barcelona: Herder, 2002.

Chul, Park. 'La libertad femenina en los entremeses de Cervantes: *El juez de los divorcios* y *El viejo celoso*.' *ACerv* 35 (1999): 111–26.

Clavero, Bartolomé. 'Delito y pecado: Noción y escala de transgresiones.' *Sexo barroco y otras transgresiones premodernas*. Ed. Francisco Tomás y Valiente et al. Madrid: Alianza Universidad, 1990. 57–89.

– *Mayorazgo: Propiedad feudal en Castilla (1369–1836)*. Madrid: Siglo XXI, 1989.

Cohen, Walter. *Drama of a Nation: Public Theater in Renaissance England and Spain*. Ithaca, NY: Cornell UP, 1985.

Comba, Juan. *La indumentaria del reinado de Felipe IV en los cuadros de Velázquez del Museo del Prado*. Madrid: Arte Español, 1922.

Cook, Alexandra Parma. *Good Faith and Truthful Ignorance: A Case of Transatlantic Bigamy*. Durham, NC: Duke UP, 1991.

Correa, Gustavo. 'El doble aspecto de la honra en el teatro del siglo XVII.' *HR* 26 (1958): 99–107.

Corteguera, Luis R., and Marta Vicente. 'The Painter Who Lost His Hat: Artisans and Justice in Early Modern Barcelona.' *SCJ* 29.4 (1998): 1023–42.

– 'Women in Texts: From Language to Representation.' *Women, Texts, and Authority in the Early Modern Spanish World*. Ed. Luis Corteguera and Marta Vicente. Aldershot: Ashgate, 2003. 1–15.

Cotarelo y Mori, Emilio, ed. *Bibliografía de las controversias sobre la licitud del teatro en España*. Madrid: Revista de Archivos, Bibliotecas y Museos, 1904.

Covarrubias Orozco, Sebastián de. *Tesoro de la lengua castellana o española*. Ed. Felipe Maldonado. Madrid: Castalia, 1995.

Cruickshank, Don. 'Calderón's King Pedro: Just or Unjust?' *Spanische Forschungen* 25 (1970): 113–18.

– '"Pongo mi mano en sangre bañada a la puerta": Adultery in *El médico de su honra*.' *Studies in Spanish Literature of the Golden Age Presented to E.M. Wilson*. Ed. R.O. Jones. London: Tamesis, 1973. 45–62.

Cruz, Anne J. 'Deceit, Desire, and the Limits of Subversion in Cervantes' *Interludes*.' *Cerv* 14.2 (1994): 119–36.

Cruz, Jesús. *Gentlemen, Bourgeois, and Revolutionaries: Political Change and Cultural Persistence among the Spanish Dominant Groups, 1750–1850.* Cambridge: Cambridge UP, 1996.

Dadson, Trevor J. 'Official Rhetoric Versus Local Reality: Propaganda and the Expulsion of the *moriscos.*' *Rhetoric and Reality in Early Modern Spain.* Ed. Richard Pym. London: Tamesis, 2006. 1–24.

Dagenais, John. '*Cantigas d'escarnho* and *serranillas*: The Allegory of Careless Love.' *BHS* 68 (1991): 247–63.

Davis, Natalie Z. *Fiction in the Archives: Pardon Tales and Their Tellers in Sixteenth-Century France.* Stanford, CA: Stanford UP, 1990.

– 'On The Lame.' *TAHR* 93.3 (1988): 572–603.

– *The Return of Martin Guerre.* Cambridge, MA: Harvard UP, 1983.

– 'Women on Top.' *Society and Culture in Early Modern France.* Stanford, CA: Stanford UP, 1975. 124–51.

De Armas, Frederick. *Cervantes, Raphael, and the Classics.* Cambridge: Cambridge UP, 1998.

– 'Painting with Blood and Dance: Titian's *Salome* and Cervantes's *El retablo de las maravillas.*' *Ekphrasis in the Age of Cervantes.* Ed. Frederick de Armas. Lewisburg, PA: Bucknell UP, 2005. 217–33.

– *Quixotic Frescoes: Cervantes and Italian Renaissance Art.* Toronto: U of Toronto P, 2006.

De la Cierva, Ricardo. *Yo, Felipe II. Las confesiones del Rey al doctor Francisco Terrones.* Barcelona: Planeta, 1989.

Del Río Barredo, María José. *Madrid, Urbs Regia: La capital ceremonial de la Monarquía Católica.* Madrid: Marcial Pons Historia, 2000.

Del Río Parra, Elena. 'La figura del secretario en la obra dramática de Lope de Vega.' *Hisp* 85.1 (2002) 1: 12–21.

Derrida, Jacques. *Of Grammatology.* Trans. Gayatri Chakravorty Spivak. Baltimore, MD: Johns Hopkins UP, 1976.

Dillard, Heath. *Daughters of the Reconquest: Women in Castillian Society, 1100–1300.* Cambridge: Cambridge UP, 1984.

Domínguez Ortiz, Antonio. *Las clases privilegiadas en el antiguo régimen.* Madrid: Istmo, 1985.

– *Sociedad y Estado en el Siglo XVIII.* Barcelona: Crítica, 1976.

Donnell, Sidney. *Feminizing the Enemy: Imperial Spain, Transvestite Drama, and the Crisis of Masculinity.* Lewisburg, PA: Bucknell UP, 2003.

Dopico Black, Georgina. *Perfect Wives, Other Women: Adultery and Inquisition in Early Modern Spain.* Durham, NC: Duke UP, 2001.

– 'Public Bodies, Private Parts: The Virgins and Magdalens of Magdalena de San Gerónimo.' *JSCS* 2.1 (2001): 81–96.

DuBoys, A. *Historia del Derecho Penal en España*. Madrid: n.p., 1872.

Dunn, Peter. 'Honour and the Christian Background in Calderón.' *BHS* 37 (1960): 75–105.

Eagleton, Terry. *Sweet Violence: The Idea of the Tragic*. London: Blackwell, 2003.

Edelman, Lee. *No Future: Queer Theory and the Death Drive*. Durham, NC: Duke UP, 2004.

Egginton, William. *How the World Became a Stage: Presence, Theatricality, and the Question of Modernity*. Albany: SUNY Press, 2003.

Eng, David. 'The Value of Silence.' *TJ* 54 (2002): 85–94.

Erauso, Catalina de. *Historia de la monja alférez escrita por ella misma*. Ed. Jesús Munárriz. Madrid: Hiperión, 2000.

– *Lieutenant Nun: Memoir of a Basque Transvestite in the New World*. Trans. Michele Stepto and Gabriel Stepto. Boston, MA: Beacon Press, 1996.

Erickson, P., and Clark Hulse, eds. *Early Modern Visual Culture: Representation, Race, and Empire in Renaissance England*. Philadelphia: U of Pennsylvania P, 2000.

Espinosa, Juan de. *Diálogo en laude de las mujeres*. Ed. Angela González Simán. Madrid: CSIC, 1946.

Evans Grubbs, Judith. *Women and the Law in the Roman Empire: A Sourcebook on Marriage, Divorce, and Widowhood*. London: Routledge, 2002.

Feliciano, María Judith. 'Muslim Shrouds for Christian Kings? A Reassessment of Andalusi Textiles in Thirteenth-Century Castilian Life and Ritual.' *Under the Influence: Questioning the Comparative in Medieval Castile*. Ed. Cynthia Robinson and Leyla Rouhi. Leiden: Brill, 2005. 101–31.

Felman, Shoshana. 'Forms of Judicial Blindness: Traumatic Narratives and Legal Repetitions.' *History, Memory, and the Law*. Ed. Austin Sarat and Thomas R. Kearns. Ann Arbor: U of Michigan P, 2002. 25–94.

– *The Juridical Unconscious: Trials and Traumas in the Twentieth Century*. Cambridge, MA: Harvard UP, 2005.

Ferguson, Margaret, A.R. Buck, and Nancy E. Wright, eds. *Women, Property, and the Letters of the Law in Early Modern England*. Toronto: U of Toronto P, 2004.

Fernández Terricabras, Ignasi. *Felipe II y el clero secular: la aplicación del Concilio de Trento*. Madrid: Sociedad Estatal para la Conmemoración de los Centenarios de Felipe II y Carlos V, 2000.

Feros, Antonio. 'Clientelismo y poder monárquico en la España de los siglos XVI y XVII.' *EHS* 19 (1998): 17–49.

– *Kingship and Favoritism in the Spain of Philip III, 1598–1621*. Cambridge: Cambridge UP, 2000.

Ferrer Vals, Teresa. *Nobleza y espectáculo teatral (1535–1622)*. Valencia: Universidad Nacional de Educación a Distancia, 1993.

Fineman, Martha A. *The Neutered Mother, the Sexual Family, and Other Twentieth Century Tragedies*. New York: Routledge, 1995.

Finlay, Robert. 'The Refashioning of Martin Guerre.' *TAHR* 93.3 (1988): 553–71.

Fischer, Susan. 'Historicizing *Painter of Dishonour* on the "Foreign" Stage: A Radical Interrogation of Tragedy.' *BHS* 77 (2000): 183–216.

Flieger, Jerry Aline. *The Purloined Punch Line: Freud's Comic Theory and the Postmodern Text*. Baltimore, MD: Johns Hopkins UP, 1991.

Fothergill-Payne, Louise, and Peter Fothergill-Payne, eds. *Parallel Lives: Spanish and English National Drama,1580–1680*. Lewisburg, PA: Bucknell UP, 1991.

Foucault, Michel. *The History of Sexuality*. Trans. Robert Hurley. 3 vols. New York: Random, 1976–84.

Fox, Dian. *Kings in Calderón: A Study in Characterization and Political Theory*. London: Tamesis, 1986.

Fra Molinero, Baltasar. *La imagen de los negros en el teatro del Siglo de Oro*. México: Siglo XXI, 1995.

Freud, Sigmund. 'Analysis Terminable and Interminable.' *Therapy and Technique*. Trans. Joan Riviere. New York: MacMillan, 1963.

– 'The Economic Problem of Masochism.' *The Standard Edition of the Complete Psychological Works of Sigmund Freud*. Trans. James Stratchey. London: Hogarth P, 1961. 19:159–70.

– *The Uncanny*. London, Penguin, 2003.

Friedman, Edward. 'Sign Language: The Semiotics of Love in Lope's *El perro del hortelano*.' *HR* 68.1 (2000): 1–20.

Fuchs, Barbara. *Exotic Nation: Maurophilia and the Construction of Early Modern Spain*. Philadelphia, PA: The U of Pennsylvania P, 2009.

— 'Virtual Spaniards: The Moriscos and the Fictions of Spanish Identity.' *JSCS* 2.1 (2001): 13–26.

Garber, Marjorie. *Vested Interests: Cross-Dressing and Cultural Anxiety*. New York: Harper, 1992.

García García, Bernardo. 'Los hatos de actores y compañías.' *El vestuario en el teatro español del Siglo de Oro*. Ed. M. de los Reyes Peña. Madrid: Cuadernos de Teatro Clásico de la CNTC, 2000. 165–90.

García Lorenzo, Luciano. 'Más allá (y más acá) de la puesta en escena.' *Diez años de la Compañía Nacional de Teatro Clásico, Cuadernos de Teatro Clásico*. Vol. 9. Madrid: CNTC, 1996. 55–9.

García Lorenzo, Luciano, and M. Muñoz Carabantes. 'El teatro de Calderón en la escena española (1939–1999).' *BHS* 77.1 (2000): 421–33.

García Reyes, Juan A. de Jorge. *El matrimonio de las minorías religiosas en el Derecho español*. Madrid: Editorial Tecnos, 1986.

García-Santo Tomás, Enrique. 'Fortunes of the *Occhiali Politici* in Early Modern Spain: Optics, Vision, Points of View.' *PMLA* 124.1 (2009): 59–75.

Gaylord Randel, Mary. 'The Order in the Court: Cervantes's *Entremés del juez de los divorcios*.' *BCom* 34.1 (1982): 83–95.

– 'La poesía y los poetas en los entremeses de Cervantes.' *ACerv* 20 (1982): 173–203.

Gillett, J. E. 'Torres Naharro and the Spanish Drama of the Sixteenth Century.' *Homenaje a Bonilla y San Martín*. Madrid: n. p., 1930. 2:437–68.

Gilligan, Carole. *In a Different Voice: Psychological and Women's Development*. Cambridge, MA: Harvard UP, 1993.

Ginzburg, Carlo. *The Cheese and the Worms: The Cosmos of a Sixteenth-Century Miller*. Trans. John Tedeschi and Anne Tedeschi. Baltimore, MD: Johns Hopkins UP, 1980.

Girard, René. *Violence and the Sacred*. Trans. Patrick Gregory. Baltimore: Johns Hopkins UP, 1977.

Glick, Robert, and Donald I. Meyers, eds. *Masochism: Current Psychoanalytic Perspectives*. New York: Routledge, 1993.

Godzich, Wlad, and Nicholas Spadaccini, eds. *Literature among Discourses: The Spanish Golden Age*. Minneapolis, MN: The U of Minnesota P, 1986.

González Arce, José Damián. *Apariencia y poder: La legislación suntuaria castellana en los siglos XIII y XV*. Jaén: Publicaciones de la Universidad de Jaén, 1998.

González-Cruz, Luis F. 'El soneto: Esencia temática de *El perro del hortelano*, de Lope de Vega.' *Lope de Vega y los orígenes del teatro español*. Ed. Manuel Criado de Val. Madrid: EDI-6, 1981. 541–5.

González Echevarría, Roberto. *Love and the Law in Cervantes*. New Haven: Yale UP, 2005.

González Ruiz, Julio. *Amistades peligrosas: El discurso homoerótico en el teatro de Lope de Vega*. New York: Peter Lang Ibérica, 2009.

Gossy, Mary. 'Uncannily Queer Iberia: The Past and Present of Imperial Panic.' *La Corónica* 30.1 (2001) http://college.holycross.edu/lacoronica/qi/qi-main.htm.

Greer, Margaret. *The Play of Power. Mythological Court Dramas of Calderón de la Barca*. Princeton, NJ: Princeton UP, 1991.

– 'Spanish Golden Age Tragedy: From Cervantes to Calderón.' *A Companion to Tragedy*. Ed. Rebecca Bushnell. London: Blackwell, 2005. 351–70.

– 'A Tale of Three Cities: The Place of the Theatre in Early Modern Madrid, Paris and London.' *BHS* 77 (2000): 391–419.

Guzmán, Pedro de. *Bienes del honesto trabaio y daños de la ociosidad*. In *Bibliografía de las controversias sobre la licitud del teatro en España*. Ed. Enrique Cotarelo y Mori. *RABM* (1904): 349–51.

Habsburgo-Lorena, Catalina de. *Las Austria: Matrimonio y razón de Estado en la monarquía española*. Trans. María de Irigoyen. Madrid: La Esfera de los Libros, 2005.

Hall, Stuart. *Culture, Media, Language: Working Papers in Cultural Studies, 1972–79*. Ed. Stuart Hall et al. London: Hutchinson, 1980.

Heath, Malcolm. 'Aristotelian Comedy.' *CQ* 39 (1989): 344–54.

Hermenegildo, Alfredo. *La tragedia en el Renacimiento español*. Barcelona: Editorial Planeta, 1973.

Hernández-Araico, Susana. *Ironía y tragedia en Calderón*. Potomac, MD: Scripta Humanistica, 1986.

Hesse, Everett. 'Honor and Behavioral Patterns in *El médico de su honra*.' *RomF* 88 (1976): 1–15.

Hokenson, Jan Walsh. *The Idea of Comedy: History, Theory, Critique*. Madison, NJ: Farleigh Dickinson UP, 2006.

Howard, Jean. *The Stage and Social Struggle in Early Modern England*. New York: Routledge, 1994.

Huerta Calvo, Javier. *El nuevo mundo de la risa. Estudios sobre el teatro breve y la comicidad en los siglos de oro*. Palma de Mallorca: José de Olañeta, 1995.

– *El teatro medieval y renacentista*. Madrid: Playor, 1984.

– *El viaje entretenido: Historia virtual del teatro español*. Madrid: Gredos, 2003.

Hunt, Alan. *Governance of the Consuming Passions: A History of Sumptuary Law*. New York: St Martin's Press, 1996.

Hutcheson, Gregory, and Josiah Blackmore, eds. *Queer Iberia: Sexualities, Cultures, and Crossings from the Middle Ages to the Renaissance*. Durham, NC: Duke UP, 1999.

Izquierdo Martínez, José María. *El Derecho en el teatro español apuntes para una antología jurídica de las comedias del Siglo de Oro*. Pamplona: Analecta Editorial, 2006.

Janko, Richard. *Aristotle on Comedy: Towards a Reconstruction of* Poetics II. Berkeley: U of California P, 1985.

Johnston, Robert. 'The Spectator's Mirror: Mencía of Calderón's *El médico de su honra*.' *IJHL* 2.2 (spring 1994): 39–48.

Jones, Cyril A. '*Honor* in Spanish Golden-Age Drama: Its Relation to Real Life and to Morals.' *BHS* 35 (1958): 199–210.

– 'Spanish Honour as Historical Phenomena, Convention, and Artistic Motive.' *HR* 33 (1965): 32–9.

Jordan, Constance. *Renaissance Feminism: Literary Texts and Political Models*. Ithaca. NY: Cornell UP, 1990.

Jordan, Mark. *Authorizing Marriage? Canon, Tradition, and Critique in the Blessing of Same-sex Unions*. Ed. Mark Jordan, Meghan T. Sweeney, and David M. Mellott. Princeton, NJ: Princeton UP, 2006.

Juárez Almendros, Encarnación. *El cuerpo vestido y la construcción de la identidad en las narrativas autobiográficas del Siglo de Oro*. London: Tamesis, 2006.

Junceda Avello, Enrique. *Ginecología y vida íntima de las reinas de España*. Vol. 1, *De Isabel la Católica a la Casa de Borbón*. Madrid: Ediciones Temas de Hoy, 1991.

Justinian, *Institutes*. Trans. J. Baron Moyle. London: Clarendon Press, 1906.

Kagan, Richard. *Lawsuits and Litigants in Castile 1500–1700*. Chapel Hill: U of North Carolina P, 1981. LIBRO: http://libro.uca.edu/lawsuits/lawsuits.htm.

Kallendorf, Hilaire. *Conscience on Stage: The* Comedia *as Casuistry in Early Modern Spain*. Toronto: U of Toronto P, 2007.

Kamen, Henry. *El Gran Duque de Alba: Soldado de la España imperial*. Trans. Amado Diéguez. Madrid: La Esfera de los Libros, 2004.

– *Philip of Spain*. New Haven: Yale UP, 1999.

Kartchner, Eric. *Unhappily Ever After: Deceptive Idealism in Cervantes's Marriage Tales*. Newark, DE: Juan de la Cuesta, 2005.

Kenworthy, Patricia. 'The *Entremeses* of Cervantes: The Dramaturgy of Illusion.' PhD dissertation, University of Arizona, 1976.

– 'La ilusión dramática en los *Entremeses de Cervantes*.' *Cervantes: Su obra y su mundo; Actas del 1 Congreso internacional sobre Cervantes*. Madrid: Edi-6, 1981. 235–8.

Kezar, Dennis. Introduction. *Solon and Thespis: Law and Theater in the English Renaissance*. Ed. Dennis Kezar. Notre Dame, IN: U of Notre Dame P, 2007. 1–16.

King, Lloyd. 'The Role of King Pedro in Calderón's *El médico de su honra*.' *BCom* 23 (1971): 44–9.

Kirby, Carol Bingham. 'Theater and History in Calderón's *El médico de su honra*.' *JHP* 5 (1981): 123–35.

Lacarra Sanz, Eukene. 'Changing Boundaries of Licit and Illicit Unions: Concubinage and Prostitution.' *Marriage and Sexuality in Medieval and Early Modern Iberia*. Ed. Eukene Lacarra Sanz. New York: Routledge, 2002. 158–96.

Lauer, Robert. 'The Pathos of Mencía's Death in Calderón's *El médico de su honra*.' *BCom* 40.1 (1988): 25–40.

Lavrín, Asunción, ed. *Sexuality and Marriage in Colonial Latin America*. Lincoln: U of Nebraska P, 1989.

Lee, David Russell. *Child-Life, Adolescence and Marriage in Greek New Comedy and in the Comedies of Plautus*. Menasha, WI: Collegiate P, 1919.

León, Fray Luis de. *La perfecta casada*. Ed. Mercedes Etreros. Madrid: Taurus, 1987.

– *The Unknown Light: The Poems of Fray Luis de León*. Trans. Willis Barnstone. Albany: SUNY Press, 1979.

Levine, Laura. *Men in Women's Clothing: Anti-Theatricality and Effeminization,*
1579–1642. Cambridge: Cambridge UP Archive, 1994.

Lezra, Jacques. *Unspeakable Subject: The Genealogy of the Event in Early Modern*
Europe. Stanford, CA: Stanford UP, 1997.

Linklater, Kristin. *Freeing Shakespeare's Voice.* New York: Theatre
Communications Group, 1993.

– 'Vox Eroticus.' *American Theatre Magazine,* April 2003, n. p.

Loftis, John. 'Henry VIII and Calderón's *La cisma de Inglaterra.' CompLit* 34
(1982): 208–22.

MacCurdy, Raymond. 'A Critical Review of *El médico de su honra* as Tragedy.'
BCom 31 (1979): 3–14.

Malcolm, Alastair. 'Public Morality and the Closure of the Theatres in the
Mid-Seventeenth Century: Philip IV, the Council of Castile and the Arrival
of Mariana of Austria.' *Rhetoric and Reality in Early Modern Spain.* Ed.
Richard J. Pym. London: Tamesis, 2006. 92–112.

Mansfield, Nick. *Masochism: The Art of Power.* Westport, CT: Praeger, 1997.

Maravall, José Antonio. *Teatro y literatura en la sociedad barroca.* Madrid:
Seminarios y Ediciones, 1990.

Mariana, Juan de. *Tratado contra los juegos públicos.* In *Bibliografía de las contro-*
versias sobre la licitud del teatro en España. Ed. E. Cotarelo y Mori. RABM
(1904): 429–37.

Mariscal, George. *Contradictory Subjects: Quevedo, Cervantes, and Seventeenth-*
Century Spanish Culture. Ithaca, NY: Cornell UP, 1991.

Maroto Camino, Mercedes. '"Esta sangre quiero:" Secrets and Discovery in
Lope's *El perro del hortelano.' HR* 71.1 (2003): 15–30.

Martín, Francisco J. 'La "novella" en los *Entremeses* de Cervantes.' *Texto y*
espectáculo. Ed. José L. Suárez García. York, SC: Spanish Literature
Publications, 1995.

McAreavey, John. *The Canon Law of Marriage and the Family.* Dublin: Four
Courts P, 1997.

McKendrick, Melveena. 'Honour/Vengeance in the Spanish "Comedia:"
A Case of Mimetic Transference?' *MLR* 79.2 (1984): 313–35.

– *Identities in Crisis. Essays on Honour, Gender, and Women in the* Comedia.
Kassel: Editions Reichenberger, 2002.

– *Playing the King: Lope de Vega and the Limits of Conformity.* London: Tamesis,
2000.

— 'Representing their Sex: Actresses in Seventeenth-Century Spain.' *Rhetoric*
and Reality in Early Modern Spain. Ed. Richard J. Pym. London: Tamesis,
2006. 72–91.

– *Theatre in Spain, 1490–1700.* Cambridge: Cambridge UP, 1989.

- *Woman and Society in the Spanish Golden Age Drama: A Study of the* mujer varonil. Cambridge: Cambridge UP, 1974.

Menocal, María Rosa. *The Arabic Role in Medieval Literary History: A Forgotten Heritage*. Philadelphia, PA: The University of Pennsylvania Press, 2003.

Miller, Nancy. *Subject to Change. Reading Feminist Writing*. New York: Columbia UP, 1988.

Milton, John. *Complete Prose Works of John Milton*. New Haven: Yale UP, 1953.

Morcillo Gómez, Aurora. 'Shaping True Catholic Womanhood: Francoist Educational Discourse on Women.' *Constructing Spanish Womanhood: Female Identity in Modern Spain*. Ed. Victoria Lorée Enders and Pamela Beth Radcliff. Stony Brook, NY: SUNY Press, 1999. 51–70.

Moreiras, Alberto. 'Nation Formation.' *JSCS* 2.1 (2001): 5–11.

Morel Fatio, A. 'La Puerta de Guadalajara.' *RBAMAM* 1 (1924): 417–23.

Moreno y Garbayo, Natividad. *Colección de Reales Cédulas del Archivo Histórico Nacional*. Vol. 1 *(año 1366 a 1801)*. Madrid: Servicio de Publicaciones del Ministerio de Educación y Ciencia, 1977.

Muñoz, José Esteban. *Disidentifications: Queers of Color and the Performance of Politics*. Minneapolis: Minnesota UP, 1999.

Muñoz García, María José. *Las limitaciones a la capacidad de obrar de la mujer casada: 1505–1975*. N. p.: Servicio de Publicaciones de la Universidad de Extremadura, 1991.

Navarro, Emilia. 'Manual Control: "Regulatory Fictions" and Their Discontents.' *Cerv* 13.2 (1993): 17–35.

- 'To Read the Bride: Silence and Elision in Cervantes' *The Jealous Extremaduran*.' *Novel: A Forum on Fiction* 22 (spring 1989): 326–37.

Neuschäfer, Hans-Jörg. 'El triste drama del honor: formas de crítica ideológica en el teatro de honor de Calderón.' *Hacia Calderón: Segundo Coloquio Anglogermano*. Ed. Hans Flasche. Berlin: Walter de Gruyter, 1973. 89–108.

O'Connor, Thomas A. *Love in the 'Corral': Conjugal Spirituality and Anti-Theatrical Polemic in Early Modern Spain*. New York: Peter Lang Ibérica, 2000.

Oehrlein, Joseph. *El actor en el teatro español del Siglo de Oro*. Madrid: Castalia, 1989.

Oostendorp, H.T. 'El sentido del tema de la honra matrimonial en las tragedias de honor.' *Neophilologus* 53 (1969): 14–29.

Parker, Alexander. '*El médico de su honra* as Tragedy.' *Hispanófila* 2 (1975): 3–23.

- 'The Tragedy of Honour: *El médico de su honra*.' *The Mind and Art of Calderón: Essays on the* Comedias. Cambridge: Cambridge UP, 1988.

Parker, Andrew, and Eve Sedgwick. 'Introduction: Performance and Performativity.' *Performance and Performativity. (Essays from the English*

Institute S). Ed. Andrew Parker and Eve Sedgwick. New York: Routledge, 1995. 1–10.

Pérez Castañeda, María Ángeles, and María Dolores Couto de León. *Pruebas para ingreso de religiosas en las Órdenes de Santiago, Calatrava y Alcántara.* Madrid: Archivo Histórico Nacional. Ministerio de Cultura. Dirección General del Patrimonio Artístico. Subdirección General de Archivos, 1980.

Pérez Priego, Miguel Ángel. *Teatro Medieva: Castilla.* Vol. 2. Barcelona: Crítica, 1997.

Perry, Mary Elizabeth. *Crime and Society in Early Modern Seville.* Hanover, NH: UP of New England, 1980. LIBRO: http://libro.uca.edu/perry/seville.htm.

– *Gender and Disorder in Early Modern Seville.* Princeton, NJ: Princeton UP, 1990.

Portús, Javier. 'Retratos familiares en el siglo de oro español.' *El matrimonio en Europa y el mundo hispánico. Siglos XVI y XVII.* Ed. Ignacio Arellano y Jesús María Usunáriz. Madrid: Visor Libros, 2005. 257–70.

Postigo Castellanos, Elena. *Honor y privilegio en la Corona de Castilla: El Consejo de las Ordenes y los Caballeros de Hábito en el Siglo XVII.* Valladolid: Junta de Castilla y León, 1988.

Pym, Richard. 'Law and Disorder: Anti-Gypsy Legislation and Its Failures in Seventeenth-Century Spain.' *Rhetoric and Reality in Early Modern Spain.* Ed. Richard Pym. London: Tamesis, 2006. 41–56.

– Ed. *Rhetoric and Reality in Early Modern Spain.* London: Tamesis, 2006.

Quevedo y Villegas, Francisco de. *Obras completas.* Ed. Luis Astrana Marían. Vol. 1. Madrid: Aguilar, 1945.

Rawlings, Helen. '*Arbitrismo* and the Early Seventeenth-Century Spanish Church: The Theory and Practice of Anti-Clericalists Philosophy.' *Rhetoric and Reality in Early Modern Spain.* Ed. Richard Pym. London: Tamesis, 2006. 25–40.

Real Academia Española. *Diccionario de la lengua castellana.* Vol. 4. Madrid, Imprenta de la Real Academia Española, por los herederos de F. del Hierro, 1734.

Reed, Cory A. 'Cervantes and the Novelization of Drama: Tradition and Innovation in the *Entremeses.*' *Cerv* 11.1 (1991): 61–86.

Regueiro, José M., 'Textual Discontinuities and the Problem of Closure in the Spanish Drama of the Golden Age.' *Cultural Authority in Golden Age Spain.* Ed. Marina Brownlee and Hans Gumbrecht. Baltimore, MD: Johns Hopkins UP, 1995. 28–50.

Rennert, Hugo. *The Spanish Stage in the Time of Lope de Vega.* New York: Hispanic Society of America, 1909.

Restrepo-Gautier, Pablo. '"Y así, a todos, os recibo a prueba:" risa e ideología en *El juez de los divorcios* de Cervantes.' *ACerv* 32 (1994): 221–39.

Reynolds, Philip L., and John Witte, eds. *To Have and To Hold. Marrying and Its Documentation in Western Christendom, 400–1600*. Cambridge: Cambridge UP, 2007.

Rincón, José. *El matrimonio, misterio y signo. Siglos IX--XIII*. Pamplona: Ediciones Universidad de Navarra, 1971.

Ringrose, David R. *Spain, Europe, and the "Spanish Miracle," 1700–1900*. Cambridge: Cambridge UP, 1996.

Ríos Izquierdo, Pilar. *Mujer y sociedad en el siglo XVII a través de los* Avisos *de Barrionuevo*. Madrid: Horas y Horas, 1995.

Rodríguez, Pedro. *El Catecismo Romano ante Felipe II y la Inquisición española: Los problemas de la introducción en España del Catecismo del Concilio de Trento*. Madrid: Ediciones Rialp, 1998.

Rodríguez Cuadros, Evangelina. *Calderón*. Madrid: Editorial Síntesis, 2002.

– 'El hato de la risa: identidad y ridículo en el vestuario del teatro breve del Siglo de Oro.' *El vestido en el teatro del Siglo de Oro*. Ed. M. de los Reyes Peña. Cuadernos de Teatro Clásico 13–14. Madrid: CNTC, 2000. 109 37.

Rosetti, Guy. '*El perro del hortelano*: Love, Honor, and the *Burla*.' *Hispanic Journal* 1.1 (1979): 37–46.

Rossi de Castillo, Silvia. 'Presencia de la lírica tradicional en los *Entremeses* de Miguel de Cervantes.' *Cervantes – Actas del Simposio Nacional Letras del Siglo de Oro Español*. Ed. Carlos Orlando Nallim et al. Mendoza: Instituto de Literaturas Modernas-Facultad de Filosofía, Universidad Nacional de Cuyo, 1994. 63–76.

Ruano de la Haza, José María. *El corral del Príncipe (1583–1744)*. Ottawa: U of Ottawa, n. d. http://aix1.uottawa.ca/%7Ejmruano/Corral.html.

– 'Hacia una metodología para la reconstrucción de la puesta en escena de la comedia en los teatros comerciales del siglo XVII.' *Criticón* 42 (1988): 81–102.

– 'Hacia una nueva definición de la tragedia calderoniana.' *BCom* 35 (1983): 165–80.

– 'Más sobre la 'tragedia mixta' calderoniana.' *BCom* 37 (1985): 263–6.

– 'Noticias para el gobierno de la Sala de Alcaldes de Casa y Corte.' *BCom* 40.1 (1988): 67–74.

– *La puesta en escena en los teatros comerciales del Siglo de Oro*. Madrid: Castalia, 2000.

Ruano de la Haza, José María, and John Jay Allen. *Los teatros comerciales del siglo XVII y la escenificación de la Comedia*. Madrid: Castalia, 1994.

Rubin, Gayle. 'The Traffic of Women: Notes on the Political Economy of Sex.' *Toward an Anthropology of Women*. Ed. Rayna Reiter. New York: Monthly Review P, 1975.

Ruiz Pérez, Pedro. 'Casarse o quemarse: orden conyugal y ficción barroca.' *El matrimonio en Europa y el mundo hispánico. Siglos XVI y XVII*. Ed. Ignacio Arellano y Jesús María Usunáriz. Madrid: Visor Libros, 2005. 39–54.

Rupp, Stephen. *Allegories of Kingship: Claderón and the Anti-Machiavellian Tradition*. University Park: Pennsylvania State UP, 1996.

Saffar, Ruth El. 'Anxiety of Identity: Gutierre's Case in *El médico de su honra*.' *Studies in Honor of Bruce W. Wardropper*. Ed. Dian Fox, Harry Sieber, and Robert Ter Horst. Newark, NJ: Juan de la Cuesta, 1989. 103–24.

Sage, J.W. *The Context of Comedy in Lope de Vega's* El perro del hortelano *and Related Plays*. London: Tamesis Books, 1973.

Said, Edward. *Beginnings: Intentions and Method*. New York: Columbia UP, 1985.

Samson, Alexander. 'Diego Hurtado de Mendoza and the Jewess of Venice: Tolerance, Interfaith Sexuality and *converso* Culture.' *Rhetoric and Reality in Early Modern Spain*. Ed. Richard Pym. London: Tamesis, 2006. 57–71.

Samudio Aispúrua, Edda. 'Un matrimonio clandestino en Mérida en el ocaso del período colonial.' *PH* 4.1 (2003): n. p.

San Román, Francisco de Borja. *Lope de Vega, los cómicos toledanos y el poeta sastre: Colección de documentos inéditos de los años de 1590 a 1615*. Madrid: Archivo Histórico provincial de Toledo, 1935.

Sariola, Sakari. *Power and Resistance: The Colonial Heritage in Latin America*. Ithaca, NY: Cornell UP, 1972.

Schechner, Richard. *Performance Theory*. New York: Routledge, 2003.

Scott, James C. *Domination and the Arts of Resistance: Hidden Transcripts*. New Haven: Yale UP, 1990.

Scott, Joan W. 'The Evidence of Experience.' *Questions of Evidence: Proof, Practice, and Persuasion across the Disciplines*. Ed. James Chandler, Arnold Davidson, and Harry Harootunian. Chicago: U of Chicago P, 1991. 363–87.

Sears, Theresa Ann. *A Marriage of Convenience: Ideal and Ideology in the* Novelas ejemplares. New York: Peter Lang Ibérica, 1993.

Sedgwick, Eve. 'Queer Performativity: Henry James's *The Art of the Novel*.' *GLQ* 1.1 (1993): 1–16.

Seidel Menchi, Silvana. 'La svolta di Trento. Ricerche italiane sui processi matrimoniali.' *El matrimonio en Europa y el mundo hispánico. Siglos XVI y XVII*. Ed. Ignacio Arellano y Jesús María Usunáriz. Madrid: Visor Libros, 2005. 145–66.

Sells, Michael. 'Love.' *The Literature of al-Andalus*. Ed. María Rosa Menocal, Raymond Scheindlin, and Michael Sells. Cambridge: Cambridge UP, 2000. 126–58.

– *Stations of Desire: Love Elegies from Ibn 'Arabi and New Poems*. Jerusalem, Israel: Ibis Editions, Literature of the Levant, 2001.

Sentaurens, Jean. *Séville et le théâtre de la fin du Moyen Age à la fin du XVIIe siècle.* Talence: Presses Universitaires de Bordeaux, 1984.

Shergold, N.D. *A History of the Spanish Stage: From Medieval Times Until the End of the Seventeenth Century.* Oxford: Clarendon P, 1967.

– *Representaciones palaciegas: 1603–1699.* London: Tamesis, 1982.

Shergold, N.D., and J.E. Varey. *Comedias en Madrid: 1603–1670. Repertorio y estudio bibliográfico.* London: Tamesis, 1989.

Sicroff, Albert. *Los estatutos de limpieza de sangre: Controversias entre los siglos XVI y XVII.* Trans. Mauro Armiño. Madrid: Taurus, 1985.

Sifuentes-Jáuregui, Benigno. *Transvestism, Masculinity, and Latin American Literature: Genders Share Flesh.* New York: Palgrave, 2002.

Silk, Michael S. *Aristophanes and the Definition of Comedy.* Oxford: Oxford UP, 2002.

Simerka, Barbara. *Discourses of Empire: Counter-Epic Literature in Early Modern Spain.* University Park, PA: Penn State UP, 2003.

Smith, Dawn L. 'Cervantes and His Audience: Aspects of Reception Theory in *El retablo de las maravillas.*' *The Golden Age* Comedia*: Text, Theory and Performance.* Ed. Charles Ganelin and Howard Mancing. West Lafayette, IN: Purdue UP, 1994. 249–61.

– 'Cervantes and His Critics.' *Eight Interludes.* Trans. and ed. Dawn Smith. London: Orion House, 1996. 166–76.

– 'Who is the Protagonist? Three Interpretations of the Wife-Murder Play.' *IJHL* 2.2 (spring 1994): 7–11.

Solomon, Michael. *The Literature of Misogyny in Medieval Spain: The* Arcipreste de Talavera *and the* Spill. Cambridge: Cambridge UP, 1997.

Soufas, Teresa. 'Calderón's Melancholy Wife Murderers.' *HR* 52 (1984): 181–203.

– *Dramas of Distinction: A Study of Plays by Golden Age Women.* Lexington: UP of Kentucky, 1997.

– *Women's Acts: Plays by Women Dramatists of Spain's Golden Age.* Lexington: UP of Kentucky, 1997.

Spiller, Michael. *The Development of the Sonnet.* London: Routledge, 1992.

Stallybrass, Peter. 'Patriarchal Territories: The Body Enclosed.' *Rewriting the Renaissance: The Discourses of Sexual Difference in Early Modern Europe.* Ed. Margaret Ferguson et al. Chicago: U of Chicago P, 1986. 123–42.

– 'Worn Worlds: Clothes and Identity on the Renaissance Stage.' *Subject and Object in Renaissance Culture.* Ed. Margreta de Grazia, Maureen Quilligan, and Peter Stallybrass. Cambridge: Cambridge UP, 1996. 289–320.

Steele, Brian D. 'In the Flower of Their Youth: "Portraits" of Venetian Beauties ca. 1500.' *SCJ* 28.2 (1997): 481–502.

Stern, Charlotte. 'The *Coplas de Mingo Revulgo* and Early Spanish Drama.' *HR* 44 (1976): 311–32.
– 'Fray Iñigo de Mendoza and Medieval Dramatic Ritual.' *HR* 33.3 (1965): 197–245.
– 'Some Thoughts on the Early Spanish Drama.' *BCom* 18 (1966): 14–19.
– *The Medieval Theater in Castile*. Binghamton: Medieval & Renaissance Texts & Studies, 1996.
Stewart, Devin. 'Ibn Zaydûn.' *The Literature of al-Andalus*. Ed. María Rosa Menocal, Raymond Scheindlin, and Michael Sells. Cambridge: Cambridge UP, 2000. 306–17.
Stoll, Anita. *Vidas paralelas: El teatro español y el teatro isabelino: 1580–1680*. London: Tamesis, 1993.
Stoll, Anita, and Dawn Smith, eds. *The Perception of Women in Spanish Theatre of the Golden* Age. Lewisburg, PA: Bucknell UP, 1992.
Stone, Lawrence. *Family, Sex and Marriage in England (1500–1800)*. New York: Harper & Row, 1977.
– *Road to Divorce: England 1530–1987*. Oxford: Oxford UP, 1990.
Stone, Marilyn. *Marriage and Friendship in Medieval Spain: Social Relations According to the Fourth Partida of Alfonso X*. New York: Peter Lang, 1990.
Strong, Roy C. *Portraits of Elizabeth I*. Oxford: Oxford UP, 1963.
Strosetzki, Christoph. 'El matrimonio en J.L. Vives y Ch. Fourier.' *El matrimonio en Europa y el mundo hispánico. Siglos XVI y XVII*. Ed. Ignacio Arellano y Jesús María Usunáriz. Madrid: Visor Libros, 2005. 27–38.
Strother, Darci. *Family Matters: A Study of On- and Off-Stage Marriage and Family Relations in Seventeenth-Century Spain*. New York: Peter Lang Ibérica, 1999.
Stroud, Matthew D. *Fatal Union: Towards a Pluralistic Approach to the Wife-Murder Plays in Golden Age Spain*. Lewisburg, PA: Bucknell UP, 1990.
– *The Play in the Mirror: Lacanian Perspectives on Spanish Baroque Theater*. Lewisburg, PA: Bucknell UP, 1996.
– *Plot Twists and Critical Turns: Queer Approaches to Early Modern Spanish Theater*. Lewisburg, PA: Bucknell UP, 2007.
– 'Rivalry and Violence in Lope's *El castigo sin venganza*.' *The Golden Age Comedia: Text, Theory, and Performance*. Ed. Charles Ganelin and Howard Mancing. West Lafayette, IN: Purdue UP, 1994. 37–47.
Sullivan, Henry W. 'Love, Matrimony and Desire in the Theatre of Tirso de Molina.' *BCom* 37.1 (1985): 83–99.
– 'The Problematic of Tragedy in Calderón's *El médico de su honra*.' *RCEH* 5 (1981): 355–71.
Surtz, Ronald. *The Birth of a Theater: Dramatic Convention in the Spanish Theater from Juan del Encina to Lope de Vega*. Madrid: Editorial Castalia, 1979.

Taylor, Scott K. *Honor and Violence in Golden Age Spain*. New Haven, CT: Yale UP, 2008.

Tejada y Ramiro, J. *Colección de cánones y de todos los concilios de la Iglesia Española*. Madrid: Pedro Montero, 1853.

Tejero, Eloy. 'De la visión del matrimonio desde la Revelación a su inserción en el derecho natural.' *El matrimonio en Europa y el mundo hispánico. Siglos XVI y XVII*. Ed. Ignacio Arellano and Jesús María Usunáriz. Madrid: Visor Libros, 2005.

Tenorio Gómez, Pilar. *Las madrileñas del mil seiscientos: imagen y realidad*. Madrid: horas y HORAS, la Editorial, 1993.

Ter Horst, Robert. 'From Comedy to Tragedy: Calderón and the New Tragedy.' *MLN* 92 (1977): 181–201.

Testón Núñez, Isabel. *Amor, sexo y matrimonio en Extremadura*. Badajoz, Spain: Universitas, 1985.

Thompson, I.A.A. *War and Government in Habsburg Spain (1560–1620)*. London: Athlone P, 1976.

Thompson, Peter. *The Triumphant Juan Rana: A Gay Actor of the Spanish Golden Age*. Toronto: U of Toronto P, 2006.

Tomás y Valiente, Francisco. 'Delincuentes y pecadores.' *Sexo barroco y otras transgresiones premodernas*. Madrid: Alianza, 1990. 11–31.

– *El Derecho Penal en la Monarquía Absoluta (siglos XVI–XVIII)*. Madrid: Tecnos, 1969.

– *La tortura en España: Estudios históricos*. Barcelona: Ariel, 1973.

— *Manual de historia del derecho español*. Madrid: Tecnos, 1983.

Traub, Valerie. *Desire and Anxiety: Circulations of Sexuality in Shakespearean Drama*. New York: Routledge, 1992.

Treggiari, Susan. *Roman Marriage: Iusti Coniuges from the Time of Cicero to the Time of Ulpian*. Oxford: Oxford UP, 1991.

Tyler, Tom R. *Why People Obey the Law*. New Haven, CT: Yale UP, 1990.

Varey, J.E. and N.D. Shergold. *Comedias en Madrid, 1603–1709: Repertorio y estudio bibliográfico*. London: Tamesis, 1989.

– *Teatros y comedias en Madrid, 1600–1650: Estudios y documentos*. London: Tamesis, 1971.

Vasvári, Louise O. 'Intimate Violence: Shrew Taming as Wedding Ritual in the Conde Lucanor.' *Marriage and Sexuality in Medieval and Early Modern Iberia*. Ed. Eukene Lacarra Sanz. New York: Routledge, 2002. 21–38.

Velasco, Sherry. *The Lieutenant Nun: Transgenderism, Desire, and Catalina de Erauso*. Austin: U of Texas P, 2001.

– *Male Delivery: Reproduction, Effeminacy, and Pregnant Men in Early Modern Spain*. Nashville, TN: Vanderbilt UP, 2006.

Vélez-Quiñones, Harry. 'Deficient Masculinity: "Mi puta es el Maestre de Montesa."' *JSCS* 2 (2001): 27–40.

– *Monstrous Displays: Representation and Perversion in Spanish Literature*. New Orleans, LA: UP of the South, 1999.

– 'Response to "Sex and Social Control."' *LC* 30.1 (fall 2001). http://college .holycross.edu/lacoronica/qi/qi-main.htm.

Vicente, Marta, and Luis R. Corteguera. 'Women in Texts: From Language to Representation.' *Women, Texts, and Authority in the Early Modern Spanish World*. Ed. Marta Vicente and Luis R. Corteguera. Aldershot: Ashgate, 2003. 1–15.

Villalba Pérez, Enrique. *La administración de la justicia penal en Castilla y en la Corte a comienzos del siglo XVII*. Madrid: Actas, 1993.

Villarino, Edith, and Elsa Fiadino. 'Relación entre códigos no verbales/código verbal en los *Entremeses* de Cervantes.' *Cervantes–Actas del Simposio Nacional Letras del Siglo de Oro Español*. Ed. Carlos Orlando Nallim et al. Vol. 1. Mendoza: Instituto de Literaturas Modernas-Facultad de Filosofía, Universidad Nacional de Cuyo, 1994. 77–92.

Vivas Tesón, Inmaculada. 'Un breve apunte civil acerda de la situación de la mujer casada.' *Artículos doctrinales: Derecho Civil* (Origen: *Noticias Jurídicas*). November 2004. http://noticias.juridicas.com/articulos/ 45-Derecho%20Civil/.

Vives, Juan Luis. *Manual de formación de la mujer cristiana (Institutio Foeminae Christianae). Deberes del marido (De oficio mariti). Obras completas*. Vol. I. Trans. Lorenzo Riber. Madrid: Aguilar, 1947. 985–1175.

Wagschal, Steven. *The Literature of Jealousy in the Age of Cervantes*. Columbia: U of Missouri P, 2007.

Wardropper, Bruce. 'Ambiguity in *El viejo celoso*.' *Cervantes* 1 (1981): 18–27.

– 'Poetry and Drama in Calderón's *El médico de su honra*.' *RomRev* 49 (1958): 3–11.

– 'El problema de la responsabilidad en la comedia de capa y espada de Calderón. ' *Actas del II Congreso Internacional de Hispanistas*. Ed. Jaime Sánchez Romeralo and Norbert Poulussen. Nijmegen: Instituto Español de la Universidad de Nimega, 1967. 689–94.

Wayne, Valerie. 'Some Sad Sentence: *Vives's Instruction of a Christian Woman.' Silent but for the Word: Tudor Women as Patrons, Translators, and Writers of Religious Works*. Ed. Margaret Patterson Hannay. Kent, OH: Kent UP, 1985. 15–29.

Weber, Alison. 'Lope de Vega's *Rimas sacras*: Conversion, Clientage, and the Performance of Masculinity.' *PMLA* 120.2 (2005): 404–21.

Weber de Kurlat, Frida. '*El perro del hortelano*, comedia palatina.' *NRFH* 24.2 (1975): 339–63.

Whicker, Jules. '"Seguid la guerra y renovad los daños": Implicit Pacifism in Cervantes's *La Numancia*.' *Rhetoric and Reality in Early Modern Spain*. Ed. Richard J. Pym. London: Tamesis, 2006. 131–44.

Wilde, Oscar. 'Woman's Dress.' *Selected Journalism*. Oxford: Oxford UP, 2004. 3–5.

Wilson, Margaret. 'Lope as Satirist: Two Themes in *El perro del hortelano*.' *HR* 40.3 (1972): 271–82.

– *Spanish Drama of the Golden Age*. Oxford: Pergamon, 1969.

Woolf, Virginia. *Orlando: A Biography*. New York: Harcourt, Brace & Co., 1928.

Wright, Elizabeth. *Pligrimage to Patronage: Lope de Vega and the Court of Philp III. 1598–1621*. Lewisburg, PA: Bucknell UP, 2001.

Zabaleta, Juan de. *El día de fiesta por la tarde*. Ed. Cristóbal Cuevas García. Madrid: Clásicos Castalia, 1983.

Zayas y Sotomayor, María de. *Parte segunda del Sarao y entretnimiento honesto (Desengaños amorosos)*. Ed. Alicia Yllera. Madrid: Cátedra, 1983.

Zimic, Stanislav. 'La ejemplaridad de los entremeses de Cervantes.' *BHS* 61 (1984): 444–53.

– 'El juez de los divorcios de Cervantes.' *ANeophil* 12 (1979): 3–27.

Zizek, Slavoj. 'Courtly Love, or, Woman as Thing.' *The Metastases of Enjoyment: Six Essays on Woman and Casualty*. London: Verso, 1994. 89–112.

Zubieta, Mar. 'Entrevista a Lorenzo Caprile, figurinista de *Don Gil de las calzas verdes*, de Tirso de Molina.' *Don Gil de las calzas verdes de Tirso de Molina: Versión y dirección Eduardo Vasco*. Textos de teatro clásico de la CNTC 44. Madrid: CNTC, 2006. 38–41.

Index